AMERICA
UNCHAINED

AMERICA
UNCHAINED

A Freewheeling Roadtrip In Search
Of Non-Corporate USA

Dave Gorman

EBURY
PRESS

For Anna Devonshire

3 5 7 9 10 8 6 4 2

Published in 2008 by Ebury Press, an imprint of Ebury Publishing

A Random House Group Company

The Random House Group Limited Reg. No. 954009

Addresses for companies within the Random House Group
can be found at www.randomhouse.co.uk

A CIP catalogue record for this book is available from
the British Library

The Random House Group Limited supports The Forest Stewardship
Council (FSC), the leading international forest certification organisation.
All our titles that are printed on Greenpeace approved/FSC certified
paper carry the FSC logo. Our paper procurement policy can be found at
www.rbooks.co.uk/environment

Mixed Sources
Product group from well-managed
forests and other controlled sources
www.fsc.org Cert no. TT-COC-2139
© 1996 Forest Stewardship Council

Printed in the UK by CPI Mackays, Chatham, ME5 8TD

ISBN 9780091899332

To buy books by your favourite authors and register for offers visit
www.rbooks.co.uk

Acknowledgements

I'd like to thank Jake Lingwood, (not the) Ken Barlow, Sarah Bennie, Di Riley, Hannah Telfer, Ed Griffiths and everyone else at Ebury – especially the Mondeo family who do the hard yards. Thanks to Rob Aslett, Amanda Hill, Dan 'Harold' Lloyd, Lucy Groom and all at Avalon too. More4, Channel 4 and ATV were all ace, and my thanks are due to Richard Allen Turner, Andy Auerbach, Peter Dale, Sally Debonnaire, Debbie Mcleod, Prash Naik, Andrew Newman, Grainne Perkins, Jon Thoday and no doubt many more.

Penny de Groot, Carla 'the MCG' McGilchrist, Stephen Pettinger, Gareth 'G-Unit' Upton, Joseph 'the' Wildman and Audra Woodruff were invaluable in so many different ways and are greatly appreciated.

Thanks to all at Editworks but especially Mark Sangster for his boundless enthusiasm and humour. Dru Masters' genius means I can transport myself back to the journey at the flick of a switch any time I want. Which is often. Ta Dru.

Thanks to the Reverend Simon Stevens for lending me some of his theological expertise (and allowing me to publish one of his emails).

Thanks to Matt Welton for looking over my shoulder and offering an encouraging nod whenever it was most needed, especially when I was dropping my shoulder on purpose in the hope that he would. To Mum for some of the same and to David 'Smiedty' Smiedt also. Louise Devonshire let me borrow something of incredible valuable to her; thanks Lou. I tried not to break it.

The kindness of strangers is a wonderful thing and with my lack of mechanical knowledge it was a resource we relied on often. To everyone who helped us along the way – especially the amateur mechanics of America – thank you.

But the biggest thanks have to be spared for the two people who shared so much of the journey; Stef 'Do you do mashed potato?' Wagstaffe and Andy 'Do you have any local beers?' Devonshire. Thanks.

'Man is born free and everywhere he is in chains.
McDonalds and Starbucks are just two examples.'

Jean Jacques Rousseau

The Man™: A generic name for the owners of multinational chain stores, brands and trademarks.

Mom & Pop: A generic name for the owners of small, independent and usually family run businesses.

Part one
In The Beginning

Chapter 1
On your marks...

'**O**pen wide,' said the doctor, taking a good long look at the back of my throat. 'Hmmm. You've been using your voice a lot, haven't you?'

'Yeb,' I said. I tried to tip my head back a bit more to help the build up of saliva to escape. When your tongue is fighting a losing battle against something that looks like a lolly stick but is, apparently, a tongue depressor, swallowing is difficult and only gravity can help. 'Sebber obe a ee or aw uns.'

'Seven shows a week?' said the doctor, his voice rich with concern, 'that's a lot.'

'Or aw uns!' I repeated, keen that he understood the seriousness of the situation.

'For four months? Whew... what kind of show is it?'

'A on a oh.'

'Well, no wonder you've done some damage,' he said. He removed the depressor and the mirror from my mouth. My jaw ached. 'A one-man show will do that to you, especially with a schedule like that. I'm afraid you have a nodule.'

'A nodule?'

The word rattled around the back of my head. I searched my memory for something nodule-related. Nodule? The word was lurking there, for sure. Wasn't it nodules that threatened Elton John's career? 'That sounds very serious,' I said, trying to be as brave as the Rocket Man but still wincing in anticipation of the yet-to-be-revealed implications.

'Excuse me?'

'I said that it sounds very serious.'

'Oh, right. Sorry, I think your English accent threw me,' said the doc, a man who could successfully interpret the half-formed grunts of a man whose tongue he was wrangling but not the *actual* words of an Englishman. 'Basically a nodule is a callus on the back of the throat. You've got one and it's cracked; it's an open wound. So it hurts. I can give you something to alleviate the pain in the short term. It will still hurt. If you perform tonight you will make it worse but you won't do any permanent damage. But afterwards you need to rest your voice. How many shows do you have left on this tour?'

'Just tonight.'

'Well then, your last show is going to be painful. After that, I recommend you don't talk for a few days. Keep hydrated. Avoid alcohol and anything that dries you out.'

'Like flying?'

'Yes. Like flying.'

'That's going to be hard,' I said. 'I fly home tomorrow.'

'Seattle to London?' he asked. I nodded. He grimaced. 'I'll give you some lozenges. But mainly, you need rest. How long before you're on stage tonight?'

'Half an hour.'

A few days later I found myself ignoring the medical advice by taking my nodule out for a few drinks. It was unwise but it seemed rude not to. After all, the BBC was throwing me a welcome home party so the least I could do was enter into the spirit of things.

To spare my blushes nobody was referring to it as the 'Welcome-Dave-back-from-a-four-month-tour-of-the-States Party'. Instead it was referred to by the codewords: 'The BBC Radio Light Entertainment Christmas Party'. They'd even printed that phrase on the invitations, bless 'em, but I knew what we were really there for and I was flattered.

To help with the subterfuge they'd invited a whole load of people that I'd never even met – many of whom seemed to have connections with BBC Radio Light Entertainment – but amongst the couple of hundred people there, there must have been a dozen or so close friends and colleagues.

Most of my conversations that day started in the same way: 'Hey, you're back from the States,' Chris, Carl, Dunc, Carrie, Dutch, Gert, Smudger, Tush, Jo or Joe would say. 'How was the tour?'

'Great,' would say I, because that's what you say in that situation. 'Really great. So... what have I missed? Give me the gossip.' And our conversations would meander on from there.

'Hey, you're back from the States,' said a voice. I turned to see the smiling face of Geoff McGivern.

Geoff is an actor. He's the kind of man whose face you recognise without being able to pin down exactly where you know him from and if you're a keen listener to Radio 4 the same is true of his voice. He's been in loads of stuff but is nowhere near as famous as his talent merits. He's in his fifties but he has a glint in his eye that belongs to a much younger man. He's a brilliant presence on a stage and a warm and garrulous presence in a bar too. He's also... well, a touch eccentric, evidenced by the fact that he lives full-time in a hotel in King's Cross – a part of town where hotel rooms are more likely to be rented by the hour. I'd met Geoff fleetingly on a couple of occasions and always been enthralled by him but I wouldn't have expected him to remember me.

'Yes,' I said, 'I'm back. What have I missed? Give me the goss, Geoff.'

'I've been reading your column in the *Guardian*,' he said, which I hadn't missed and wasn't gossip.

While I'd been touring the States I'd been contracted to write a weekly tour diary of sorts for the *Guardian* newspaper. Geoff leant in towards me as if he had something secret to divulge. 'You've been having a *fucking* miserable time, haven't you?'

I stared at Geoff in disbelief. I wanted to hug him. I had indeed been having a miserable time. What's more, I'd spent most of the miserable time lying to myself and to others about it, telling everyone that everything was fine, burying the underlying unhappiness a little deeper each time. I'd even spent the last couple of hours telling a number of close friends that it had been '*Great. Really great*', but somehow Geoff – a man I barely knew – could see through me.

When I'd been writing those columns I'd made a conscious effort not to put in any whining. I was aware that I was in a very privileged position: I was being paid to travel the world, performing a one-man show that I'd written and directed, so being a grump about it didn't feel seemly.

The truth was that I'd had a big falling out with the tour's promoters very early on and that for four months we had then had to work together without really wanting to. There wasn't any glamorous side to this tour, just badly thought-through travel arrangements, largely unpleasant hotels and a lot of ill will between me and the people I was working for. I didn't think *Guardian* readers would want to know about this. After all, they had muesli to eat on a Saturday morning and that's hard enough to swallow as it is.

So instead I'd pitched each article as a quirky but affectionate view of our American cousins. I didn't discuss the work side of the tour at all if I could help it. Instead I would spend a few hundred words discussing the architecture of American sandwiches or the curious appeal of their impenetrable sports.

'How on earth did you know that?' I asked Geoff, slightly frightened by his mystic powers. 'I *was* having a miserable time but I was really trying not to think about that when I wrote those columns. I thought I'd hidden all the misery.'

'Oh it was there,' said Geoff. 'Between the lines.'

I looked him in the eye. The glint was there but it wasn't the glint of a younger man... it was the glint of a wizard.

Again I wanted to hug him. This time, I did.

'Tell me all about it,' said Geoff comforting me with a gentle pat on the back of the head. Then, with a whisper, 'But go easy on your voice. It sounds like you have a nodule.'

★

Over a couple of glasses of white wine I poured out my recent woes to the wise and wonderful Wizard McGivern. I told him about the tour's behind-the-scenes arguments, the assumptions made (by both parties) and the realities then discovered. I explained the loneliness of life on the road: thousands of miles from home without anything other than the most fleeting of friendships to sustain you, and I explained the things I'd done to get through the days and keep myself sane. (I played a lot of crazy-golf in Aurora, Illinois. I dare say I even got quite good at it. But crazy-golf was not the answer. It never is.)

'There's more to it than this,' said Geoff sagely, 'so you fell out with the promoters, you stayed in some bad hotels. You've been on tour before, Dave, you know what it's like.'

He was right. Of course he was. He was a wizard. Some of my complaints were particular to this tour but most of them were just the usual grumbles that emerge when you're living life out of a suitcase. But there *was* something else lurking there also. There was a deeper malaise that made those four months in America such an unhappy experience. I had come to a shocking and troubling discovery: I didn't much like America.

Now if you happen to be American, please don't throw the book out of the window just yet. I promise you, I'm on your side.

I'm afraid to say there is a lot of lazy America-bashing in popular culture these days and I have no truck with it. I've seen a few too many bad comedians raising a laugh from a British audience by characterising Americans as a bunch of idiots who have dismantled the English language and are devoid of irony – none of which is true.

How on earth could America have incubated the comic minds responsible for *The Simpsons*, *Seinfeld*, *Larry Sanders*, *South Park* and *Spinal Tap* (and that's only the S's) if it *was* the land that irony forgot?

Every time I hear this trite non-observation trotted out I want to apologise to my American friends. Hell, I'll even apologize because, do you know what, the 'i-z-e' ending is the original spelling. Americans are still doing it the way it was when we parted company and it's we Brits who have changed the language. 'Soccer' is a word that started in the English public school system – bizarrely, as an abbreviation for *Association Football* – so you can blame posh English kids for that one and don't even get me started on the 'pants' debate.

Americans clearly 'get' irony, they just don't tend to use it quite so often in day-to-day conversation because, unlike us Brits, they aren't afraid to say what they actually mean and will happily discuss emotions. (Incidentally, if you ever accidentally find yourself in a comedy club and hear the *America = Zero Irony* equation being traded for a laugh, take a good look at the people laughing loudest. They're probably wearing blue jeans and Nike trainers. Ironic?)

Over the last few years I've spent quite a lot of time in the States and I've normally enjoyed it. On two separate occasions I have lived in New York for a three-month stretch and I've never failed to adore that city. I've learnt to love Los Angeles too over the years. It took several short stays there to work it out but slowly it has revealed its charms.

The trouble is, New York and LA don't really tell you what life in the rest of America is like. To judge America on those two cities alone is to admire a man's bookends without reading any of his books.

I had been to other parts of the States too, but only really to big cities and even then, only on such brief stays as to be meaningless. This tour however took me to smaller towns and for longer durations. Even so, it still took me a while to identify what it was that felt wrong about the place. Then one night, through a camera lens, it suddenly came into sharp focus.

Photography has become something of a serious hobby for me. It is, I believe, the perfect pastime for the solo traveller. If you are feeling lonely, a hotel room is only going to intensify that feeling. Propping up a bar by yourself does pretty much the same thing, only with the disadvantages of having liquid depressives on tap. Photography gives you an excuse to be somewhere else, it can be done at any time of the day and it makes perfect sense – in fact, it's better – if done alone.

So there were many occasions when, awake at 3 a.m., the stage-adrenaline still coursing through my veins, I would take my camera and tripod, jump in the hire-car and go off in search of something interesting to photograph.

In LA one night I had decided to take photographs of motels. Not just any old motels, no, motels designed in the architectural style known as *Googie*. You might not be familiar with the term but I guarantee you have seen a few Googie buildings in your time and if you weren't just a little bit charmed by them I don't believe you have a pulse.

Basically Googie describes the kind of buildings that look as if the space age cartoon family the Jetsons might have lived in them. It's full of bold angles, cantilevered roofs, fins, bubbles, domes, starbursts, boomerangs, bold signs, bright colours and pop-culture imagery designed to grab the attention of passing motorists. Seattle's famous Space Needle is as Googie as things get, it just looks like a flying saucer and that's that. It's what American coffee shops, bowling alleys, car washes and motels all seemed to look like in the 1950s and '60s and I think it's pretty darned dandy.

Just as so many American cars of the post-war era were adorned with tailfins and other space-rocketesque stylings, buildings too reflected the mood of the day. The mood – I wasn't there so I'll have to assume – was optimistic. You don't need to be a psychologist to work out that a building that reminds you of a space rocket is looking to the future.

Every now and then as I explored a small American town I would alight upon some all but forgotten Googie gem and happily snap away, recording the exotic structure and, perhaps more importantly, keeping me away from my depressing hotel room for a little while longer.

It's a style that originated in Southern California, and Los Angeles is still one of the best places to find examples. Which explains why, on this particular occasion, I could be found mooching around the seedy end of La Cienega Boulevard in the early hours of the morning setting up my tripod beneath the flicker of some barely functioning neon signs that looked like they were about to give up the ghost.

The motels I was photographing might have been built in a style that I found genuinely impressive but most were in a sorry state. Many had long ago turned out the lights while others appeared to still be in business but were surely only limping along like a pack of wounded animals wondering which one would be picked off next.

It was then that I realised I was photographing the America I liked and admired but that it wasn't the America I'd been living in. For months I'd been staying in a series of chain hotels. There were Best Westerns, and Comfort Suites, Quality Inns and Howard Johnsons, Fairfield Inns and Best Values and others that I've managed to forget. It doesn't really matter what they were called, they were all so disturbingly alike and their overriding quality can best be described as... *adequateness.*

They all – well, nearly all – provided clean linen and hot water but not much else. In particular they were lacking character, the one quality that these nearly dead Googie motels seemed to possess by the space-age bucket load.

The hotels I was staying in felt like they came out of a kit. As if they'd taken three weeks to build and weren't expected to last for more than 10 years. They provided an identikit experience for the American traveller, ticking the boxes that ensure most people's requirements are met – a percolator in your room, a running machine somewhere in the building and Internet access at a price – but having no soul. Besides, I don't want my hotel room in Green Bay, Wisconsin to feel just like the room I stayed in, in Aurora, Illinois... I want it to have some uniquely Green Bay quality to it.

The America I grew up admiring from afar seemed to be a place where anything was possible. Anyone could pursue a goal, set up a business, make it work and feel proud of themselves. Is that as possible to do now as it once was? Can a regular guy set up a hotel and compete with the budget chains, for instance? How easy is it for a local coffee shop to thrive when a new Starbucks opens somewhere in America every five nanoseconds? In the time it's taken you to read this sentence 83 Starbucks have been opened. Probably.

You don't notice these things so much in the big cities. Of course, New York is teeming with Starbucks and McDonalds, The Gap, HMV and all the other global chains you'd expect to see but it seems to have everything else as well. In a city with a population of eight million people I suppose even the most niche of businesses appears to be sustainable. However, if you reduce that population by a factor of 50 it obviously gets harder – and perhaps impossible – to survive.

I started to wonder how many old-fashioned, independent businesses *were* surviving in small-town America. Maybe they were out there... maybe they were just harder to find? Maybe I just hadn't seen them? Or maybe they were no longer there? Would my tour have been possible without the major chains? Could I have found places to stay, places to eat, drink, caffeinate and be entertained without handing my dollars over to The Man™?

A plan started to form. I wanted to know if it was possible to live life in America without the chains. But more than that, I wanted to do America on my own terms. I'd spent four months on tour there feeling like an indentured slave; going wherever I was sent and doing whatever I was told. I wanted to put an end to this. I wanted to go home and put it all behind me. But then I wanted to return and do things differently. I wanted to believe that the America I'd recently experienced was just the plastic veneer it had seemed to be and that if I looked a little deeper I would find the real America, an America of substance.

I wanted to find out. I wanted to see if it was possible to live life in America without the faceless chains... I wanted to discover Unchained America.

Chapter 2
...Get set...

The hotel receptionist stared at me with what seemed like undue suspicion.

'So... you want a room?' he asked, his tone of voice suggesting that he found the idea faintly absurd.

'Yes,' I said, my eyes flitting about the tiny lobby to check that it was indeed a hotel reception. I'd hate to think I was requesting a room from some kind of avant-garde LA butchers. Reassured that my environment was radiating nothing but hotel-ness, I ploughed on.

'But not just one room. My colleague would like a room for the night also. We'd like a room each. Between us, we'd like two rooms.' I paused. 'Please.'

'Two rooms?'

'Uh huh.'

'And there are just two of you?'

'That's right.'

'And when you're in the rooms the two of you are planning to...?'

He left the question mark there just floating in the space between us. I waited a short while hoping he would add another word or two. He didn't. My jet-lagged brain struggled to work out what he wanted to know. What did he think we might be planning to do?

'Um... sleep. In them. I guess,' I guessed.

'So you're not going to...?'

Again the question was left unfinished. Not going to... what? The list of things we were not going to do was long. Infinite, even. It always is. I mean the list of things I'm doing right now is pretty short: I'm writing, I'm thinking, I'm compiling a list of the things I'm doing right now and... well, that's about it. On the other hand, the list of things I'm *not* doing is huge. I'm not swimming the channel, I'm not clipping my toenails, I'm not clipping *your* toenails and, well, you get the idea...

I looked this most cryptic of hoteliers in the eye in the hope that his true meaning would be revealed. He didn't meet my gaze for long. Instead his eyes darted away from mine taking a giveaway glance just over my shoulder. Instinctively I turned to see what it was that had caught his attention and at last I understood his suspicion.

The hotel receptionist had found himself staring through the glass door straight into the lens of a large video camera. Holding the camera was Stef, an attractive, thirty-something blonde. The ring in her nose was glinting with each blink of the hotel's neon sign.

No wonder he was suspicious. It wasn't my behaviour that was unsettling him at all. There's nothing unusual about walking into a hotel and asking for a room for the night, but filming the exchange is, I have to admit, a little odd.

'Ah yes... the camera,' I said, 'yeah. Sorry about that... Nothing to worry about... We're making a film, that's all.'

'A film?'

'Yes.'

'Just you... *and the lady*?' he asked.

'Yes,' I said matter-of-factly before I realised what he seemed to be implying. Me? Making a film in a cheap hotel bedroom? With a lady?

'Oh no,' I gabbled, 'it's not *that* sort of film.'

I think I've probably got a bit ahead of myself and raised more questions than I've answered. Let me explain...

The idea itself was simple. You could have written it on the back of a fag packet but being a non-smoking stationery-whore I wrote it down in a nicely bound notebook instead:

> ➤ *Go to America*
> ➤ *Buy a car*
> ➤ *Drive from one coast to the other*
> ➤ *While doing so, try not to spend any money in chain businesses*
> ➤ *Sell the car*
> ➤ *Go home*

It didn't start off as an idea for a documentary film. It was something I wanted to do for myself and that was it. In fact, long before the idea of a documentary was even floated, my plans for the trip were underway. These plans were twofold: I'd bought a ticket for a flight to LA and in the firm belief that no man should own more than one car in this world (and the even firmer belief that I needed some money to fund the purchase of an American motor), I'd sold my car in London. That was really all the planning I could do. After all, the whole point was that once the journey was underway I didn't want to know where I was going next.

The idea that it might make a documentary came from my agent, Rob. For some reason I can't work out, the idea of me going away for a few weeks and *not* being paid for it seemed to offend him. It's odd, isn't it? I mean, it's almost as if he was on some kind of percentage.

To begin with, the notion of making a film made me uncomfortable. I'd travelled round America doing what I was told once, now I wanted to go and do it the way I wanted. This journey meant something to me and I didn't want it to suddenly turn into a job. I didn't want to present a travel programme. I didn't want to have a four-man film crew following me everywhere and intimidating people along the way. I didn't want to have a team of researchers working out where I was going next because not-knowing-where-I-was-going-next was the most exciting part of the journey. In short, I didn't want to surrender control of the journey to anyone.

But Rob tried hard to persuade me. For every objection I raised, Rob came back with a 'what if'. What if I *was* in charge? What if there was no crew? What if it was just one person? What if, what if, what if?

What it boiled down to was a suggestion for what Rob called, 'a *proper* documentary'. In other words, no contrived set-ups, no pre-planned route, no schedule to stick to and most importantly no doing as I was told. My journey could unfold as circumstances dictated… all we had to do was find someone who was able to come along for the ride and document it. And then someone else who was prepared to buy the finished product.

A few days later Rob introduced me to a producer called Andy, a mild-mannered man with the benign features of an off-duty vicar. Over a hearty lunch in my favourite East London caff, Andy laid out how he thought the project could work as a film and what equipment he thought would be needed.

'The only thing that would definitely have to change,' he explained, 'is that you'd probably need a bigger car.'

'How do you mean?'

'Well, even with a one-person crew there's a lot of kit. You've got an extra body in the car already but with all the kit they're gonna need, it's like having another couple of people. So if you were thinking of getting a small car, it probably won't work.'

'I don't think that's a problem,' I said. 'It's got to be an American car and it's got to be at least as old as me… they didn't make small cars in America back then, did they?'

'Probably not…'

If that was the only thing that Andy thought might change I was ready to be persuaded. Now all we had to do was find someone who was prepared to actually film it.

'I'd do it myself,' said Andy, 'but I've got a young daughter and I'm already committed to filming something else over here. But we'll find someone…'

Over six or seven days the two of us met with nine or ten filmmakers. While Andy assessed their filmmaking knowledge and abilities I would spend each encounter working out whether or not I could happily spend four weeks in a car with them. It's quite tricky working that out over the course of a cup of tea.

There were some that Andy thought could do the job but that I thought would drive me mad. There were some that I thought were great but had Andy shaking his head. There was one we both liked but who obviously didn't like me and another who I don't think had ever made a film before and who seemed a little too excited as the words, 'If one of us went missing in the middle of America... well, no one would know... right?' fell from his mouth. And then there was Stef.

Stef was British but had been working in American TV for a few years. She lived in New York with her boyfriend but luckily for us she happened to be back in Blighty visiting her folks when a friend of a friend of a dentist of a friend had told her about the potential film and so we were able to get together for a chat.

We met in a small Italian café in the centre of town. Andy and I had got there first and were nursing our cuppas when in she bounced. She had Tigger-like energy, dry Northern wit, a no-nonsense attitude and, Andy reassured me, an impressive CV. More important than all of that, like me, she seemed to be more interested in making the journey than she was in making the film.

'So when you say "no chains",' she asked, 'what exactly do you mean?'

'Well,' I said, 'obviously no Holiday Inns, no Best Westerns, Comfort Suites or whatever. No McDonald's, no Burger King – not that that'll be hard – no Starbucks, obviously... that kind of thing.'

'What about petrol stations? Because if you do all that but you're not looking for independent petrol stations then, well, there's no point in doing it with half measures, is there? It's got to be all or nothing, hasn't it?'

'Yes it has,' I grinned, 'yes it has.'

I didn't sleep well that first night in LA. My head was spinning. It was partly the inevitable result of an eight-hour flight and an unsettled body clock, but mainly it was the anticipation that comes when you're on the brink of something big and new. My mood hung in a strange place; a delicate balance of excitement and worry.

Still restless at 3 a.m., I decided to step out for some air. Photography is my friend at times like this so I took my tripod and camera with me and set up to take a few shots of the motel. The Hollywood Downtowner's huge animated neon sign made me smile. It was gaudy and commercial yet somehow innocent and appealing at the same time. With the dead-still night air around me, I stooped to look through the viewfinder. This was exactly what I'd been doing many months ago when the seed of the idea was first planted and it felt right. My worry ebbed away and the excitement took over. Everything felt right.

Chapter 3
... Wait for it ...

I managed to get a couple of hours sleep that night but not much more than that. By nine in the morning, I'd showered, brushed my teeth, breakfasted on a pastry that may or may not have once met an apricot, brushed my teeth again, had a coffee, brushed my teeth once more and now I wanted to get going.

I wanted to go and knock on Stef's door. I wanted to wake her up, pour coffee down her throat and then go out and buy a car. I wanted to be heading east already. I wanted to be driving into the glorious unknown. I wanted this coast-to-coast journey to have truly begun. I wanted it now.

I tried to read but I couldn't focus on the page in front of me. I tried to watch TV but just felt assaulted by the multi-channel nothingness on offer. I tried listening to music but nothing my iPod shuffled to seemed to sit with my mood. Maybe I ought to programme a special music-for-impatient-people playlist. One day. Not now.

A small part of me was annoyed that Stef wasn't up and ready and raring to go but the larger part of me knew that it was an entirely unreasonable thing to expect. I wanted her to be as excited by the whole thing as I was. I wanted *everyone* to be as excited by the whole thing as I was. But I knew I had to wait and so, like a nine-year-old boy waiting for his parents to rise on Christmas morning, I waited. And brushed my teeth. Twice.

When Stef did appear – at a perfectly reasonable 10.15 – I smiled my minty fresh smile and offered her a coffee.

'No thanks,' she said, 'I've already had three cups of tea this morning.'

'Have you? Oh. So you've been up for a while then?'

'Hours,' said Stef. 'I've done a complete inventory on the camera equipment, labelled all the mics, repacked the camera bag so that I know where everything is and called round a few suppliers because I think part of the tripod is missing.'

'Ah,' I said, as the small part of me that had been consumed with impatient anger suddenly died of guilt.

'How about you?' she asked, 'are you wiped out by the flight or do you want to go and buy a car?'

We toured various second-hand car lots that day but despite my eagerness to get going we just couldn't find the right car to get going in.

My mum always worries about the fact that I've reached my mid-thirties but am still single because, 'you'll end up having to choose between 21-year-old girls who don't understand you and 45-year-old divorcees' and for the first time in my life I think I could sort of see her point, albeit with reference to a very different market.

There seemed to be two kinds of second-hand cars available in LA; those that were nearly new or classics and neither seemed right for the job. The nearly news were easily dismissed; it simply had to be a car with some age to it. I was here to look for the America of my childhood – or at least of my childhood imagination – so somehow a three-year-old Hyundai just didn't seem to fit the bill.

But when we trawled classic car lots they brought us no joy either. For a start, 90 per cent of the classic cars we looked at were beyond our means but even with budgetary concerns put to one side they were just too… well, too Californian. A big old '50s Cadillac might be great if you want to put the roof down and fish for admiring glances on the boardwalk but is it really a car you want to drive 3,000 miles across country in? It's fine in the California sun, but do you want to head to the rain-and-wind-swept East Coast in one? How about crossing the Nevada desert? Yes we were looking for an older car but we wanted a warhorse and in LA all we could find were show ponies.

One day of searching in vain rapidly turned into two and then three and with each glorious LA sunset my frustration grew. As far as anyone back home was concerned, my journey had begun when I got on the plane and left Heathrow but I was still waiting for it to truly begin and hating this sense of limbo.

Still, I suppose it did prove to be useful bonding time for Stef and me. We barely knew each other after all and yet here we were, preparing to make a 3,000-mile road trip together. I learned two very encouraging facts about Stef during our LA stasis.

Firstly, I liked the fact that she was as determined to do things properly as I was. As frustrating as our fruitless car hunting was, I knew I was rejecting cars for the right reasons. It would have been far worse if my travelling companion had stood behind the camera tutting impatiently and asking me, 'Well, what's wrong with *this one* then?' Luckily, we appeared to be of one mind on the automotive front. We instantly knew when a car was wrong and, I hoped, we'd instantly know when a car was right.

The second encouraging thing I learned about Stef was that she loved mashed potato. I've never seen anyone display such passion for the foodstuff before. In fact, she loved it so much that she ordered it three nights running. If that doesn't sound extreme wait until I tell you that the restaurants she ordered it in were Vietnamese, Mexican and Thai respectively. None of them had mashed potato on the menu and yet all of them were persuaded to serve the stuff up. I don't know about you but I reckon that makes Stef the perfect road-trip companion. I obviously wanted to avoid trouble on our travels but if we did get into a tight spot I wanted someone like her on my side. I mean, who's more likely to persuade a redneck trucker to help change a tyre? Me, or a woman who can persuade a Vietnamese restaurant to do mashed spuds? Exactly.

Of course if we were going to get a flat tyre we first needed to get ourselves a car. Now, there's obviously no fooling you. You're not stupid and you know there's only a little bit of book to your left and a fair old chunk of book to your right. You know this means there's obviously some kind of story to tell and so you've probably worked out for yourself that we did end up purchasing a car. And indeed we did. It's just that it wasn't in LA.

Strictly speaking, Coronado isn't really an island, it's a peninsula connected to the American mainland by a long strip of land called the Silver Strand. Technicalities aside, it is referred to by all the locals as 'the island' and as we came over the crest of the impossibly grand bridge that connects it to the bustling city of San Diego it certainly looked like one to us.

The north of the island is a naval base and well known as a training area for US Navy SEALs. But the rest of the island has a wonderfully villagey feel and the relaxed, laid-back atmosphere that seems to accompany all such sun-kissed seaside resorts.

We were on our way to meet Grant, a man who, like many Coronado residents, had first moved there on Navy business but who had then fallen in love with the place and stayed for his retirement.

I'd seen the advert for his car online, we'd exchanged a couple of emails and one brief phone call and I'd been persuaded that this was the right car for me. Luckily, I'd managed to press-gang Gareth, an LA-based friend of mine, into giving us a lift on the 140-mile journey necessary for us to view, test-drive and hopefully buy our chariot.

I was a little nervous about meeting Grant. There's something gladiatorial about the buying and selling of cars. It's a manly exchange and I'm not a very manly man. But Grant was a former Navy SEAL and surely that meant he was amongst the manliest of the manly.

SEALs are employed in counter-terrorism, direct action and what is euphemistically referred to as 'unconventional warfare'. I have no idea what the phrase 'unconventional warfare' really means, but I was pretty sure I was on my way to meet a man who could kill me in seven different ways armed only with a flip-flop.

As Gareth steered us through the wide open Coronado streets towards Grant's home, I prepared myself for a man with a hard shell of a personality, a man who would do business with a steely gaze and a firm handshake but would give no quarter. I couldn't have been more wrong.

Grant turned out to be a cheerful, avuncular presence with a twinkle in his eye and a charming sense of old-fashioned manners that meant he could only bring himself to refer to Stef as Stephanie – a trait that made me giggle as much as it made her bristle. Grant was a contradictory package. His frame appeared to come from two separate bodies. Beneath his colourful Hawaiian shirt was the paunch of a man who was thoroughly enjoying his retirement but sticking out of his plain blue shorts were the thin, muscular legs of a man who had stayed in shape.

When we got chatting I discovered he'd even retired twice; once from the Navy and then again from his second career as a lawyer. (I think the lawyer was wearing the Hawaiian shirt while the shorts belonged to the Navy man.)

Grant was there on the driveway to greet us as we pulled in and so was she. 'She' was a 1970 Ford Torino and it was love at first sight. I've never been much of a car man. I didn't inherit my father's petrol-head genes so I wasn't expecting to love the car that would make this trip with me. I didn't really think it was possible... but here I was, being absolutely smitten.

A Torino is what Starsky and Hutch used to drive and staring at her front end the lines were so recognisable I could immediately hear that 1970s wakka-wakka theme music playing in my head. But, just as her present owner had two personas, so did she and side on she was altogether different. This, my friend, was the Ford Torino *estate*. She was long, certainly longer than anything I've ever driven, and she was homely. She had timber panelling down each side which for me, set her apart as something quintessentially American. We don't really have station wagons in Britain but if you could look the term up in my mental dictionary you wouldn't find words there to define it, just a picture of this car. Coming towards you she was a souped-up, action-packed cop car while in profile she was a soccer mom's school-run dreamboat. She was a thing of beauty and even before I'd taken her for a test drive, I knew I was going to buy her. She was a show pony *and* a warhorse. She was perfect.[1]

Grant gave me a tour of the car, explaining how to check the various dipsticks and how and when to top up the various fluids that would keep her ticking over properly. He showed me the switches to press and knobs to turn to make things move. There was the electric rear window that has to be completely lowered before you can open the tailgate, the secret compartment in the trunk that can convert to a rear-facing seat, the eyelids that open when you turn the headlights on; a feature that provides little discernible benefit but was hugely appealing to the nine-year-old boy inside me because... well, because who wouldn't like a car that has eyelids?

The more Grant talked about the car, the more it became obvious that he loved her too. I couldn't help but wonder why he had decided to sell.

'Basically, I'm too old and I own too many cars,' he sighed. 'That's the whole reason. If I had a nice place with an eight-car garage we wouldn't be having this discussion. I have this old Mustang here that I really want to do up and, well, I guess she has to go.'

---

[1] Incidentally, if you're wondering how I decided the car was a 'she' rather than a 'he' – or perhaps just an 'it' – well it's just one of the many areas in life where I agree with the French. It's *la* and not *le voiture* for a reason; cars are feminine and that's all there is to it.

I looked at the metallic-blue Mustang sitting on the other side of Grant's driveway. It was the kind of car that is meant to set a man's pulse racing... it did nothing for me.

'So how long have you had her?'

'Since new: 1970. When I graduated from SEAL training, I was given a platoon on my way to Vietnam and my then wife said she wasn't going to let me go there unless I got her a new car so... there she is. I paid for it with my demolition and parachute pay; the SEALs get extra.'

The more obvious Grant's emotional connection to the car became, the more I started to worry about our plans for it. A 3,000-mile journey is a lot to ask of a 36-year-old car. I'd nodded and ummed and ahhhed while Grant had shown me how to care for her but I wasn't sure I'd taken it all in. Where did the coolant go again? How do I know when she needs more oil? How much additive do I add to a full tank of fuel? And why?

'Did I explain on the phone what we're planning to do with the car?' I asked, keen that he knew what he was letting her in for. 'We want to take her cross-country.'

'Oh yeah, you said. The whole non-corporate thing? You know, that really turns me on.'

'Really?' I asked, as surprised by Grant's apparent delight in the idea as I was by his choice of words. 'Turns me on'? It's a phrase I expect to hear from the lips of a '60s peacenik not a military man.

'Oh yeah... you know, down here, near San Diego, often times what happens is cars don't really sell. They go to auction and people end up buying them and taking them over the border and, well, this car has a big engine, it can probably outrun the border patrol and it's got enough seats in it that I would really worry that it would be used to smuggle people across the border or some other nefarious thing like that. But what you're planning to do, I think that's a phenomenal mission for this car. I'm stoked about this. I really hope you want to take it after our test drive.'

I took her for a spin around the island with Grant sitting in the passenger seat. The V8 engine purred beautifully and my, was she powerful. Staying within the sedate Coronado speed limit meant constantly reining her in. I'd let my foot off the brake as we left a set of lights but the engine would never fully open up before another set were upon us and I was having to apply the brakes once more. She cruised boat-like along the coast road and I just wanted to keep on going, head towards San Diego, the mainland and go.

But of course that would have made me a car thief. So instead we went back to Grant's place, worked out a price and sealed the deal with a handshake.

'Now, it's getting a little late,' said Grant, 'and I have some things I want to talk through with you about the car. I've driven over 120,000 miles in this thing so I think I'll have some useful advice for you. My suggestion is that you stay the night and head off in the morning, is that agreeable with you?'

'Absolutely,' I said. I wanted to get on with things but I was enjoying Grant's company, I wanted his advice and I couldn't begrudge him a few more hours of owning this beautiful car. 'Is there an independent hotel on the island?'

'Oh, you don't need a hotel. You and Stephanie can stay at mine.' Grant smiled an I-might-be-older-than-you-but-I'm-not-a-fuddy-duddy smile. He almost winked. 'I have a spare room.'

'I think Stef and I will need two...'

'Really? Are you two not...?'

'No, we're not,' I explained. 'We're just colleagues. I think a hotel would be best.'

The most famous hotel in the area is the Hotel del Coronado. It was built towards the end of the nineteenth century and is considered by many to be one of the world's top resorts. With its turrets and towers, red roofs and pristine white walls it looks like a cluster of luxury dovecotes. Over the years it's accommodated the great and the good seeing at least nine US presidents stay there as well as countless movie stars. In fact the place is a movie star in its own right having appeared in the Billy Wilder classic *Some Like It Hot*.

We didn't stay there.

We spent the night across the road in the much smaller, considerably humbler, but, for my money, equally charming Villa Capri. We didn't get there until late, mind, having spent the evening drinking rum and eating chips and dips in Grant's cosy front room while he told us all about the motoring adventures he'd had in his beautiful Torino.

It seemed Grant and the Torino had covered almost every square inch of the states that make up the West Coast, as he'd travelled on every imaginable route between Coronado and a second home on an island off the coast of Seattle. He had many tales to tell and I found myself drinking them in. I felt incredibly fortunate; we were buying a car from this man, but he was throwing his wisdom in for free.

'I think the hardest part about what you're doing is going to be fuel,' he said, sucking in his cheeks. 'You should be able to get 15 miles per gallon, and maybe even as much as 18 or 19, and with 22 gallons in the tank... well, you do the math.'

'We'd get around...' the cogs and wheels turned inside my slightly rum-addled brain, '300, maybe 340 miles.'

'Yeah... so, if you're only going to buy gas from independent gas stations, I think you need to adopt Destroyer tactics...'

'What do you mean by that?'

Grant's eyes brightened. He wanted to explain and was clearly delighted that I'd asked. 'One of the things the United States Navy developed in World War Two was the whole concept of refuelling at sea.'

'Yeah?'

'A Destroyer can run at full speed for about 30 hours max before they run out of fuel so they got the idea that they should fuel whenever they could.'

'Uh huh.'

'I was a Destroyer Officer in Vietnam and we took on fuel at every opportunity, even if we were down only 15 per cent. That way, whenever we were called upon, we were ready.'

'I get you.'

'When I was driving this car,' he said, 'I wasn't fussy about who was selling me the gas, but you are, so I think if you see an independent gas station, you have to take it. No matter how full you are; top off.'

'Destroyer tactics,' I said with a nod in the direction of my Commanding Officer.

'Destroyer tactics,' said Grant.

I almost saluted him.

As I put my head down in the Villa Capri that night I was aware that the anxiety I'd felt during the nights in LA was now gone. Now there was no doubt the journey was about to begin. There was even an independent gas station on the island so at least our first 300-odd miles promised to be trouble free. The LA-based car hunting had left me feeling restricted and contained. It was as if time had stood still. I wanted momentum; surely the most important ingredient of any road trip. I wanted to be moving but the fates had stood in my way, and now, with a deft sidestep down towards San Diego, I'd brushed them aside. The journey was about to begin.

We breakfasted in a seafront diner and then headed straight to Grant's. We loaded up the car and exchanged keys, cash and parting words.

'How do you feel, Grant?' asked Stef, because that's what documentary makers always ask.

'I have a lot of mixed emotions,' he said, and I swear there was a tear in his eye. 'I have nothing but happy memories of this car. It's sort of like seeing your kid go off to college.' He paused. There was a tear in my eye too. 'You're real sad to see 'em leave,' he continued, 'but real happy that they're going on to something more important.'

'How do you feel, Dave?' asked Stef.

You see? I told you. That's what they say.

'Come on, let's get going,' I said because I didn't want to talk about it. I *was* feeling emotional but I was feeling ridiculous for feeling emotional too.

We jumped in the car. I put the key in the ignition. I pumped the gas once, twice and then turned the key. She roared into life. I pulled slowly out of the drive and paused to wave at the faintly forlorn figure I could see waving back at me in the rear-view mirror.

'Right, let's go,' said Stef.

I put my foot down.

'Yeeeeeee haaaaaaa!'

Chapter 4
Go!

DAVE: Yeeeeeee haaaaaaa!
TORINO: Vrrrrmmmmm clack, clack, clack, clack, clack, clack, clack, clack.
DAVE: Can you hear that?
STEF: Yeah.
TORINO: Clack, clack.
DAVE: She's clacking.
STEF: Yeah.
TORINO: Clack.
DAVE: She wasn't clacking when I took her for a test drive.
STEF: No.
TORINO: Clack, clack, clack.
DAVE: Something's broken, isn't it?
STEF: Yeah.
TORINO: Clack.
DAVE: We've only driven a hundred yards.
TORINO: Clack.
STEF: Shit.
TORINO: Clack, clack, clunk.
DAVE: Shitting shitty shit.

Now might be a good time for me to tell you the car's number plate. 1JWV666. Yup: 666. I mean, I'm not really a superstitious sort but surely that should have been a sign. We'd just bought the Devil's car. We had the number plate of the beast.

Grant's muscular legs lowered his bulky frame down to floor level so that he could take a look at the base of the car. My own legs creaked as I did the same.

'I'm really embarrassed, guys,' he said with a little huff and a puff from the effort, 'nothing like this has ever happened to this car before. I had it checked out and...'

'It's okay,' I reassured him, 'I did kind of bomb away from the house. I'm sure if I hadn't gone for a "yee-ha" it would have been okay.'

'You were quite fast,' agreed Grant as he stretched his arm out under the car and blindly felt at something or other. 'Here it is,' he exclaimed, 'the tailpipe's come loose. There's a bracket here that should be holding it up.'

I stretched out my own hand and felt at the rusty base. Sure enough, the exhaust pipe was hanging free.

'It'll drive for a while sure but you need to get it fixed,' said Grant, his hand continuing to roam. 'Actually... y'know what, it's rusted right through here. Ain't that the thing... you're gonna need a new tailpipe.'

★

'You're gonna need two new tailpipes and a muffler,' said Larry.

Larry was the proprietor of Jack's Mufflers, a business located in the University Heights district of San Diego. Grant had assured us that this was *the* place to be if you wanted your exhaust looked at by an independent, one-off, unchained business. Larry had owned the place for nearly 30 years having bought it from the guy who bought it from the guy who somewhere down the line had bought it from Jack way back when.

Larry had broad shoulders, a barrel chest and hands that looked as big as my head. His face seemed to carry a half smile at all times, while his eyes were set in an almost permanent squint. Perhaps the half smile/perma-squint is what happens to your face when you spend most of your time working in bright Californian sunshine with a lick of dust kicking about your feet.

Our Torino was high up on the hydraulic ramp that sat in the parking lot attached to the small box-like building that was Jack's Mufflers and Larry was casting his expert eye over the bottom of our car; tapping the pipes and listening to the notes they played as he went.

'Two tailpipes and a muffler?' I asked with a sigh. It didn't sound good. Looking at the underside of the car it was obvious the tailpipes were contoured quite specifically to the model. The chances of someone having 1970 Ford Torino station wagon parts in stock seemed slim and I could easily see us being trapped in the starting blocks for another few days. 'How long are we going to have to wait for that?'

Larry's squinty eyes flickered while he calculated the delay. 'I'd say, you're looking at one, maybe one and a half hours.'

'Hours?' I asked, full of genuine surprise. 'One and a half *hours*? As in, 90 minutes?'

'Yeah.' Shrug. 'About that.'

This was great news. I couldn't hide the look of relief that came over me. Damn. Surely that's lesson number one in the

Negotiating with Mechanics manual; never let your expression tell a mechanic that you're prepared to pay whatever he asks or he'll ask for whatever he wants. (I think lesson two says something about toying with your hair, giggling and showing some cleavage but then it's possible I've been reading the wrong edition.)

'So how much is that going to set us back?' I asked, trying to affect the look of a man who'd often gone through the frankly tedious task of buying tailpipes for his 36-year-old car and so knew exactly how much these sort of things should cost. I'm pretty sure I fell somewhat short and instead only managed to pull off the look of dumb-foreigner-who's-out-of-his-depth-and-would-happily-cut-off-a-finger-in-order-to-have-a-working-car-right-now. It didn't matter because Larry clearly wasn't the kind of man to take us for a ride.

'You've got $32.95 for each tailpipe,' he said, jotting it all down on a scrap of paper, '$58.95 for the muffler, three clamps, labour, tax... I make that $230.99. Is that okay?'

It all seemed entirely reasonable to me, especially when I did some rough calculations and converted it into pounds sterling. It seemed even more reasonable when I saw Larry go to work.

I couldn't believe that Larry would have the specific parts in stock. And I was right. He didn't. But Larry had something far more valuable in stock: the ability to manufacture the parts himself.

I watched in awe as he held up our useless old rusted tailpipe. His eyes scanned its complex series of twists and turns before he then set about replicating them in one of the shiny new pieces of steel tubing he'd pulled from the shelf. He'd stop every now and then, hold the pieces side by side and make another tiny adjustment. He used a bending machine – a Heath Robinson style conflation of clamps and vices – but the measurements were all made by eye and it was an artful hand that pulled the metal this way and that. I was transfixed. It was like watching a skilled potter at the wheel. Larry was clearly at one with the tailpipe.

'Is this normal?' I asked over the buzz and hum of the machinery. 'The hand bending?'

'For me, sure,' said Larry, his eyes not leaving the pipe. 'About 80 per cent of my work is custom. Basically for economic purposes. If I had to have everything I was going to put on a car sitting here on a shelf, I'd have to have a huge shop. If you went to one of the chains they'd probably have to order the parts. Unfortunately, most guys these days don't know how to use this machine... it's kind of a lost art.'

'So what happens when you retire?'

'Well, my son can do this but he's not really interested in running a business. It's got harder now, all the city rules and regulations. I'll try to sell the place, keep it going, you know.' Larry paused to compare the two pipes, one rusty and broken, one shiny and new, but in all other respects, identical. He dropped the rusty one and carried the other towards the car but stopped halfway as a thought landed and his shoulders dipped with regret. 'It'll probably end up being a 7-11.'

Ninety minutes later the Torino was being lowered back down to the dusty floor of the parking lot.

'It's a pretty cool car you got here,' said Larry as he wrote out my receipt. 'It's in pretty good shape. This is exactly what you used to take a trip across country in. You threw everyone in the station wagon and off you went. Right on.'

'That's exactly why we bought it,' I beamed, delighted to have my choice affirmed by a man who clearly had gasoline running in his veins.

The more Larry had talked about his business, the more convinced I was that there was some higher purpose to our journey. I was doing this because I thought the unchained businesses would show me the true spirit of America and even before we'd left the West Coast we'd found someone who seemed to do exactly that. We shook hands.

'Larry, I'm really pleased to meet you.'

'Right on.' Larry tossed the car keys my way. 'You're lucky that bracket went when it did.' He smiled, much more than a half smile. 'If you hadn't noticed that tailpipe was rusted through, you could have had carbon monoxide in the car. You could have fallen asleep halfway across the United States. Right on.'

Oh boy. The car was trying to kill us. 1JWV666.

You don't need a convertible to feel the wind in your hair. You don't even need wind. Or hair. It's not a physical sensation, it's a state of mind. And right then it didn't matter that our windows were closed, I could feel the wind in my hair.

Our days of car hunting in LA had left me feeling penned in and restrained but now as we thundered along at 65 miles per hour I felt released. I felt free.

I couldn't stop myself from smiling. The car was cruising along with ease, we had a fully functioning exhaust system and a full tank of gas. More importantly, I had a full tank of confidence too. At that moment in time, nothing could intimidate me.

I looked around me, at Stef and her camera, at the mass of luggage piled up in the back but mostly I looked ahead at the vast task that lay before us. We had no plans. No prescribed route. No hotels booked. I could do anything. I could go anywhere.

My smile widened, becoming a grin and then a beam and when it couldn't get any broader it grew louder instead as it transformed into a satisfied *ack-ack-ack* chuckle.

'What're you laughing at?' asked Stef, her camera finger twitching in case she'd missed something.

'This,' I explained, gesturing at everything and nothing. 'It's ridiculous, isn't it? Nobody knows where we are. We haven't got any plans. All we know is that we're going to try and cross one of the largest countries in the world. We have something like 3,000 miles to drive and we could go any which way... we could take that exit there. Or that one. Or that one up ahead. None of it's wrong. All of it's right. It's entirely up to us. It's exciting, isn't it?'

'Yeah.'

'And stupid,' I giggled. 'We haven't even looked at a map.'

'You're right,' said Stef with a nervous laugh. 'It is very, very stupid.' She paused. 'Do you think we'll succeed? Do you think we'll actually get all the way across without the chains? Do you think it can be done?'

That was the question that stopped my chuckles. That was the question that focused my mind.

To succeed we'd need to find independent, unchained businesses in three key areas: food, lodgings and gas.

As we whizzed along I-15 the signs did not look good. And signs were pretty much all we could see. Signs advertising the businesses we were setting out to avoid: Burger King, McDonald's, Dairy Queen, Wendy's, Pizza Hut. Best Western, Holiday Inn, Red Roof Inn, Comfort Suites, Country Inn. Shell, Chevron, Arco, Costco. Food, lodgings and gas; but none of it for us. Water, water everywhere but not a drop to drink.

When the road rose up on stilts to take off over the heads of the urban sprawl the businesses below refused to be ignored. Instead their signs followed the road, popping up on ridiculous stalks, appearing in little clusters, each sign taller than the last, vying for the motorist's attention like so many trees competing for sunlight in a densely packed forest.

Despite all the evidence of the chains surrounding us, I can't say I was particularly worried about food and drink. I was pretty sure independent diners could be found in pretty much any community. We wouldn't necessarily always eat in style but I didn't imagine we'd ever have to go without.

Hotels were likely to be a bit trickier, but again I didn't foresee any major problems so long as we were prepared to leave the main highways and drive a few extra miles if needed. If it came to it, we could always sleep in the car.

Gas however was starting to look like an insurmountable hurdle. I couldn't remember the last time I'd seen an unbranded petrol station in the UK although I have some faint memory of my family filling up at one once when I was a child. Amazingly there had been one on the island of Coronado – but nobody we'd met so far, not Grant, not Larry nor any of his other customers were able to tell us of any more.

'Oh, they definitely exist,' said Stef, after I'd voiced my concerns. 'I've used one. It was in California as it happens.'

'Really?'

'Yeah. I was with a TV crew and we stopped at this little station run by a guy with no teeth. Once he'd charged us for the gas he asked us if we'd pay $10 to watch him wrestle an alligator. You don't get that from BP.'

'What did you do?'

'What do you think we did?' said Stef with a derisory snort.

'Was it any good?'

'Not really,' said Stef, 'I think the alligator had fewer teeth than he did.'

'So, this independent, unchained, Californian gas station... where was it exactly?' I asked, hope drifting through the back of my mind. 'Anywhere near the I-15? Was it between San Diego and LA, by any chance?'

'No. It was somewhere up near San Francisco,' said Stef. 'And it was about 10 years ago now. I doubt it's still there, to be honest.'

'Right,' I said, hopes dashed. 'So we need to find a host of unchained gas stations and the only one either of us know about is, what, some 500 miles north...'

'Yeah.'

'... and in the last century?'

'Yeah.'

'We haven't got a chance, have we?'

'No.'

'But we've got to give it our best shot,' I said. 'If we run out of gas and there's no way of carrying on without using a chain, then that's what we do and that becomes part of the story. But we're not stopping at a chain just because we're low... if it happens it has to be because we had no choice, not because we gave in. It's noble to try and fail but we can't concede.'

'So we're going to drive until we run out of gas?'

'I hope not.' I put my foot down and eased past the much younger car to my right. 'But if we have to...'

★

From San Diego to the eastern outskirts of the Greater Los Angeles area the landscape barely changed. It would melt from low-rise housing to retail outlets and industrial units and then back to low-rise housing again without any discernible breaks. We were never nowhere. There was never nothing. But once LA was behind us, things started to change.

The road started to climb subtly. Down to the left an impossibly long train zigzagged through the view. It crossed my field of vision from right to left then left to right and then right to left again as it snaked its way up the side of a mountain in the distance. Somewhere out of view the train driver had long ago escaped the smell of the city while somewhere, seemingly miles behind him, the still unseen rear of the train was yet to shake the last of it off.

This muscular locomotive with its hundreds of freight containers in tow was our last visual link to the city, an umbilical cord anchoring us to the familiar. I wanted to break that link. I wanted to be driving into unfamiliar territory. I put my foot to the floor and the powerful V8 engine took the climb in its stride, cresting the hill and breaking through the gravitational pull of the city.

Instinctively, I looked to the fuel gauge to see how we were coping. We should have had more than half a tank of gas but the needle didn't seem to agree. As the verdant San Gabriel Mountains gave way to the Mojave Desert my concern started to grow. We must have passed a hundred gas stations we couldn't use and now there were none at all. Once we'd driven past the town of Victorville the steady supply of exits dried up. The next town, Barstow, was some 30 miles away. All of a sudden, 30 miles didn't seem like such a trivial distance. That was almost two gallons worth. That was nearly 10 per cent of our total capacity. I gulped. Unfortunately, so did the car. Ten miles. Gulp. Twenty. Gulp, gulp.

'We ought to find some gas,' I said, trying to sound more relaxed than I really was.

'Okay,' said Stef, trying to sound more relaxed than she really was too. She pointed ahead at what seemed to be a village in the distance, 'I guess that must be Barstow, shall we go and see what's there?'

The prosaic name of the road we pulled on to should have been a clue: Outlet Center Drive. What had looked like a village from the freeway was just an outlet mall, home to Factory Brand Shoes, Perfumania, Levis, Timberland and many more. Damn. If anywhere was unlikely to sell unbranded gas it was this place, a temple devoted to the worship of brands.

How far had this taken us off route? Had we just wasted a third of a gallon? Less? More? I turned round and headed back to and then under the interstate as we headed off to try the opposite direction.

'We should still have half a tank,' I said. The needle told me we had around a quarter. 'There's no need to panic yet.'

'No problem,' said Stef in her best oh-I'm-not-panicking-yet voice. 'I'll keep my eyes peeled.'

The sun had bleached all the colour out of this landscape and a dusty pallor hung in the air as we drove timidly through emptiness. There was some promise of life when the desert gave way to fields of crops, each patrolled by huge wheeled watering systems irrigating the land into compliant submission. The people who farmed this land must have been nearby but there was no sign of them.

Left and right turns were chosen at random: Locust Street, Acacia Road, Hope Street (I kid you not, a dead end). Turn around. Acacia Road again.

When we saw it, the sign was everything the signs on the interstate were not. No neon. No brightly coloured logo. Not sitting atop a you-can-see-me-from-20-miles-away stalk. But there, by the side of the road, tied to a telegraph pole, it was; a piece of wood the size of an estate agent's sale board. On it, scrawled in marker pen, were the potentially magical words, 'Hinkley Gas Station and Mart, next left.'

'Oh, happy days!' I exclaimed, 'I hope it's independent.'

'I hope it's bloody open!' said Stef.

I put my foot down.

Hinkley Market Gas Station was a thing of beauty. Not in the traditional sense, but then I'm not sure there is a traditional sense in which gas stations are ever considered beautiful.

The painted wooden sign nailed over the door was peeling and cracked, the colours, red, yellow and blue, all muted by age. In large letters it spelled out, 'Hinkley Liquor & Gas' and beneath that, 'Checks Cashed * Fountain * Deli * Snacks.' Liquor before gas. Cashing checks more important than sodas and sandwiches.

On top of the one-storey building – and almost as tall again – was a large triangular sign, a sort of inverted shark fin. I guess this Googie-esque feature was originally meant to hold a neon sign of some kind but that had long gone. Now it was painted the colour of the desert sand and nailed to it was another weather-beaten wooden sign, this one giving a faint nod to native American folk art with it's shape and turquoise colour. It said simply: 'Mart.'

A couple of cars were parked outside on the dusty forecourt while to the left of the building sat a small concrete island with two lonely, vintage pumps; one for diesel, one for gas.

The rush that came as I filled up the car is difficult to describe. Pumping gas had never made me feel this good before. But then, finding gas had never been such a challenge before. Suddenly, our task didn't seem quite so stupid. It felt like we'd just lit one 50-watt bulb in 3.7 million square miles of darkness. But for now it was enough. It was enough to give me hope. It was only day one of our journey but suddenly the impossible seemed possible.

This was going to be brilliant.

Chapter 6
Four weeks later

This was shit.

I looked around the bland, beige hotel room. I closed the heavy drapes. I wanted privacy. Strange, really, given that I was about to film myself.

I had already set the camera up on a tripod. The legs were fully extended which meant that I had to stand on a chair in order to see the viewfinder and ensure that I'd framed things properly.

The camera was angled downwards, taking an eagle's-eye view of the shiny, low coffee table and stain-resistant, two-seater sofa. Something didn't look right. The symmetry was ruined by a dark-blue folder sitting on the coffee table. You know the kind of thing. You get them in a lot of hotels. A wipe-clean leatherette binder containing a few sheets of A4 telling you what time breakfast is served, what number to dial if you want an outside line and so on.

I stepped down from my chair and picked up the folder. The lettering on the front of it – gold and embossed – confirmed for me just how satisfyingly wrong everything was. This, it reminded me, was a Best Western Hotel. This, it boasted, was a part of the world's largest hotel chain. It was everything I'd set out to avoid. Perfect. I tossed the folder aside and then stood back up on the chair to check the shot once more.

There were too many buttons on the camera. I didn't have a clue what they did. If only there was a director to help me set this up. Then again, if the film still had a director, this wouldn't be happening at all. I pressed a random switch to see what would happen. The picture took on an alien, yellow hue. I pressed the switch again and things returned to normal. Hmmm. Best not to meddle. Satisfied that it looked as good as my amateur talents would allow, I pressed the red button. I heard the motor turning. A red light blinked. It was recording. It was time for the ceremony to begin.

On the desk behind the camera I had three paper bags. One from McDonald's, another from Wendy's and a third from Burger King. The three largest burger chains in the world. Certainly the three most visible in Moab, Utah. In each bag there was a burger and a large portion of fries. One by one I took the three burgers from their bags and laid them out on the coffee table. Besides each burger I placed the corresponding cardboard scuttle of salty, stringy, fried potato.

Like a Samurai warrior laying out his blade before committing hari-kiri, I arranged everything just so. It had to be neat. It had to be perfect. The project was dead and buried. Now it was time to take its soul. The chains had won. Rules had been broken. Now every rule must be broken.

In the parking lot outside the car sat idle. The petrol slopping around in its fuel tank had come from the nearby Shell station. If it's good enough for the car, it was good enough for me. Chains? Bring 'em on.

Fuck.

It wasn't just the rules of the project that were going to be broken. I wanted to punish myself. I wanted to hurt myself. My own personal rules would be broken too. I'm a vegetarian.

I sat down on the sofa and stared up at the camera. I breathed in deeply. As the fatty aroma circled through my nostril hairs I felt the back of my throat tighten. The camera was taking a wide shot but I wanted to make sure every detail of my humiliation was recorded for posterity. I wanted a close-up. For that, I had a small handheld video camera. My own. With only three or four buttons, it was so simple a child could use it.

I hit record.

Alone. Two cameras recording.

I picked up the first burger. Macky Dees. Meat, if you're not used to it, can be quite a shock to the system. The taste – if you can call it that – hit me and my stomach convulsed. My body told me to spit the rubbery patty out but I refused to let it happen. My cheeks bulging, I kept the mush in my mouth. I chewed and I gagged and I chewed and I gagged and I chewed and then, ach, I swallowed.

Ugh.

A few fries. Or was it a portion of salt with some potato on the side? Another bite. Burger in my right hand. Camera in my left. Let it see the food being chewed, crushed, ground and pulped. Let it see the sweat on my brow. Let it see the sorrow in my eyes. Chew. Gag. Chew. Gag. Chew. Swallow. Ugh.

I ate quickly. I didn't want to give myself time to contemplate what I was doing. In 10 minutes it was all gone. Fast food.

Five minutes later it made a sudden reappearance. Very fast food.

Three burgers and three portions of fries in 10 minutes. It's probably enough to turn the stomach of even the most robust carnivore but for a lily-livered, namby-pamby vegetarian like me, the unfamiliar tastes and textures, the fat, the smell, the shock; everything was violently rejected.

The first warning sign: my saliva was changing, becoming more viscous. The second warning sign: a volcanic rumble deep in my belly. With the video camera still in my hand I rushed to the bathroom. I knelt on the hard tiled floor and... nothing happened.

Was it a false alarm?

No.

From nowhere it suddenly erupted.

Bleeeeeuuuuuuuurghhhhhhh. Agggggh. Wendy's. Where's the beef?

Bleeeeeuuuuuuuurghhhhhhh. Agggggh. Burger King. You got it.

Bleeeeeuuuuuuuurghhhhhhh. Agggggh. McDonald's. I'm lovin' it.

Stomach acid burned at the back of my throat. Something lodged itself into the cavity between nose and mouth and I had to employ a violent hacking cough to remove it. It felt like someone was dragging a cheese grater across my gullet and dousing my epiglottis in bleach.

A stream of sick hit the toilet at high velocity. As a quarter pound of barely digested food blasted its way out of me, the sound – like machine-gun bullets hitting water – echoed around the porcelain bowl. A splash of sick-infested toilet water bounced up and hit me in the eye.

I hugged the bowl. Waiting for the aftershock. A hotel toilet and me. Me and a hotel toilet. How many strangers had parked their arses where my face was now? How much shit and piss had flowed down this hole? I dry heaved. I felt pathetic. I *was* pathetic. Good. Unchained America? Fuck that. If I couldn't have my idea, nobody could.

Exhausted, a tiny tear rolled down my cheek.

From: Jake Lingwood (Ebury Publishing)
Subject: Chapters 1 to 6
To: Dave Gorman

Dave,

Thanks for the manuscript so far.

You know there's a four-week jump in the narrative don't you? I'm sure you do but I just thought I'd check. You are going to explain, aren't you?

Your ever-faithful editor,

Jake

From: Dave Gorman
Subject: Re: Chapters 1 to 6
To: Jake Lingwood (Ebury Publishing)

Yes.

Part two
The Bit Where I Explain What Happened In Those Four Weeks

Chapter 7
Bears like jam sandwiches

I guess there are two big things that need to be explained. The whole journey from coast to coast was meant to be over in less than a month so you might well be wondering why, four weeks after setting off, I'd only got as far as Moab, Utah.

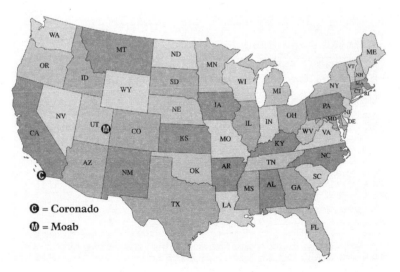

© = Coronado
Ⓜ = Moab

And then, given the stated aims of my journey, it's only reasonable that I tell you quite how I came to end up sitting in the world's largest hotel chain, eating burgers bought from America's three biggest burger chains while petrol bought from a global brand gas station was sitting in the tank of my car, outside.

In a way the two things are kind of connected. But they are complicated. As things panned out, our route from Coronado to Moab wasn't a simple one. The drive from Coronado to Moab is 787 miles. Over four weeks that would be less than 30 miles a day; I could have walked this journey in that time. I didn't walk it. And we did considerably more than 30 miles a day. Most days, anyway. It's just that our route was, well, a little more complex than necessary. Let me start with the first of our wrong turns.

It came as we left the Hinkley Market Gas Station. I admit it was my fault. I did something very stupid: I had an idea.

I'd brought a little notebook with me in order to record the mileage and monitor our fuel consumption. I know it sounds kind of anal but I knew that finding gas was going to be the most challenging aspect of our trip and so I thought it was wise to know as much as possible about the car's performance. That way we'd know more about when to start looking for gas... and when to start panicking. And besides, I am kind of anal.

While Stef was braving the gas station's toilet facilities (and believe me, brave is the word) I sat in the car and made my notes. Page one of the notebook looked like this:

Coronado Mileage:	122,060
Hinkley Mileage:	122,278
Total mileage:	218
Gasoline used:	13.66 gallons
Miles per gallon:	15.95

Which was good news. The needle had told us we were down to a quarter. And now, through the magic of maths, I knew that the needle was lying. We knew from Grant that we had a 22-gallon tank. If we'd used up three quarters of our 22-gallon capacity we'd have had to put in over 16 gallons in order to fill her up. The truth was that when the needle said we were down to a quarter we still had a good eight gallons to go and that added up to more than 120 miles of driving. That was definitely worth knowing.

The obvious place to stash the notebook was in the glove compartment – after all, I hadn't brought any gloves – and so, having made my notes, that's what I went to do. Which is when I discovered that the glove compartment was stuffed full of maps. I was surprised. I know maps aren't a particularly surprising thing to find in a glove compartment but then I also knew they hadn't been there when I'd first taken the car for a test drive. I assumed that my canny, filmmaking co-pilot had stashed them there just in case. I was wrong.

I pulled the top one from the pile. It was a map of California. On the front cover, in neat handwriting, were the words, 'I thought these might be useful. Grant.' Aw... he was still looking after us. What a lovely man. It was like having an Obi Wan Kenobi hologram pop up to offer us guidance. (The classy, Alec Guinness variety rather than the Ewan McGregor version, obviously.) The force was with me.

I unfolded the map and started tracing our route. The sun was setting fast and I figured that working out where to go next would be easier if I knew where we actually were. As my eyes located the word Hinkley, I found them drawn irresistibly to another place name just two or three inches to the north.

It was a place that Grant had mentioned a couple of nights earlier when we'd sat around drinking rum and listening to his many tales of motoring between California and Washington. He had an atlas out and ran his chubby finger along a road, speaking aloud each town his digit passed. Occasionally, as he mentioned a place the sound of it would spark a memory for him and he'd take his finger from the map and relax into an anecdote, telling us about the best fish restaurant he ever visited on this stretch of coast or the resort where his kids had enjoyed the best swimming on another.

It was on an inland route north that his finger had carried us through this place and the name of it was bound to set off a small germ of an idea. The place was Independence. I mean, we

were making a film about independence after all. And yet I
didn't think too much of it. A little pulse of electricity had
flowed from one synapse to the other as I recognised the slight
coincidence in the word but then I dismissed it because it
seemed so far from our expected route east.

Of course that was before we'd got to Hinkley. That was
before I found myself looking at the place on a map once more
and now it was only a couple of inches away. Independence? It
was just too tempting.

A couple of inches? That can't be so far, can it? Highway 395
was just, ooh, a thumbnail to the west and from there
Independence was a couple of thumb-joints north. It was *literally* just a thumb and a bit.

Of course I knew there was no reason why a town called
Independence should be any more or less independent than
anywhere else but even so, there was something kind of right
about it as an idea.

If we could get to Independence tonight, we could take a
look round it in the morning and *then* we could start heading
east. It might be fun. It was certainly in the spirit of our adventure. I couldn't think of a good reason not to do it.

Just in case Stef *could* think of a good reason not to do it, I
decided not to tell her. I thought it would be a nice surprise.

There was no fooling Stef.

'Dave?'

'Yeah?'

'I do know that we're not going east, y'know.'

It was dark now and the road, just one lane in either direction, was unlit. An enormous convoy of 15 huge trucks, nose to
tail, with barely a second's gap between them, whooshed past
us going the other way, shaking the car violently and reminding
me that I really did need to stay awake.

'You've noticed then?'

'It's bloody obvious,' said Stef. 'I-15 goes off that way,' she
gestured somewhere off into the darkness behind us and to the
right. 'You're heading west, aren't you?'

'Um…' I considered lying. There was no point. 'Yes.'

'Why?'

'Okay… I know it sounds a bit cheesy… but we're not far from a town called Independence. I thought we could stay there tonight and then see how independent Independence is in the morning. What d'y'reckon?'

'Nice,' said Stef with an appreciative nod. And then more cautiously, 'Do you think we should call London? Tell Andy we're changing the plan?'

'Nah, if we do that, he'll only tell us not to,' I said. 'Remember, we're not making this trip in order to make a film, we're making a film about a trip that was happening anyway. And if it was just me, I'd be heading to Independence.'

Which is why, on day one of our travels, we were already heading in the wrong direction.

We didn't get to Independence that day. That thumb and a bit of map turned out to be rather longer than I'd imagined. One day, when I'm in charge, I'll enact a law that will make all maps operate on a 1:1 scale. We'll all have to get very good at folding but at least this sort of mistake will be avoided.

As it goes, a thumb and a bit of this particular map added up to roughly 150 miles. On an unlit, two-lane highway with a lot of trucks heading in both directions we were lucky if we were averaging 50mph and I simply didn't have another three hours of driving in me.

After a couple of hours of staring hypnotically at the dim yellow triangle of light cast by our primitive headlamps I was propping my eyelids open with matchsticks and starting to worry. We hadn't seen a hotel in ages.

Then all of a sudden there were lights up ahead. Lots of them. We'd reached a town called Lone Pine and the main drag was decorated with sign after sign advertising motel after motel. After driving through so much black void this strange little festival of neon seemed out of character with the surrounding area. It was as if someone had plucked a tiny stretch of the Las

Vegas strip out of the ground and then dropped it in the middle of nowhere.

Independence was only 12 miles away but the promise of a bed for the night was just too tempting. We'd driven through three other towns without seeing anywhere to stay so there was no reason to assume Independence would be any different. Besides, we wanted to see the place by daylight so there was no reason why we shouldn't seize the opportunity to sleep now and then make the 10-minute drive first thing in the morning.

We did stay in Lone Pine that night but we didn't drive to Independence first thing the next morning.

Lone Pine sits at the foot of Mount Whitney, the tallest mountain in the whole of the mainland United States. In the pitch black of night we'd been oblivious to the mountain's presence, only the procession of brightly lit motels had been visible. In the morning it was as if a curtain had been lifted to reveal the most spectacular and theatrical of sets.

It certainly explained quite why so much accommodation was available in this otherwise unremarkable location; who wouldn't want to look at something as beautiful as Mount Whitney? There can't be many people who have checked into a hotel here without being aware of its presence. It seemed ridiculous that something so large had gone unnoticed the night before, even if it was pitch black. How do you hide 14,505 feet of mountain? Simple, you just turn the lights out.

Our hotel, the Dow Villa ('family owned and operated since 1957', thank you very much) was decorated with hundreds of photos depicting scenes and characters from westerns. Wherever you looked a gnarly faced actor-cum-cowboy looked back at you in black and white. I can't say I recognised most of them but while they possessed rugged, lived in, cowpoke faces it was obvious they were only screen cowboys because they all had perfect teeth. Most prevalent amongst them – and the only one I recognised – was John Wayne, indeed in one particular stretch of corridor it felt less like a hotel and more like a shrine to The Duke and his oeuvre.

I had assumed that our hotelier was just a big fan of the genre but as I strolled along the high street it became clear that this cowboy fixation wasn't the sole preserve of the Dow Villa. The whole town seemed to be cowboy crazy. Reading a sign in a shop window I soon discovered why.

In the 1920s Hollywood discovered Lone Pine and TV shows and movies have been filmed there ever since. Snow-capped peaks, desolate deserts, mountain lakes and rocky streams... Lone Pine has them all which means it can pass for the plains of Mexico, the South American Andes or any Wild West location you care to mention and all within a manageable distance of the movie industry's LA base. The photos that lined the walls of the Dow weren't just random pictures; they came from movies shot in Lone Pine itself and depicted the many stars who'd stayed there.

Once upon a time the big studios were churning westerns out on a virtual conveyor belt and it was clear that Lone Pine had blossomed at the same time. Nowadays the appetite for chaps in chaps has diminished and consequently the place looks a little tattier around the edges but every now and then a TV commercial or mini-drama still rolls into town. When you look at the landscape you can understand why. I only had to wander two or three blocks from the main drag and I immediately felt like a truly gritty *True Grit* bit part player.

Visiting Lone Pine and not taking a closer look at Mount Whitney seemed a little absurd and there was a road that wound its way around the mountain at least part of the way. But as Stef and I discussed it over breakfast I still wasn't convinced that we should do it.

'The thing is,' I explained, 'we're obviously going to use petrol going up and down a mountain. If we do that and then end up running out a couple of miles shy of an independent gas station we'll have failed and it won't be because there aren't enough Mom and Pop stores out there, it will be because we wanted to look at a mountain.'

Stef stared at me incredulously, obviously trying to work out if I was serious or not. Behind my shoulder the imposing glory of Mount Whitney looked on.

'Come on Dave,' said Stef with a withering shake of the head, 'it's the tallest mountain in America...'

'Only the contiguous states...'

'The what?'

'The 48 states that are, y'know, joined up...' I said with perhaps annoying pedantry. 'Y'know, not including Alaska or Hawaii.'

'Right. So unless I've misunderstood your definition of coast-to-coast this is the tallest mountain it's possible for us to see on this journey, and you're seriously considering not going to have a closer look?'

'Well...'

'What's the point in driving across America if we don't stop to look at things?'

'Well...'

At which point a gingham-shirted waitress sealed the deal.

'Honey,' she said as she refilled my cup of morning coffee, 'you simply have to take yo' lady up the portal.'

I sniggered as a dozen smutty punchlines suggested them- selves. This time it was Stef's turn to explain that we weren't actually a couple. The waitress ignored us both.

'But Whitney Portal is only a 10-minute drive up the moun- tain and it sho' is beautiful...'

It was fantastic up there. The drive was full of 'wow's and 'cor's and 'would you look at that's as we took in the changing scenery. The desert sand gave way to bulbous clusters of rock that had an almost liquid sheen. We traced the path of a now dry creek and marvelled at the tenacity of the scrawny trees that were somehow clinging on to its arid banks.

The road started to creep up, the incline getting steeper and steeper, the Torino's automatic gearbox comfortably taking the change in its stride. Behind us Lone Pine already looked tiny; like a toy town that had been played with a bit too often and lost a few pieces behind the sofa.

Where the side of the mountain had weathered away it revealed a many-layered cross section. Each strip of differently hued earth and rock; once the earth's shell, now just calling cards from eons ago, once horizontal, now thrown almost vertical by whatever violent, tectonic clash it was that had forced this mountain up out of the ground in the first place.

The sun was still bright but the air was growing cooler. And thinner. We started passing through the shadows cast by strong pine trees and somewhere a trickle of melted snow water could be heard but not seen.

Of course the road only takes you so far and only serious climbers get to truly conquer a mountain like this. We were content to stand and stare. We pulled into a small parking area and stretched our legs. A sign warned us not to leave food in the car in case the smell proved to be irresistible to bears. We had some English tea bags buried deep in the trunk but the only food was a jar of the peculiarly British delicacy: Marmite. Even if the scent of it did reach ursine nostrils I couldn't imagine the salty yeast extract appealing to an all-American bear. Bears like jam sandwiches. I've seen that in cartoons. Marmite? I doubt it.

While the car had made the climb with ease our troubles started when we made our way down.

'Dave?'

'Yeah?'

'What's that smell?'

It was a smell that instantly summoned a childhood memory of running a *Scalextric* car for too long causing the copper elements to overheat. Adding to the sense that all was not well there was a small but steady trickle of smoke bubbling out from under our bonnet.

'I'll pull over.'

I lifted the hood – so much more glamorous than opening the bonnet – and recoiled as the trickle of smoke became a plume of poisonous air; the acrid smell of hot metal watering my eyes.

I have absolutely no mechanical know-how whatsoever but I've seen mechanics at work and so I did my best to do what I thought was appropriate in the situation. Firstly, I walked a full circle around the car while biting my lower lip. Then I stood and I scratched my head while sucking air through my teeth. Then finally, I lowered myself to the ground and examined the rust speckled wheel arch. A rust speckled wheel arch stared back at me.

'Nope,' I said with a shake of the head. 'No idea.'

'Have you been working the brakes a lot?'

'Um… yeah,' I confessed. The car was so powerful and left to its own devices it wanted to go far faster than was safe on the steep road with its tight twists and hairpin bends.

'I think you might have burnt the brakes out,' said Stef.

'Ah.'

'What do you think we should do?'

'Well the brakes haven't actually failed,' I said. 'They just *smell* funny. Every time I've put my foot on the pedal they've responded… so maybe we should just carry on.'

'Hmmm,' said Stef. It was a 'hmmm' that clearly meant 'You've got to be bloody well kidding if you think I'm getting back into that death trap, pal.'

'Or…'

'Go on…'

'Or we can try and call a local garage…'

Stef tossed me her mobile phone. I looked at the screen. No reception.

'Maybe I'll just film you driving off,' she suggested.

'That will leave you halfway up a mountain with no mobile phone reception,' I said. 'You won't know if I'm coming back to get you or dead in a ditch.'

'True,' she said. 'But at least I won't be dead in a ditch.'

There was a pause. Stef sighed. Staying there really wasn't an option.

If you're a fan of rollercoasters I can heartily recommend driving down a very tall mountain with brakes that might or might not be working. It's exciting in an oh-my-God-I-think-I'm-going-to-die kind of way.

Whenever the road was straight I would leave the brakes alone and with the powerful engine pushing and gravity pulling our huge bulk we would gather speed at an alarming rate. Then, as late as I dared, I would go for the pedal and hope that the brakes would react.

All the while I did my best to hide my fear and present myself as calm, collected and in charge. Stef was displaying more than enough nerves for the two of us. While she constantly urged me not to overuse the brakes, every time our pace picked up her own right foot would instinctively move towards the non-existent brake pedal that all anxious passengers seem to imagine sits in their footwell.

Luckily the real brakes did what the sweaty palmed driver told them to, albeit in their own smoky, smelly way, and we soon found ourselves parked outside Lindsey Automotive. Two mechanics ambled towards us.

I explained our predicament.

'Yup, sounds like you've glazed yo' pads,' said the more whiskery of the two men. The teeth he was missing added the odd surprising whistle to his voice.

'It happens a lot coming down the mountain,' added his colleague, a man with less facial hair but a full set of gnashers. 'I've seen cars come off that road with no brakes before now. Believe me, you don't wanna do that. There's a lot of rocks to hit back there. You got more chance o' hittin' a rock than not. It's all rocks out there.'

'You shoulda used a lower gear,' added Whiskers, 'you can't jus' ride the brakes the whole way down.'

'Right,' I said. 'A lower gear.'

I started to blush with the uncomfortable realisation that this was my fault. I'm embarrassed to say it but the simple truth is I had no idea lower gears were even available to me.

Almost all of my driving has been in cars with stick-shift gears. The first time I'd driven an automatic was in a rental car on a trip to the States some years earlier. I remember sitting on the car company's forecourt, staring in bafflement at the gearstick, trying to work out what it all meant. The labelling – PRNDL – made it look like some vowel-less text message that my old-fashioned brain couldn't decode. On seeing my confusion the hire-car rep had given me the most basic of instructions, saying, 'R is for reverse, N for neutral, and D for drive. Ignore everything else.'

So that's what I'd done and because these words of wisdom had seen me through so many hours of trouble-free Stateside driving it had never occurred to me that the P (park) or L (low) might actually come in handy one day. I'd simply – very simply – done as I was told: I'd ignored everything else.

As it was our Torino didn't have an L. Instead it had a 1 and a 2. Which means it actually offered the luxury of not one but two lower gears. Gears that a sensible driver might want to engage if they were, ooh, I don't know, just as an example let's say, driving a powerful V8 engine down the side of a very tall mountain.

When it came to it my brain hadn't even acknowledged such options existed. As far as I was concerned the only options available to me had been R, N and D. As we careened down Mount Whitney I just did what I knew how to do. We weren't going backwards so I wasn't in Reverse. We weren't in Switzerland so I wasn't in Neutral. We *were* going forwards, so I *was* in Drive.

Standing outside the garage I processed the information that I was responsible for our predicament and started to squirm because it obviously left me with no way of holding my own in our conversation with these two mechanics.

It's not like I was going to be able to pass myself off as an engine-savvy man of the world when it was obvious to everyone that I didn't understand all of the options available on my own gearstick. For the second time in two days I threw myself on the mercy of the mechanically minded.

'So... is it something you can fix?' I asked.

'Uh huh,' said Mr All-His-Teeth, with a nonchalant we-can-fix-anything shrug, 'but you'll have to bring it back tomorra mornin'. It's too late today.'

'Really?' I asked, taking an anxious glance at my watch.

'It must be about beer o'clock,' said Whiskers. The chuckle he awarded his own joke soon turned into a full-blown laugh before morphing into an uproarious, painful cough.

We'd obviously been up the mountain for much longer than I'd thought. I'm sure it wasn't long after coffee o'clock when we'd set off.

We didn't have much choice. Our car was going to spend another night in Lone Pine and so were we.

'Come on, Dave,' said Stef, 'let's go and check back in... then let's go and get something to eat.'

'Is it mashed potato o'clock?' I asked.

'Yeah.'

'Well we'd better get going then,' I said with a shrug, 'but keep your eye on the time because I'll need to be in a bar by rum-30.'

Chapter 8
Better get some jerry cans

When it came to settling our bill at Lindsey Automotive there was no need to ask who was in charge. Sonny was the master of his domain and he absolutely looked the part. He had a slow and capable demeanour but his crisp white shirt told you that he wasn't likely to spend much time fiddling with greasy engines. His pristine appearance – perfectly pressed shirt, neatly trimmed moustache and tinted spectacles – were in stark contrast to his cluttered office, which was full of Betty Boop memorabilia, car parts, yellowing paperwork and photos of the local high school's female basketball team that he evidently coached. He reminded me of an officer in the English military, maintaining his own standards despite the chaos of the war going on around him. Where I expected to see campaign medals pinned to his chest I instead saw his name embroidered on his shirt, while on his upper arm was the American flag.

Like everyone else we met he assumed Stef and I were a couple. I don't think it was because we looked particularly coupley, I think Sonny just found it easier to imagine Stef was there as my wife than it was to contemplate a woman having a job. I don't remember asking him for any advice of the non-automotive variety but I do remember receiving it and it soon became apparent that Sonny was a man full of down-home wisdom, soundbites and an almost endearing, old-fashioned I-love-women brand of sexism.

'I love my wife,' he said with a smile, 'but a marriage is like a bad job. Sometimes you don't want it but you can't quit because you need it.'

'Right,' I said with a polite nod. It wasn't going to make it into many Valentine's Day cards but I suppose it did have a certain practical sense to it.

'When we're driving along,' he continued, warming to his theme, 'I'll be thinking, "I could use some ice cream" and then she'll say, "why don't we get some ice cream?" Or I'm thinking, "I'd like some Mexican food" and the next thing is she says, "why don't we get Mexican food?" You see, eventually the two of you become one.'

'Right,' I said again.

I suppose it is kind of sweet that a couple can become psychically aware of each other's foody desires.

'We were made different for a reason,' said Sonny, an opening clause to a sentence that's always going to set off my liberal alarm bells. 'Think about it.' I did. 'I don't want to go home and find my partner has a beard, that's *disgusting*.'

Sonny sat back in his chair, his body language spelling out a satisfied QED. He clearly felt his point had been made but actually he'd just confused me with what seemed to be a deft verbal body-swerve. I could have sworn that sentence had started out heading towards a women-aren't-built-to-go-to-work conclusion but somehow it had suddenly veered into same-sex-relationships-are-disgusting instead.

'Well, it's not really disgusting, is it? I mean, it doesn't ring my bell, but each to their own.'

That's what I *wanted* to say. Instead, I said nothing. I didn't want to get into an argument with anyone – especially with a man who hadn't yet written out our bill. Besides, while I disagreed with Sonny, I still *wanted* to like him. So, with nothing to say, I instead found myself returning Sonny's gaze with what I hoped was a neutral expression that would neither counter nor endorse his world view.

But, just as I had the car in the wrong gear the day before, so I had my face in the wrong gear then and Sonny clearly thought I needed further persuasion.

'Just *think* about it,' he insisted. 'That's *disgusting*. Isn't it? Think about it.'

I did my best impression of a man who was thinking about it and then I decided to change the subject. We'd already explained the particular nature of our journey and so I steered the conversation back that way.

'So,' I started, 'what do you think our chances are of going across the country, filling up the car, not running out of fuel and only visiting independent gas stations... Do you think it can be done?'

Sonny gave the question some thought. His head shook slowly while he weighed up the pros and cons. After a moment or two's consideration he dispensed his verdict.

'No.'

'I think we'll have to hit some real small towns to find them,' I said. I was fishing for information, hoping Sonny would back up my hunch by listing a couple of nearby small towns in which unbranded gas stations were still surviving. It didn't happen.

'You'd better get some jerry cans,' he said, 'and put some gas in 'em.'

It wasn't really what I wanted to hear.

For the second time in three days a garage had kept us on the road then presented us with a surprisingly reasonable bill. Maybe it just looked cheap because of the exceedingly friendly exchange rate that meant we were getting a lot of dollar for our pound or maybe US mechanics really are more reasonable than their UK counterparts. Or maybe we just got lucky with the two we'd visited. Then again, maybe all mechanics would charge less if they knew the transaction was being filmed. Perhaps I'm being too cynical? Probably.

It obviously wasn't ideal having to have the car fixed every other day but, while it was slowing us down, at least it was providing us with a regular ego-boost in the form of car-appreciation. There was no getting away from the fact that the

Torino turned heads, and when the heads in question belonged to people who dealt with cars for a living it definitely made me feel good about our choice of motor. Mechanics just seemed to swoon in her presence and as a rule the oilier a man's hands, the more effusive his praise would be.

Clean-fingered Sonny was complimentary – 'That's a real nice dinosaur you're driving' – but our grease monkey, Mr Whiskers, was positively gushing – 'Man, that's a beautiful, beautiful car' – and even left a note on the dashboard offering to buy her from us when our journey was complete. That never happened when I put my old Vauxhall Corsa in for a service.

'You don't want to get a jerry can, do you?' asked Stef as we trundled away.

'Nah,' I said. 'I think that's sort of... cheating. Anyone could drive anywhere if they carry their own fuel, that wouldn't prove anything.'

'Yeah, but what if...'

'No,' I said and then, with a motivational, let's-go, clap of the hands, 'now come on, it's 12 miles to Independence, we've got newly cleaned and repacked brake pads, a jar of Marmite, a thousand English teabags, a quarter tank of gas, it's sunny and I'm wearing sunglasses... let's go.'

Fifteen minutes later and we got to Independence.

Sixteen minutes later and we had left Independence.

In fact driving through Independence took less than a minute.

'Population of Independence: 574,' I said, reading the information from the sign that welcomed us to the town, 'There's a Shell gas station,' I continued, 'a Chevron station... and I think we're now leaving Independence.'

Read that sentence back to yourself. That's how long it took to drive through Independence. There were two gas stations. Neither of which we could use. Arse.

'Was that it?' asked Stef. 'Have we come on a detour for... for... for *that?*'

'It was a bit disappointing, wasn't it?'

I felt like a six-year-old kid who'd just unwrapped a

Christmas present to discover it was nowhere near as exciting in real life as it had looked in the catalogue.

'What do we do? D'you wanna go back?' asked Stef.

'What, for another 30 seconds of Independence?' I snapped, angry at myself for bringing us here.

It was my stupid idea to take a detour to Independence in the first place. We'd taken this detour because of me. And what had it brought us? Well, combined with my incompetent driving, just some burnt-out brakes, another day of going nowhere and a repair bill.

'So what are we going to do?' asked Stef. 'I mean, we're heading north now and for no reason?'

'Hang on,' I said, 'let's park up, take a look at the map and work out the best way of getting back on track.'

With the 'Welcome to Independence' sign still visible behind us, I unfolded our map on the dashboard. In that small space, folding the map down to a manageable section was a bit of a struggle but as I did so I found a place name leaping out at me.

'Tch, that's odd,' I said.

'What's that?' asked Stef.

'The first thing I see when I try to sort out this map is another town called Independence.'

'Really?' shrugged Stef, 'is it east of here?'

'No,' I said, still struggling to arrange the map in a way that showed us exactly where 'here' was. 'It's in Oregon. That's north, isn't it?'

There was a pause while we both had the same thought.

'You know how we're heading north at the minute...?'

'No,' said Stef, firmly.

'I'm just saying that we could keep going north if we wanted to... y'know... to Independence...'

'It's in Oregon, Dave... it'll mean going hundreds of miles out of our way...'

'It can't be *that* far,' I said, folding, unfolding and then folding the map again so as to leave both Independi in view. 'I'd say it's about... ooh... say, a forearm worth.'

Oh dear. Was it really that simple? Somehow, because our original 160-mile diversion had proved unsatisfactory I'd managed to persuade Stef that we should launch into a second diversion. And this one was going to prove somewhat larger. Because that forearm worth of map was equivalent to roughly 600 miles of America. That's as the crow flies. As the motorist drives it's more like 780 miles. But as this idiot drives it would be more like 1,100 miles. This time we knew full well that we weren't going to do it in one day. We weren't expecting it to take us the best part of a week.

Our next fuel stop came in the town of Bishop, roughly 40 miles north of Independence. Just as well because the fuel gauge was saying empty. I knew from our Hinkley experience that the gauge wasn't exactly accurate and simple arithmetic told me that we must have had plenty of juice in the old girl yet but even so, when you look at the dash and see your car telling you she's empty it's impossible not to be just a little nervous.

Salvation came in the form of the Paiute Palace, a Native American casino with its own unbranded gas station attached.

'Is a casino not a bit too... y'know, corporate?' asked Stef as I filled the tank.

I shrugged. 'It's not part of a chain, is it? It's a one-off. We're not going to find another Paiute Palace Gas Station anywhere in the world. And besides, the Paiute people were Mom and Pop long before Mom and Pop came here.'

Hinkley Mileage:	122,278
Bishop Mileage:	122,517
Total mileage:	239
Gasoline used:	16.57 gallons
Miles per gallon:	14.42

Getting less than 15mpg was a bit of a disappointment but then she had spent a lot of time ticking over, burning fuel and going nowhere, at Lindsey's. In general terms I thought it more good news. The car had told us she was empty and yet we'd only had to add 16 and a half gallons. That meant that a reassuring five and a half gallons had still been sloshing around in the tank and that was worth about 80 miles.

As we left Bishop we were faced with a choice of routes. We could stay on I-395 or take Highway 6, both of which were effectively heading north. We chose Highway 6 because it seemed smaller.

We knew that on smaller roads we would see fewer businesses but our hope was that more of those we did see would be independent. If the multinational chains flock to the expensive pockets of land that sit besides the interstate then we hoped they had left the roads less travelled alone.

It was a theory that seemed to hold water as 37 miles later we came across another independent: the Benton Gas Station.

It felt ridiculous stopping to add less than three gallons of gas and it felt even more so when the girl behind the counter found herself unable to ask me for the $6.51 without sniggering at the tiny transaction but I knew I was doing the right thing. After all, this was what Obi Grant Kenobi had recommended. I was using Destroyer tactics.

Bishop Mileage:	122,517
Benton Mileage:	122,554
Total mileage:	37
Gasoline used:	2.24 gallons
Miles per gallon:	16.52

As we'd travelled north through California the towns had grown further apart and less populated but as Highway 6 carried us into Nevada this was taken to a new extreme. With volcanic rock surrounding us the land took on an almost alien aspect. It felt like we were driving on the moon one minute and then, as we came over the crest of a peak, it would transform instantly into Mars. There was a real joy in looking out at such a magical – and almost untouched – landscape where the only evidence of mankind's presence was the road itself.

For every hundred miles we drove we would pass only four or five cars. Every now and then we'd see a weather-beaten trailer-home sitting in some desolate spot a hundred yards or so from the road, perhaps being kept company by some beaten-up pick-up truck or other. Who lived in these places? Where did they buy a loaf of bread and a pint of milk? Where did their children go to school? What did they do for a living?

We passed into what had once been mining country. Minerals, gemstones, coal, gold and silver had all been carved out from beneath this most unpromising of surfaces. We started to see remnants of that time in the shape of abandoned pits; black-hole gateways to subterranean hells, each propped up with bent and twisted wooden frames.

It was easy to imagine the lawless world that surrounded such unforgiving work. Where men had risked their lives mining, others had followed to mine the miner's pockets not with picks but with gambling, alcohol and prostitution. These days the three vices remain; all are legally available 24 hours a day in parts of Nevada but the mines are dead[2].

Now that the mining is no more some of the towns have disappeared completely while others, like Mina and the even more ghostly Luning, limp on. The population of Luning was less than 80. The town has two businesses. Both brothels.

Our route through Nevada was dictated by the paucity of options. There were times when we would stare down a long straight road and know there were no turnings for 70 miles. If only all of life was so simple. And beautiful too.

Those roads provided breathtaking views. There's something special about an empty road going on and on and on to the horizon where the sun burns the world away into a dancing, shimmering heat haze that reflects the crystal blue sky, literally blurring the line between heaven and earth.

But more intense than the visual spectacle is the tingling sense of disconnection that comes with it. I don't think I've ever felt so *other*.

---

[2] It is however illegal to drive a camel on Nevada's highway... I suppose you have to ban *something*.

For so much of the time, there was nothing through the windscreen that was identifiable either as America or 2006. When so little that surrounds you defines where or when you are then the only thing you know for certain is *who* you are and you feel it in every pore of your being.

'Has your phone got any reception?' asked Stef, her words nudging into my self-indulgent, wallowing thoughts. It seemed an odd question.

I looked down at my phone and was genuinely hoping that the answer was no. I didn't want to be connected to the world. My head was swimming with the joy of being so unconnected. Nothing. Good.

'No,' I said with a smile.

'So what happens if we break down? What happens if we run out of gas in the middle of the bloody desert?'

'You see, this is where you and I differ, Stef,' I said, 'I *like* the fact that we're on our own. I like the fact that this is so anywhere *and* nowhere. This is exciting. I'm feeling really alive but you're more... '

'... worried about dying?'

'Yeah.'

'You're right,' she nodded, 'but I think one of us should be. I mean worrying about dying is one of the things that stops it from happening. It's not as if this car has proven itself to be especially reliable.'

Which, I suppose, is fair enough.

'Fair enough,' I sulked.

Now you might think you've got the measure of things by now. You might be thinking the only reason it took four weeks for me to reach that Best Western hotel room in Moab, Utah is that I kept taking us on ever more ludicrous detours. You'd be wrong. That wasn't the only reason.

There were three of us on this journey – Stef, the car and me – and in our own ways we each have to shoulder some of the responsibility.

Chapter 9

That's the thing with zombies

I'm pleased to say that throughout our Nevada run the car didn't misbehave. We didn't break down and we didn't run out in the middle of the bloody desert. We didn't even come close.

It seems the small towns of Nevada are blessed with a plentiful supply of unbranded, independent gas stations. We filled up whenever the opportunity presented itself and never had to add more than 10 gallons to do so.

So many people had written off our chances of success. When I'd discussed this trip in advance my friends – Brits and Americans alike – had all said the same thing: that it wasn't possible, that there simply were no independent gas stations left. Nevada showed me they were wrong. Nevada showed me that unchained America did exist. The doubts that had occupied my mind before this journey began slowly started to wither in the desert sun and by the time we left the silver state I found I had 100 per cent confidence that our unchained ambitions might actually be achievable.

7.27 gal

5.19 gal

9.41 gal

6.85 gal

I was having a high old time. I loved driving the car through such classic road-trip territory and with unbranded fuel in the car and more seemingly just around the corner there was nothing to tarnish the experience. Unfortunately, the same could not be said for Stef.

While I was enjoying the scenery Stef was charged with the task of filming it... *and* filming me enjoying it. It was proving to be a more demanding task than either of us imagined. It certainly involved much more than just putting the camera to her shoulder and pointing it through the windscreen.

In a big room you can get a wider shot by simply backing away from your subject. In a confined space like, say, the cab of a car, it's not so easy. Stef was constantly twisting and turning in her attempts to find the angle she needed. She spent some of the time leaning forwards, holding the camera low down in the foot well and angling it up towards me. At other times she was leaning back and holding the camera awkwardly behind herself in order to capture both me and the road ahead. All of the time it turned out she was damaging her back. Badly.

Stef had spent most of her working life lugging heavy cameras about without any trouble. Admitting she was having a problem now wasn't easy for her, as much as anything because I don't think she wanted to admit it to herself. For a day she suffered in silence but by the time we checked into the first of our Nevadan motels it became obvious that she was in real agony and she was forced to come clean. Mind you, it was good timing on her part. The film equipment we carried with us was expensive and so we had a policy of always emptying the car each night. Stef's back being out of whack meant the job of humping all our cases indoors was left to me.

It wasn't the kind of bad back that felt better in the morning. It was the kind of bad back that got worse by the day. It was the kind of bad back that got worse when it was used, but also when it wasn't. Not only did holding the heavy camera in awkward positions exacerbate the problem, so did sitting in the same position for too long.

This meant it was impossible for us to do long days in the car and we were forced to break our journey down into smaller steps. The situation grew steadily worse and by the time we got into Oregon and the small town of Lakeview it was obvious that Stef was in real trouble. We had Mexican food that night and while the margaritas were sublime, mashed potato was not forthcoming. Stef was losing her powers. She was in desperate need of a break.

I suppose we could have taken a day off in Lakeview but while the place was pleasant enough it wasn't offering us sufficient distraction. Its proud boast is that it's the 'Tallest Town in Oregon' and it's not as though its 'tallness' was something we could go and have a look at.

What the 'Tallest Town' status means is that Lakeview – which sits at 4,800 feet above sea level – is at a higher altitude than any other town in Oregon. It didn't seem like a particularly impressive fact to begin with but when the owner of the gift shop where I bought a Lakeview fridge magnet told me that it was actually the *only* town in Oregon it became even less so.

Surely as the only town in Oregon they could claim any townly virtue they wanted. It's not just the tallest but also the shortest, widest, thinnest, biggest, smallest, smartest and most charitable town in all of Oregon... all of which is entirely meaningless. I might as well describe myself as this book's best-looking author.

Incidentally, I did ask the fridge-magnet saleswoman how it was possible for Lakeview to be the only town in Oregon and apparently it's because everywhere else that you or I might call a town is technically a city.

In Britain the term 'city' implies a certain size and importance; in America it seems as though any three huts in a row can call themselves a city if they so desire. If you don't believe me try looking up the city of Greenhorn, Oregon. It occupies 0.1 square miles and comprises only seven homesteads. Which is at least five more than it needs because according to a 2006 study it has an estimated population of just two people. At time of writing the mayor of Greenhorn is Frances Villwock. One can only imagine the hard-fought election campaign. Oh, by the way, at an altitude of 6,300 feet, the *city* of Greenhorn (pop 2) is a good 1,500 feet 'taller' than the *town* of Lakeview (pop 2,655).

No, there was no reason to hang around in Lakeview. But there was every reason to get going: we had a reservation for a two-person treehouse at the Out 'n' About Treehouse Resort in Takilma.

I'd booked the treehouse online the night before during a dangerous margarita-fuelled session. Now I don't recommend browsing the internet when drunk – trust me, I speak as a man who once bought a hot-air balloon on eBay – but on this occasion I reckon things worked out well. In fact, it would have been wrong of me not to spend some time online that night because it meant I experienced my most Robin Hood moment of the trip so far.

Our independent motel was standing cheek by jowl with the multinational chain hotel next door. Guests at the chain hotel were treated to free wireless Internet access as part of their package and because my room was close enough to the chain, so was I. Oh yeah... I wasn't just eschewing the chains, now I was stealing things from them. Albeit invisible, intangible things that nobody would ever miss. Tough luck, The Man™, I stole your megabytes and I ain't givin' 'em back. Power to the people.

Anyway, drunk as I was I managed to avoid making any fool-hardy purchases and instead used my time online to search out what I thought would be an interesting south-Oregon bolthole. After all, it was obvious that Stef needed a day off and I figured that if we were going to spend a day going nowhere we owed it to ourselves to find an interesting place to do it. The treehouse resort looked perfect.

Independent gas wasn't easy to find in Lakeview but thanks to a tip-off from the fridge-magnet lady we made a visit to the local RV park and were able to leave the town with a full tank.

That should have given us the confidence to just enjoy the start of the journey. The scenery – rolling green fields dotted here and there with deep red claret-coloured barns with Dutch bonnet roofs – was certainly beautiful but nevertheless the mood in the car was tainted.

Stef was unable to wield the camera and somehow seeing such beautiful, picture-postcard views drift by unrecorded added a sense of subdued, impotent rage to her physical discomfort. It was frustrating for me too. Every time we turned a corner and a new and surprising view prompted me to gasp an appreciative 'ooh', 'ah' or 'wow' I'd feel guilty for bringing the vista to Stef's attention. Why couldn't the scenery just be boring? Why did it scream to be filmed? Why did it have to taunt us with its beauty?

We slipped around and through the city of Klamath Falls and then motored on, skirting round the edge of Upper Klamath Lake with the sun bouncing off the water on our right and a forest of pine trees consuming the mountain to our left.

We filled up again at the Odessa Store – a tiny gas station in a woodland copse – and then continued on up and over the Cascade Mountains, putting my foot down to push us up the hills but having to hold the car back – and use a lower gear – on the way down.

In the thick of winter these mountain roads would be treacherous, perhaps unpassable. Laybys were set aside especially so that motorists could stop and put chains on their tyres for extra grip and there were signs warning us of potential road closures in the winter months. Luckily for us, this was a crisp, clear day and while the sun was fading fast there was still enough to kill the chill.

At Medford we had no choice but to join the interstate for a quick burst. Suddenly we weren't just travelling, we were time travelling. Back to the future.

When your view of the world is framed by a 1970s windscreen it starts to feel like you're living in a 1970s world. Lakes, pine trees and vintage gas pumps only serve to reinforce the illusion but joining a throng of cars on a busy interstate brought us back up to speed with a bump. Suddenly, the Torino's great,

great grandchildren were swarming around us, jostling for space, showing off their modern curves and reminding us that this was the real here and now.

There was more evidence of the twenty-first century when we exited at Grants Pass. The sky was black now but the town's proximity to I-5 meant it was lit up with all the usual signs as every fast food joint and motel chain competed for the weary motorist's dollar.

It's a scene that would have appeared normal only a week earlier but now – having avoided such sights on our back roads route from small town to small town – it looked uglier than ever before. In this forest of neon it felt like the world was screaming at me and I'd got used to one that only whispered. We stopped at an Arco gas station – not to fill up the car but to empty our bladders.

This was Robin Hood moment number two. They weren't going to have our money but they could flush away our piss. Take that, The Man™. That's direct action. We were freedom fighters! Go us!

'Are you sure you know where we're going?' asked Stef as we rolled slowly down a tiny, unlit, tree-lined lane.

'Not really,' I confessed.

Grant's Pass was far behind us now. So was the sleepy town – sorry, city – of Cave Junction. If I'd followed the directions correctly we should have been in Takilma but I had no way of verifying that as Takilma didn't actually appear on any of our maps and it didn't seem to have any buildings, landmarks or borders. Takilma didn't feel like a place so much as a state of mind.

Every road we turned into seemed narrower than the last and our dim headlights gave us very little warning of the twists and turns ahead. We hadn't seen any sign of life for the last 20 minutes but on roads this narrow and this dark we turned each corner cautiously just in case we found something coming towards us.

'Holy shit!'

Something was coming towards us. It wasn't any old something either. It was a zombie on a bicycle. Yes, you read that right. A zombie. On a bicycle.

His clothes were trailing behind him in a ragged, tattered, dirty brown mess, he had sunken cheeks, a deathly pallor to his skin and a look of fear in his red-ringed eyes. That's the thing with zombies – they're more scared of you than you are of them. Especially when their bicycle is heading towards your car.

'Holy shit!'

I yanked the steering wheel violently to the right and we headed into the verge, the tyres scrunching and mulching the gravel and leaves they found beyond the tarmac. The zombie steered the other way and we missed each other by a few feet; the living dead luckily avoiding becoming the dead dead.

The car was still. In my mirror I could see the cyclist was unharmed. All around us there was nothing but an eerie silence. Fear heightens the senses and I felt my heart pumping and my muscles tense. What for? Was I about to engage in a road-rage fight with a zombie? He didn't approach the car. He didn't even look our way. He just stayed where he was and stared into the darkness ahead of him.

'Is he all right?' I asked.

'God knows,' said Stef, wincing as she twisted her back to get out of the car.

I turned the engine off and followed, staying three or four yards behind.

Stef called out to him.

'Are you okay?'

The zombie turned slowly. As his eyes found us, he looked utterly startled as if the last thing he expected to see was a person. It was as if he'd already forgotten our near miss. There was a long pause while he processed the question.

'I'm good,' he said eventually, fixing us with a wide-eyed, deathly stare.

This was probably the most convincing zombie I'd ever seen. Yes, he was wearing a costume and make-up but this outfit hadn't been thrown together at the last minute. I stared through the cosmetics and tried to work out his real features. I was pretty sure that even in the cold light of day there would be a zombiesque aspect to his face. It was all the more convincing because of his eerie calm and spaced-out demeanour. Either he had been to some method acting zombie school or he was on some serious drugs. Or he was a real zombie. Or maybe he was a real zombie who'd been to method acting zombie school *and* taken some serious drugs. He was that good.

'Are you going to the party?' he asked in his monotone drawl.

'What?' asked Stef.

'At the school,' he said. 'The Halloween party. It's the biggest night of the year. Come along to the party.'

Halloween. Of course. It was the Saturday before the day itself and so obviously a good day for a party, and in the States, they do love a Halloween party. In Britain, Halloween is seen as something for the kids. I think most adults spend the evening at home worrying about the local ne'er-do-wells who are too old for trick or treating but meatheaded enough to put fireworks through your letterbox. In the States however *everyone* celebrates Halloween with gusto.

'Look, we just wanted to see that you were okay,' said Stef but her concern was met with another vacant stare.

'Actually we might be lost,' I said – if we couldn't help him we might as well see if he could help us – 'we're trying to find the Out 'n' About Treehouse place?'

'You just go down here...' he said, pointing back down the road in the direction we'd just come from. '... and take the second right.'

'For the treehouses?' asked Stef.

'No. The school.'

'We're *not* going to the party.'

'But it's the biggest night of the year.'

'No. We're not.' Stef sounded unusually stern. The zombie's face dropped like an eight-year-old who's just been told there's no more ice cream. 'Now, are we going the right way for the treehouses?'

'Yes,' he sulked. 'It's a left and then another left.'

We backed away slowly towards the car.

'See you at the party!'

Stef gave a withering shake of the head as the two of us watched him zombicycle away, round the corner and out of sight.

Unlikely as it may seem the zombie's directions proved to be correct and we were soon trundling down the bumpy farm track to our treehouse home for the night. We stepped outside and breathed in the still night air.

'Oh wow,' said Stef. 'Look at that!'

She was standing with her neck rolled back, staring straight up at the sky. I did the same.

'That. Is. Amazing!' I said. 'Wow. I mean... just wow!'

From any town or city you see the sky through a blanket of light-pollution but here, with near perfect darkness all around, the cloudless black sky looked blacker than ever before and every star twinkled with perfect clarity.

As my ears tuned in to what seemed to be silence I could make out the faint crackle of a wood fire and the hubbub of hushed conversation in the distance. It was the only clue we had as to which way to walk.

We stepped under the canopy of the trees and into even greater darkness. We trod gingerly through the grass, testing each step with a pad of the foot, feeling for roots and stones underfoot and anything else that might trip us. Then suddenly we found ourselves in a small clearing. At the centre was a roaring camp fire and sitting around it were seven or eight people, wrapped up warm, huddling together, palms out towards the flames, swapping stories in hushed whispers.

To our right was a large, regular family house with a notice board posted outside. A trail of fairy lights decorated a wooden walkway up to the front door. As my eyes adapted to the low light other details started to emerge. Up above us there was a network of rope bridges, looping between circular wooden platforms that hugged tall, sturdy trees. And in whichever direction I looked there were treehouses. Not just little platforms sitting in branches but proper timber houses, each one uniquely built to fit with the tree to which it clung.

They looked like gingerbread houses with eaves and shutters and other little architectural details, only in trees. It's what cartoonists always seem to imagine Tarzan living in, a jungle home decorated with quaint modern day suburban features. It was funny but not twee. Most of all it was beautiful. We'd stumbled into a magical fairy grotto.

We were too late to find any staff on site to check us in... but then when you're staying in a treehouse you don't really expect a reception that's staffed 24 hours a day. I knew there would be some instructions somewhere and that once we'd located our treehouse we'd be okay.

There was a diagram explaining the layout of the camp on the noticeboard, showing which treehouse was which and whether or not they were currently occupied. Reading by the light of my mobile phone I worked out which treehouse was ours and we set off through the woods again.

'This is amazing,' whispered Stef excitedly. 'They're like real houses!'

'I know,' I said, 'I can't wait to see what ours is like. You can have first dibs on choosing a room if you like... here we are.'

We climbed the wooden staircase, unlatched the door and stepped inside. The first thing that hit me was the smell. No need for a Glade plug-in here, the natural fresh scent of the wood was amazing. The second thing that hit me was the size of the place. It looked quite small from the outside. Of course, looks can be deceptive.

On the other hand they can be entirely accurate. This place was tiny.

'Oh dear,' I said as I took in the surroundings. It was one room, almost all of which was taken up by a double bed.

'Is this it?' asked Stef. 'One room! Good job you gave me first dibs then, isn't it? I'll take this one.'

'Oi.'

'Well, what else are we going to do?'

Around the side and base of the bed there was a little wiggle room but that was it. A stepladder went up to what was basically a shelf. The shelf turned the corner with the room forming an L shape, both lengths of which were furnished with a narrow strip of bedding. Fine for a child or two; not so fine for a grown up.

It was a room that was perfect for an adventurous mum and dad with a couple of kids who wanted to pretend they were the Swiss Family Robinson... but it was less than perfect for a couple of adults who were, well, not a couple.

I looked at Stef and she looked at me and then we both looked at the double bed. I hoped she wasn't thinking what I was thinking. Then I hoped she wasn't thinking, 'I hope he *is* thinking what I'm thinking.' Then it got worse. What if she was thinking, 'I'm not thinking what he's thinking and I really don't like the fact that he's thinking it!'?

My head was getting wrapped up in a Gordian knot of confusion as I constantly tried to second guess what Stef might or might not be thinking. Stef and I were getting on well but we were far from being lifelong buddies. We'd been thrown together for this project and that was the extent of it. We were already spending large parts of each day cooped up together in the confines of the car. With the best will in the world, neither of us wanted to spend our day off at close quarters – especially if it meant sharing a room.

But what if Stef thought I'd done this on purpose? I'd booked it after all. Would she think this was my clumsy attempt to try and get her into bed? Ai!

'Okay... um... first things first...' I said, 'I did *not* do this on purpose.'

'What?'

'This isn't some weird attempt to... you know...'

Words failed me. I desperately reached around trying to find a nice way of saying the thing I didn't want to say. And then I saw the penny drop behind Stef's eyes and a look of horror came across her face at the very idea.

'Oh God, no!' she said her hands flapping about in front of her face as if the idea was buzzing around in front of her and could be swatted like a fly. 'I didn't think you were doing that. Jeez. No! Ugh!'

'All right, all right,' I said slightly offended by the level of her revulsion. 'Neither of us was thinking *that*. That's good. But there's no need to be quite so down on the idea.' I paused. 'I mean, do be repulsed by the idea if you like, that's fine, but, but... but don't tell me about it.'

'You started it!'

'But I didn't want you to thi—'

'But I wasn't thinking ab—'

'Well, let's both stop thinking about it now and work out what we should do about this.'

There was a pause. We looked at each other and one thought landed in both our minds. We were English. There was only one thing we could do in this situation.

'Cuppa?' asked Stef.

'I'll get the tea bags,' I said, one foot already out the door.

We decided two things over our cup of tea. Firstly, that I was going to sleep on the child-sized shelf. Secondly, that this was a one-night-only situation. It didn't matter that I'd booked it for two or that we were due a day off, we weren't going to put up with this level of awkwardness for any longer than was strictly speaking necessary.

There then followed what was quite possibly the most uncomfortable lights-out routine I have ever experienced. It was physically uncomfortable because I was attempting to sleep on a narrow strip of timber some 10 feet from the ground and socially uncomfortable because no silence has ever been more squirm-inducingly awkward.

'Night then.'

'G'night.'

Silence. Too. Much. Silence.

'That was a strange day, wasn't it?'

'Yeah.'

'Long day too.'

'Yeah.'

'Anyway… sleep well.'

'You too.'

More silence. The self-conscious silence that occurs when people *try* not to make a sound. People don't normally sleep in silence. They breathe and *hmm*, they swallow and scratch. An intentional silence is so much more intense, so much more silent. So much more uncomfortable.

I had an itch. On my ankle. I tried to ignore it. I counted to 10. I counted to 10 again. I counted to 20. It was still there. I lowered my arm and tried to raise my leg to meet it halfway but instead I bumped my knee on the wooden rail that was there to keep me on my shelf.

'Ow.'

'You all right?'

'Yeah. Fine. Bumped my knee. Sorry.'

'Right.'

Pause.

'G'night then.'

'G'night.'

I lay awake testing my eyesight in the dark. Nothing. I knew the roof was only just above my head because I could feel its presence. I made a mental note not to think about coffin lids and then realised that meant I was already thinking about coffin lids. All that wood around me. I told myself to relax. I breathed in deeply, concentrating on doing it properly. Through the nose. Don't lift the shoulders. Feel your chest expand. Then out slowly, imperceptibly, silently. Relax.

'What about that freak on the bike?' asked Stef.

'Tch. Yeah.'

'Do you think he was on something?'

'Yeah. A bike.'

'Cuh!'

'Sorry.'

'Sleep well.'

'You too.'

Silence. More bloody silence.

The wind blew and the treehouse moved, creaking like a boat in water. I used the noise to cover a shift of position, turning on to my side. Hmmm, now I was facing into the room. Oh no. That meant I was facing towards the bed. Towards Stef. I couldn't see anything but what if she could? What if she could see me? Would she assume I was looking at her? That wasn't right. I couldn't lie facing Stef all night in case she thought I was... *looking*. I know I wouldn't feel comfortable if someone was looking at me. Turning to face the other way was going to be a two-part operation. I waited. Willing the tree to creak. Wait. Wait. Creak. I went for it, turning stealthily, slowly, on to my back. Coffin-lid thoughts. Wait for a creak. Wait. Wait. Wait... and turn. Finally I was facing into the wall. I told myself to sleep. It wasn't happening.

This stilted, self-conscious silence continued for a while. Down below I could hear the occasional, slow, deliberate movement that told me Stef was in a similar state of self-conscious awakeness. Two people unable to relax, too uptight to sleep, each desperate not to disturb the other.

'Dave?'

'Yeah.'

'Nothing.'

Pause.

'This isn't going very well, is it?'

'Nah.'

Oh, how much did I want to be somewhere else? Anywhere else?

'Stef?'

'Yeah.'

'Do you want to go to a party?'

★

As we reached the end of the dirt track headlights bounced around us in all directions. There were cars everywhere, parked at odd angles wherever they could find a berth between two trees. We crawled along, the car bumping and grinding through unseen potholes on the rough surface, studying the area, looking for a Torino-shaped space in the shadows. There was an enjoyably anarchic sense of chaos with an amazing cast of characters in ridiculously elaborate fancy dress costumes wandering in and out of our headlights. A family in coordi-nated purple and green alien outfits drifted by while a bumblebee crawled out of the trunk of the car in front. To my right Little Bo Peep was hugging a pirate.

'They take this seriously, don't they?' whispered Stef.

'Biggest night of the year,' I said. It was quite possibly the first time in my life I've ever quoted a zombie. 'Here, this'll do. Let's abandon ship and walk from here.'

As we neared the party Stef stopped and tugged at my arm. 'Can you smell weed?'

I inhaled a lungful of air and the sickly sweet smell of mari-juana hung heavily within it.

'I most certainly can.'

Isn't that a bit... weird? Y'know... for a school? I mean it's really strong. It's everywhere.'

The closer we got to the modern timber building, the stronger the smell grew. It was coming from all directions but the most obvious source was a group of three teenaged boys in blue jeans and heavy overcoats who were standing around chat-ting and passing a joint around. Joint or no joint it was good to see we weren't the only people without costumes.

One of the lads greeted us with easy, laid-back confidence.

'Hey, how you doing?'

'Good, thanks,' I said.

The end of the bulbous joint glowed as he inhaled heavily before offering it to me. 'Smoke?'

'No,' I said a little too quickly. I tried to soften my tone by adding a belated, 'thanks' but it came out in an overeager-to-please way that made me sound like the class square.

The three boys chuckled at my self-conscious, unhip demeanour. They were teenagers; I'm sure they were the ones who were meant to be self-conscious. In a vain attempt to redeem myself I lifted up the car keys and raised my eyebrows in an I'd-love-to-join-you-I-really-would-but-oops-poor-old-me-has-to-drive-so-unfortunately-I'll-have-to-pass-sorry-guys way. (I have very expressive eyebrows.)

The young man shrugged and offered Stef the joint instead.

'Nah,' she said, managing to pull off exactly the not-really-that-fussed-but-thanks-all-the-same tone that I was so ridiculously unable to manage. Maybe this is what happens when I'm near a school building? Maybe I'll always revert to being an awkward teenage version of myself? I hope not. If I ever have kids it will make parents' evenings hell.

'So, what's the party like?' I asked.

'Oh, it's pretty wild,' said one. He leaned in conspiratorially. 'And it's gonna get wilder.'

'This *is* Takilma,' said another as if that alone was an adequate explanation for the extreme wildness his friend was promising.

'What do you mean?' asked Stef.

The three boys shared a look of bemusement.

'You don't know about Takilma?'

'No.'

'Whoa!'

Our lack of Takilma-awareness seemed to blow their minds. Being in Takilma without knowing about its reputation was clearly as ludicrous to them as it would be to visit Niagara without knowing about the waterfall. (Which, I suppose, is only marginally more ludicrous than visiting Lone Pine without knowing about Mount Whitney.)

'Wow,' said the one who'd only just whoaed.

'This is hippie central,' explained another.

'A lot of hippies moved north when they thought California had gotten too... *straight*... y'know?'

'I see,' I said with a shrug. 'So it's going to get wilder, is it?'

'Oh yeah!'

All three of them nodded.

'Well, I guess we should take a look inside,' said Stef. 'See how much wildness we can take.'

A green-faced monster sat at a table by the door greeting newcomers with a warm smile and a collecting tin. A live band were throwing themselves around the stage playing some great Latin-tinged, upbeat reggae. The dance floor teemed with people of all ages with toddlers and teens dancing alongside their parents and grandparents. To our right a huge papier-mâché figure of a topless woman with enormous spherical breasts stretched to the ceiling. This was clearly a more liberal school than any I ever attended. I looked down and saw that next to the collecting tin where the friendly monster was stashing people's entry fees there was a help-yourself basket of condoms.

Can you imagine the reaction of a British tabloid newspaper if they found a small school in rural England hosting a party like this? A party? In a school? With children present? Where marijuana is openly smoked? And condoms are given away on the door? Imagine the headlines! How much would the *Daily Mail* hate this? How much would the *Daily Mail* love hating this?

But it didn't feel like we were walking into a tabloid scandal. No, it felt fantastic. We were walking into a room full of energised, happy people. The happiest and most energised people we'd encountered so far.

This party had originally seemed like a good idea only because sharing a room full of silent tension had seemed like such a bad idea but suddenly I realised that a party was a good idea simply because it was a party.

As the joyful atmosphere throbbed around me I felt the weight lifting from my shoulders. I needed to let loose. On stage a trumpet blared and the musicians – who'd identified them-selves as the Frankie Hernandez Band – struck up a ska beat; um-chacka-um-chacka-um-chacka-bum. My foot started tapping, my knees started bending, up, down, up, down, up, down, up. I was *almost* dancing. But not quite. A small slither of English reserve was holding me back but as I looked around the room and realised that nobody there would ever meet me again I gave in to the music, threw myself forward and started dancing properly. Um-chacka-um-chacka-um-chacka-bum.

I turned and invited Stef to join me but she just gestured towards her back and shrugged her shoulders.

Four songs later I was still on the floor having a high old time when a lady of, well, *senior* years approached. She had a flowing mane of silver hair rolling elegantly down her back and below her waist. I wasn't entirely sure if the long flowing robe was part of a witch-like costume or just a part of her everyday wardrobe. She raised her eyebrows in a dance-floor hello and then play-fully matched my steps to the end of the song.

As the singer took a slug of between-tunes beer she leaned forwards saying, 'You're a good dancer.'

'Thanks.'

I knew I was worth 10 out of 10 for effort but nothing for style.

The band launched themselves into another number and I launched myself back into my moves. I hadn't felt this good for a while. My new dance partner studied me for a few seconds and then fell into step for a few bars. After a while she changed up a gear, adding a few touches of her own – a shimmy here and a shake there – and this time it was my turn to follow suit and so I copied her.

We continued in this fashion – a dance equivalent of duelling banjos – for the full song by which time I was bushed. I was dripping in sweat and gasping for air but somehow this glam-orous gran looked as graceful as she had when our dance off began.

She leaned forwards, flirtatiously beckoning me towards her

so that she could be heard. I turned my head and offered my ear. She cupped my chin in her hand, her spidery fingers stroking through my beard.

'You must have sisters.'

Our heads rotated, my lips to her ear now.

'No. Three brothers.'

And back.

'No way... they normally have sisters. Older sisters.'

And back again.

'I'm really not sure I know what you mean by "they"?'

Back.

'Oh... well, maybe we should get to know each other better.'

'Oh, well... I'm... not um... from round here... er... I'm just... you know... passing through,' I babbled.

At which she smiled and raised her other hand to my other cheek and planted a long lingering kiss on my lips before dancing off towards the centre of the dance floor. I looked around feeling slightly adrift from reality, unsure that what had just happened had indeed just happened. I saw Stef leaning against the wall and darted over there to safety.

'It's all getting a bit too *Wicker Man* for my liking,' I said.

Stef laughed.

'What?' I was indignant.

'Don't let me get in the way,' she grinned. 'If you want to take her back to the treehouse, I'll let you take the bed.'

'Come on,' I said, 'let's get out of here... it's all getting a bit too wild for me.'

Chapter 10
Just do it, you big soft get

After staying out late and dancing myself into a state of exhaustion no amount of social awkwardness could prevent me from sleeping. I crawled on to my shelf and went out like a light.

I woke early the next morning feeling more refreshed than I had since our journey had begun. Stef was still sleeping soundly but I managed to creep down my stepladder and out of the treehouse without disturbing her or the horses that were standing like statues, deep in sleep in a small paddock besides our arboreal abode.

The camp's communal bathroom was unoccupied so I took an invigorating hot shower and then wandered over to the main house for breakfast. Several of the people who'd been sitting around the campfire the night before were in the kitchen but while they all knew each other they immediately welcomed me into their conversation. They worked together at a law firm based a couple of hours north in the city of Eugene and they'd come down to Takilma together for a short break in the country as a bonding exercise.

Apparently, while they indulged in some outdoorsy activity together they were also able to 'talk about company strategy without the hierarchical politics so often reinforced by the office environment.'

I think I must have wrinkled my nose at the corporate jargon because one of them, Bob, was quick to step in and neutralise it.

'What Paul means is that while we're here we can say things we wouldn't say in the office. I mean, he's my boss and I'd never call him a jerk when we were at work together... but here, when he starts mentioning "hierarchical politics" I can say, "Paul, you're being a jerk!"'

Paul smiled an indulgent put-upon-boss smile and the rest of the group chuckled along at Bob's cheek. There was an enjoyable mateyness to the banter and Paul expertly waited for the laughter to die before delivering a deadpan counterpunch:

'Bob?'

'Yeah?'

'You're fired.'

Which inevitably yielded yet more laughter.

'You've obviously enjoyed it here,' I said.

'Oh yeah, it's been awesome,' said Bob. 'All the fairies are nice...'

'I beg your pardon?'

'I mean the staff,' he explained, 'all the people who work here are called "tree-fairies".'

'And the activities,' said Paul, 'they're not called activities... they're activi-*trees*. They kinda like using the word tree around here...'

'Right,' I said, again wrinkling my nose, this time at the puny pun. 'Not that I think I'll be doing any of the activities... I think we're checking out today.'

'But you only turned up last night!' said Paul. 'We saw you arrive with your... wife? girlfriend... ?'

'Colleague,' I said. 'And *that's* kind of the problem. We've only really known each other for a couple of weeks. The idea of coming here was to have a day off, enjoy some space and... and, well, our treehouse is kind of small, y'know?'

'Even so,' said Paul, 'you can't come here, stay just one night and then leave. You have to *enjoy* a place like this. It's just too beautiful not to.'

They were right but I didn't feel like I had much choice. We were meant to be taking a day off so that Stef could recuperate and I knew she didn't want to stay another night. The only responsible thing to do was to wait for her to rise and then move on.

After a fine home-cooked breakfast – prepared by our 'breakfast fairy' – I wandered out and lazed in the sunshine. I sat down on one of the logs that surrounded the pile of ash that had been last night's campfire.

A few hundred yards away, Paul, Bob and the rest of the law firm were loading luggage into their small fleet of cars. I waved. They waved back. One of them pointed at the Torino and then pointed at me and I understood his silent enquiry. I nodded vigorously. He nodded an impressed nod and then offered me a big thumbs up. And then so did the rest of the group. I'm telling you, everyone loved that car.

Standing near the walkway up to the main house someone was observing this conversation in long distance mime. He watched the whole exchange, taking in both party's contributions by moving his head from left to right like a spectator at the world's slowest game of tennis.

As the legal eagles got in their cars and waved me a final goodbye wave I caught the man's eye and we exchanged real, out loud pleasantries.

'Morning.'

'Morning.'

He walked towards me and I took in his features properly for the first time. His was an enjoyably craggy face. He had a mop of hair that was greying but his bushy eyebrows were jet black, giving a clue to what once had been. He had an unkempt soup-strainer of a moustache that drooped down over his top lip. He wore glasses too and for a brief moment they combined with his eyebrows and 'tache combo to look like he was wearing a novelty Groucho Marx mask but it soon became clear that each element was moving independently and that this was indeed his face.

Beneath his bodywarmer I could see the Out 'n' About logo was adorning his dark green sweatshirt.

'I take it you work here?'

'This is my place,' he said with a smile. 'I'm Michael. Are you enjoying your stay?'

'Yeah,' I said, which wasn't as true as I wanted it to be. I was enjoying the moment much more than I was enjoying the stay as a whole. 'I'm Dave.' We shook hands. 'This is an amazing place. How long have you been here?'

'I moved out west about 30 years ago,' he sighed, 'but we've only been doing *this*,' he swung his arm around towards the treehouses, 'for about 15. You're English, right?'

'Uh huh.'

'Hmm. I started this place with an Englishwoman. We just had a basic cabin and the horseback riding. The cabin was just a cabin – on the ground – and nobody came. It was only when I made it a treehouse that people really started coming. People ask me where I got the idea and I say, "I tried a lot of things – this one worked." My money came back to me and so I was able to build another treehouse. It filled up and the money came back and so on... one of my boasts is that I have the highest concentration of treehouses in the world.'

'Well, I would have thought two was enough for that boast,' I said.

Michael thought about that for a moment – I got the impression he was never really rushed – and then, with a shrug, he said, 'Maybe.'

This laissez-faire demeanour gave no clues as to how entertaining a story Michael had up his sleeve. We walked through the camp together as he told me about how the treehouse resort – or you've guessed it, *tree*sort – had come to be and I was hanging on his every word.

'I built the first treehouse in 1990 and the building department told me I couldn't get a permit for it because it was a tree and didn't have a concrete foundation. It took me eight years of battling to get round it. They ordered me to tear it down... told me that I had to cease operations on the fifth of July or they'd start fining me. So I was still okay on the fourth of July and that's a big thing here. That's our Independence Day from *you*,' he said, pointing playfully at the Englishman in his midst, 'that's when we tell a government that's not being fair to bugger off, right?'

'Right.'

'Now they said I couldn't get a permit because I couldn't prove it was safe. So I got all my friends together and I put 66 people up in that treehouse along with two dogs and a cat. And we're not sure if a hummingbird alighted or not. We had a lot of media here, ABC, NBC, CBS and Associated Press; it was like a *tree*-ringed circus. And the treehouse didn't fall down… so I showed them it was safe.'

'Good publicity,' I mused.

'Publici-*tree*,' said Michael. 'This is when we started using these puns with the word tree. For the press. We called it a *tree* party. There were *tree* of us. It was a *tree*-vesty of justice. What the government was saying was a high *tree*-son. And we started selling *tree*-shirts.'

I didn't wrinkle my nose this time. The tree puns might have been twee – yes, twee – but now that I saw where they'd come from, now that I saw they were part of his fight for survival, they made more sense to me. They were more charming. They were, dare I say it, *tree*-mendous.

'You see, after this the building inspector said I didn't have to tear it down but he also said I couldn't have the general public in it and I couldn't rent it out. Well I said, "a kids' tree-house doesn't need a permit and they're allowed to have their friends over, right?" and he said, "yes… but they're not friends if they're renting it out."'

'Which must have been a problem when that's basically your business?'

'Well, that's when we came up with the Tree Musketeers. All for trees and trees for all. If you became a Tree Musketeer you *became* a friend of the trees and therefore a friend of mine and that meant you could stay here…'

'But you couldn't rent it out...?'

'No, so we did tree-servations. A tree-servation was a certain date that you could get a tree-shirt... which was a T-shirt with a picture of the treehouse on it and the day's date. And we could charge a lot of money for them because they were one of a kind. So if you wanted to buy 15 August 1994, say, well, back then, that tree-shirt was $60.'

'And then,' I said, amused by the audacity of the scheme, 'you could stay the night?'

'No,' said Michael, choosing his words carefully. It was clear he'd had to tiptoe through this legal minefield many times before and he knew the terrain well. No matter that it was all in the past, he knew what he could and couldn't say. 'That would be us renting it out. A tree-servation didn't *guarantee* you stayed the night... it just guaranteed you that day's tree-shirt. But if you *did* stay the night, I would sign the shirt.'

The legal distinctions weren't immediately clear to me but it didn't really matter. The fact was that for years people were able to stay in a treehouse for free and their visits just happened to coincide with them buying a T-shirt for the price of, oh, I don't know, about what you'd pay for a night in a treehouse. You've got to admit, it's brilliant.

'We got away with that for four or five years,' said Michael in his calm, slow, measured way, 'but then they came back with another lawsuit. I just defied that one for a while and ended up in court. The judge found me not guilty.'

'So was that it?'

'Well, after about eight years a lot of the county commissioners, government officials; the people who didn't want to work with me... they'd moved on. Plus we'd done a lot of engineering and a lot of study. So after eight years we finally got a permit.'

'Good for you,' I said. 'A lot of people wouldn't have fought it for that long.'

'Well, that's how you beat City Hall,' shrugged Michael. 'You outlast 'em.'

He might have been smiling. It was hard to tell through that moustache.

'So have you signed up for any of the activi-trees?' he asked.

'No, I'm just waiting for my colleague to get up,' I said. 'When Stef surfaces, I'm afraid we might have to check out.' I shrugged my shoulders in a way that I hoped suggested there were circumstances beyond my control and then, eager not to offend, I white-lied, 'I mean we love it here but we've got so much work to do and so little time so maybe we can't really afford a day off...'

'So what's your line of work?'

I couldn't think of a lie quick enough and so I told Michael the truth and explained our film. It sounded so implausible he probably assumed I was lying anyway.

'So you're meant to be going from LA to New York and you've wound up here?' he asked.

'Um... yeah. Kind of.'

'Well good for you,' he said. 'But if Stef isn't up yet, I don't see any reason why you shouldn't do something. I know John's taking some people on the zip line... do you fancy that?'

'Sure,' I said although I only had half an idea what it was I'd just agreed to.

An hour and a bit later and I was standing on a small rickety platform high in the branches of a tree that was quite definitely moving with the breeze. A densely packed forest of split top sugar pines scaled the hill behind me while a glorious sun-kissed open meadow lay straight ahead.

My arms were aching, having pulled myself up one branch at a time, all the while clinging on for dear life, unprepared to test out the safety harness, clamps, ropes and pulleys that the instructor, John, had strapped me into.

'Just don't look down,' said John.

I looked down – 52 feet down. My knees wobbled.

'I told you not to do that.'

'Sorry.'

John guided me through the last few steps. I hooked myself

on to the steel wire that dropped down and disappeared into the distance. I unhooked myself from the tree and stepped down on to a lower branch.

'Now put your gloves on,' said John. 'Remember the lesson: they're your brakes.'

I slipped on the heavy leather gauntlets and looked at the palms where friction had burned away a layer or two as previous zip-liners had gripped the wire to slow themselves down.

'Are you sure these are all right?' I asked. I'd already burnt through one set of brakes on a steep and dangerous descent. I didn't want to do that again.

'They're fine,' grinned John. 'Now... the wire's about 650 feet long. The land slopes away from here so while we're only 52 feet up at the moment you'll actually drop something like 65 feet. It's exciting, you should get up to 35 miles per hour. You ready?'

'No.'

'Are you ready?'

Gulp.

'Yes.'

'Then off you go...'

I tried to lift my legs from the branch but my right leg refused to move. I looked down at the ground again. Shitting crikey. Fifty-two feet! How come it's a short walk but such a long fall? I tried to reason with myself. I knew that climbing back down the tree would be scarier than sliding down the line. It would also be humiliating. Especially as three other people had just gone down the fast way. And one of them was eight. And a girl. My knees continued to wobble but my feet refused to budge. John offered me some gentle words of encouragement but down on the ground someone had some more abrupt advice.

'JUST DO IT, YOU BIG SOFT GET!'

The flat vowels were instantly familiar. A few hundred yards away, with two arms waving madly, was a shock of blonde hair. Stef.

'JUST GO FOR IT!' she yelled again, her laughter following on the breeze.

'LOOK,' I yelled back, 'JUST BECAUSE YOU WANT TO GET GOING, IT DOESN'T MAKE THIS ANY EASIER!'

'WE'RE NOT GOING ANYWHERE.'

'WHAT?'

'I SAID WE'RE NOT GOING ANYWHERE! THIS PLACE IS BRILLIANT! I'VE JUST HAD A MASSAGE!'

'BUT WHAT ABOUT…?'

'I'VE BOOKED US ANOTHER TREEHOUSE FOR TONIGHT. WE'VE GOT ONE EACH.'

'FANTASTIC!'

'NOW JUMP!'

And so I did.

'WOOOOOOOO-HOOOOOOOOOO! YEEEEEEEEEE-HAAAAAAAA!'

Chapter 11
The Dukes of bloody Hazzard

We left the treehouses with a fuel-related tip-off from Michael. Nine miles of twisting, turning back roads later we pulled up on the dusty forecourt of the Holland General Store; a small, weathered one-storey building with a wooden porch out front. An American flag drooped forlornly at one end while the single fuel pump – an original 1950s model – was offset to one side. We'd never have found this place of our own accord.

Above the door hung a blade from an old two-handed saw. Painted on the metal in a neat handwritten script were the words: 'Holland Store. Home to George and Jody'.

Across the way there must have been 20 tin mailboxes all nailed to small wooden posts even though there were no clues as to where the 20 homes they belonged to were hidden.

As soon as we'd parked up the front door swung open and a woman stepped out on to the porch. She was short with strawberry-blonde hair scraped back into a ponytail and she was swamped by a large black-and-blue lumberjack shirt.

'Looking for gas?' she asked

There are two states in the Union where self-service gas stations are forbidden; New Jersey is one, Oregon is the other. In both cases the law originated as a safety measure but in a world where millions of people regularly manage to dispense their own fuel without blowing themselves up I can't imagine that holds much water these days.

In the 1980s the corporate might of Arco challenged the law in Oregon but they lost the fight and so it remains illegal for customers to pump their own gas in the state to this day.

There are two techniques for pumping gas; hands-on and hands-free. The cool people do the hands-free method while I'm very much a member of the hands-on school. While I understand the mechanics that keep the trigger depressed and the fuel flowing I've never really understood how it knows when the tank is full and how it cuts the flow and so, unwilling to trust in magic, I've always kept my finger on the trigger instead. I don't know what else I'd do with my hands during the process anyway... it's not like I'm itching for some extra Rubik's cube training.

Sandy was one of the cool people. While she was refuelling our car she found good use for her hands, using them expressively to underline every word she said, a habit no doubt related to the fact that she was deaf.

'It's a lovely old store,' I said. 'How long have you been here?'

'Since July of this year.' Sandy smiled. 'My dad's been here for 21 years. My stepmother, Jody, passed away last October and my dad couldn't manage it all by himself so he called us.' She leaned forward as though she was about to reveal some precious secret. 'It's my *Little House on the Prairie* dream,' she beamed.

'So it's a real family business...'

'It sure is,' she said throwing her shoulders back with pride. 'But it's been here a lot longer.'

Sandy suddenly switched into tour-guide mode, rattling off the history of the store in a way that suggested she'd told the story many times before.

'Back in the 1890s there used to be a hotel just there...' she pointed towards the mailboxes '... it was built for the miners who were digging for gold nearby. The top floor used to be a whorehouse. The mayor's wife didn't like that and so one day she burned the hotel down. Sadly, the store caught on fire too. But they rebuilt it on the same foundations.'

I looked around at the surrounding countryside and while I could see why Sandy liked it so much here I was struggling to work out how they made a living. I suppose each mailbox must have represented at least one customer but apart from that it was hard to see where their business came from. Surely there wasn't a great deal of passing trade?

'Well, we're part of the community,' explained Sandy. 'Before you came I was preparing a shopping list for an elderly lady who lives nearby. She can't get out of her house and so we either deliver things to her or someone will come by and pick it up. I make a trip to Medford every coupla' weeks to do shopping for people who can't do it for themselves. We don't charge for that. There's a lot of trust in a small community; we still do credit, y'know when someone can't pay cash but they need, say, milk or butter, we're okay with that.'

As Sandy chatted away it became clear that the sense of community she was talking about went both ways.

'One of the locals recently donated a thousand dollars so that we could get our roof fixed. My husband's in masonry so he tore it down and put up a new one.'

'That's amazing,' I said, because it was. 'I can't imagine anyone donating a thousand bucks to help fix up an Exxon gas station.'

'Well, people are nice,' said Sandy matter-of-factly. She turned on her heels and headed indoors to the register. I followed.

On the door a handwritten sign said: 'Caution!! Old Wooden Floor. Shoes Must Be Worn!!'

Sitting in the car outside the Holland General Store we unfolded a map and worked out where we were. There was no getting away from how ridiculous the situation was. We were meant to be going from coast to coast and yet, eight days after we'd left Coronado, we were still less than 40 miles from the Pacific Ocean.

In fact, it was even more ridiculous than that. Yes, we'd travelled north from our starting position... but we'd also travelled west. West! The wrong bloody way! We'd managed the impossible! We'd set off from the West Coast and somehow we'd gone even further west! I'm sure that shouldn't be possible without getting your feet wet.

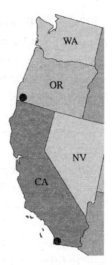

When you're making a road trip you want to keep on moving, you want to feel like you're making progress. You want to see a lot of road. We'd made slow progress through Nevada and it was frustrating for us both. Now that we'd taken a day off and Stef's back had been on the masseur's table I was keen to reignite the journey. I wanted to put some serious miles behind us.

'So... which route do you want to take?' I asked.

'What are the options?'

'Well, we're heading towards Independence, right?'

'Right.'

'And we've been heading there for days now.'

'Uh huh.'

'If we head off on small roads, going through small towns as normal, I reckon Independence is at least two days away. Or...'

'Or?'

'Or, we hit the interstate.'

Stef looked confused. Suspicious. She wanted to make sure it was a serious suggestion on my part and not a sneaky test of her resolve.

'Isn't that *exactly* what you wanted *not to* do?' she asked. 'You're the one who talks about sticking to the smaller roads...'

'Yeah... but we've got a full tank of gas. We're averaging over 16 miles per gallon now. Independence is roughly 250 miles away. If we throw ourselves up the interstate for a couple of hundred miles we can get there today...'

Once I'd floated the idea I knew there wouldn't be any real debate. We were both too eager to get going.

It was a risk, of course. If we took two days to get there but visited 20 towns along the way it would give us 20 chances of finding independent gas en route. Taking the interstate meant we'd bypass those towns and spurn those opportunities. Taking the interstate meant putting all of our fuel-eggs in one fuel-basket.

But somehow it didn't feel like a risk. We'd covered nearly 1,400 miles already without having to use a chain. What had seemed completely impossible on day one felt doable now. We were getting cocky.

Driving on the interstate is easy. Too easy. You forget that you're driving a car. When a road is full of twists and turns you're constantly adjusting the way you drive. Every time you touch a pedal you're reminded of the relationship that exists between your eyes, your hands, your feet and the road. When the road is straight and flat and carrying you along at a steady rate of knots you start to feel like a passenger. Autopilot. We've all done it.

It was only when we left the well-lit interstate – still some 10 or 20 miles shy of Independence – that I realised the night had fallen. It was only when we left the interstate that I checked the fuel gauge.

'Shit!'

'What?' asked Stef nervously, clearly aware that there was genuine concern in my voice.

'The fuel gauge says we're empty…'

'Shit.'

'Okay… don't panic,' I said, panicking.

'Well, how much fuel have we got?'

'It's okay,' I said, 'We've been here before. The needle said empty when we filled up at the Paiute Palace, remember, and we only needed 16 gallons then.'

'So how much have we got?'

'Well, when it says empty, that means we've still got nearly 80 miles left in the car.'

'So we're all right...'

'Well...'

'What do you mean by "well..."?'

'Well, we should be all right... it's just I haven't been looking at the fuel gauge. I don't know when it first said empty.'

'What?'

'Maybe it said empty 80 miles ago. Maybe we're *actually* empty.'

'Dave, pull over!'

'I can't,' I said. 'There's too much traffic and nowhere to pull over to.'

'Dave. Just pull over,' said Stef, more urgent now. 'I need to put a tape in the camera and it's dark so I need to put some lights up. If we're going to run out of gas I need to make sure it's on tape.'

'Yeah... but we're not going to run out of gas,' I said, trying to do the maths in my head. How many miles had we done? Would our fuel consumption be different on the interstate? At higher speeds?

'Pull over.'

There was a lot of traffic behind us.

'I can't.'

'There's a right turn up ahead, take that.'

'But that's not the way.'

'Just bloody take it!'

'It's not even a proper road!'

'Just take it!'

I flicked the indicator, checked the rear-view mirror, slammed my foot on the brakes and pulled abruptly on to a dusty farm track. The car bumped and rolled along the uneven track throwing a cloud of dust around us as we came to a halt. The engine idled.

'This isn't the bloody *Dukes of bloody Hazzard*, you know!' I bloody said but Stef wasn't listening. She'd already undone her seat belt and was clambering around the car, diving into bags and pulling out equipment.

From the sense of urgency you'd have thought she was a bomb disposal expert looking for her lucky wire cutters, not a film-maker looking for a tape. She pulled a cassette out of a holdall, made two or three thumbnail attempts to breach its cellophane wrapper and then handed it to me instead, barking her orders, 'Open that!'

While I attacked the tape with my teeth I could hear Stef rummaging some more. The cellophane gave way, half of it clinging magnetically to my teeth, no matter how hard I blew on it.

'Pfft, pfffft, pfft, pfft,' I spat. 'Here'th the pfft tapeff pfft.'

'Thanks,' said Stef although she didn't look round. She was kneeling on the seat, leaning into the back of the car with her arse in the air and her face and hands buried in a kit bag. 'Now put it in the camera.'

I reached into the passenger side footwell where the camera was resting and started fiddling with the mechanism to load the cassette.

'Got them!' yelled Stef triumphantly, jolting backwards and kicking me in the face with her trailing right foot.

'Ow!'

'Well, get out of the way then!'

'I will,' I said sitting back in my chair, my right hand rubbing my cheek where the blow had landed.

Stef was triumphantly holding what looked like two minia-ture flying saucers. They were silver and white plastic discs, about the same diameter as a CD but maybe an inch thick.

'They'd better be worth a kick in the face,' I said sorely.

'They're lights,' said Stef.

She slapped one of them dead centre and the fluorescent bulb inside snapped on.

Stef dropped the lamps in her lap and started pulling at a roll of double-sided sticky tape and in a matter of seconds one of them was attached to the sloping dash, the light shining up on to the ceiling and bouncing around the car.

'Okay, are we ready?' I asked, slipping the car into gear and starting to execute the three-point turn needed to get us back on the road.

'No,' said Stef, checking the view on the camera's display. 'It looks like a horror film. Can't see your eyes at all.'

'I think we should go anyway,' I said. 'We're going nowhere and we're burning fuel. We're burning fuel while you get the camera ready so that you can be filming if we run out of fuel! That's insane!'

'Well, turn the engine off then!'

'Starting the engine uses more fuel than idling.'

'Does it?'

'I have absolutely no idea,' I said. 'But someone once told me it did...'

'Well, it doesn't matter because we're nearly ready,' said Stef, all the while moving the second light around the car, checking the camera to see how it changed the shot from this angle and that.

'I just don't want to run out of gas *because* you want to be filming *when* we run out of gas!'

'You don't want to run out of gas and not have it on film either, do you?'

'Well, no... but then I don't really want to run out of gas at all!'

'Here,' said Stef, handing the spare light to me. 'Put that in your lap.' I did. She glanced at the viewfinder. 'He has eyes! Hallelujah. Right, this'll do... let's go.'

'Like this?'

'What?'

'With a light balanced on my lap?'

'Well, there's no point if we can't see you... now come on, you're wasting precious petrol... let's go.'

I completed the bumpy three-point turn and then rejoined the traffic-strewn highway for some of the most tentative and self-conscious driving I've ever done. Passing motorists stared longer than normal. And why wouldn't they stare at the 1970s car with its ghostly inhabitants lit up by the mysterious blue-white fluorescent light. With my eyes flitting between the road ahead and the fuel gauge, we headed towards Independence. Why I was bothering to check the fuel gauge, I can't tell you. It already said 'empty'... it had nowhere else to go.

Seven or eight miles later we made it to the town centre. It was a pretty-looking place, looking rather like the '50s setting in the *Back to the Future* movie franchise. There were no hover-boards in evidence though, just a series of unfussy, red-brick buildings standing in a line.

'Not gas... not gas... not gas... ' I mumbled, surveying every shop front in hope.

'At least we've got this far,' said Stef. 'If we run out now, at least there are people around and we'll be okay.'

'True.'

'But we can't push it any further... if we see a petrol station now, chain or no chain, we've got to take it, haven't we?'

'Yeah,' I shrugged a defeated shrug. 'I guess we do.'

'Well then,' said Stef brightly, 'I guess it's straight ahead and on the left.'

I looked and true enough there was the familiar outline of a modern gas station. It didn't have the charm of the Holland General Store. There were no uneven white plaster walls there. No dust and gravel forecourt. It had the modern, plastic, anti-septic look of every other urban gas station with an island of pumps all lit up by the phosphorescent glow of the lights in the tall, square canopy overhead.

'What brand is it?' I asked.

'Does it matter?'

'Not really,' I sighed. 'D'y'know what? The scary thing is that I can't see a logo, I can't see any branding and yet I know it's a Union 76 from here. I just know the colour scheme.'

'I'm sure their branding department would be delighted to hear it,' said Stef. 'That's exactly what they want, isn't it?'

'Hang on,' I said, my foot instinctively reaching for the brake pedal. 'What does that say?'

We'd got close enough to the gas station to take in the

signage now. Where I expected to see the logo – a red circle with a blue 76 inside it – there was just an unlit blue-and-white oval and the words 'Jimmy Z – Independence Gas – Locally Owned'.

'I don't believe it,' I said, my jaw slack. 'It isn't, is it?'

'I think it is, y'know,' said Stef, her eyes wide.

'There's only one way to find out.'

I pulled on to the forecourt and parked up besides a vacant pump. I'd only just turned the key to let the engine rest when I was surprised by a familiar sound; a *clank* that told me someone had just lifted the sprung, metal flap that covered our fuel tank.

'What the—?'

I unbuckled my seat belt and jumped out of the car to find a young man standing there with the fuel pump nozzle already inside the Torino. Of course. This was Oregon – land of the fuel pump attendant.

The young man had a muscular frame and a chiselled jaw that made him look like he'd just stepped off the set of *Dawson's Creek*.

'Regular or super?' he asked, his index finger flexing on the trigger.

'Hang on!' I said, 'before you do anything else, can you tell me... is this a Union 76?'

He furrowed his brow at me.

'Where's your accent from?'

'England,' I snapped. 'But seriously, I need to know whether this is a Union 76 or not?'

'England? Cool.'

'Yeah but...'

'Oh yeah, this used to be a Union 76 but it got bought out about six months ago. We're independent now.'

'Seriously?'

'Uh huh.'

'Then fill her up,' I said, the tension falling from my shoulders, relief flooding through me. 'Make it super. Give her the best you've got!' I turned to Stef – or rather to the camera's lens. 'Do you see that? I thought we were dead then. It's independent!' I punched the air in celebration. 'Get in there! You beauty!'

'That'll be 16.8 gallons,' said the teen-idol cum fuel-attendant. 'I'm sorry... I spilled a bit.'

'I can't believe that,' I said. 'We still had 5 gallons left! I was so convinced it was a 76 I wouldn't have even come here if I'd known we had 5 gallons left. Oh man... this is our lucky day!'

'How do you feel?' said Stef the director taking over from Stef the friend.

'Brilliant! How amazing is this? We've found a chain that's unchained itself! Brilliant! I love Independence! What a town! Do you see that? I told you Independence was the place to come. I told you it would be worth it. Independence is actually *more independent* now than it was six months ago. Brilliant!'

Chapter 12

Work hard and eat a lot of ice cream

Travelling together is a surprisingly bonding experience and it's fair to say the two of us had grown closer than I ever imagined possible. In the furnace of shared experience an unbreakable connection had been forged and previously dormant emotions were starting to stir. What the hell, I might as well admit it: I was in love. She was taking me to places I'd never been before and I had learned exactly how to turn her on.

She never started first time, of course, but my right foot knew how much to pump the gas and my right hand knew how long to turn the key, forcing her through the wheezy, whiney failed attempts to ensure that, on the third go, the Torino's engine would start to purr with pleasure. I thought we had an understanding.

But I thought wrong. Something had come between us. I don't know what happened overnight... only that when morning came she was threatening not to start at all.

We had stayed the night in an uninspiringly bland motel. Yes, it was an independent, unchained establishment but it had all the characteristic lack of character of the chain hotels it was competing against. It was a modern building with off-the-rack hotel furnishings and absolutely no sense of personality. It left me feeling genuinely unsettled.

I had woken at 4 a.m. in a state of confused panic, a slick coat of cold sweat upon me. Only slowly was I able to define what was real and what was not as I separated my bad dream from the here and now. In my dream I was convinced I was back on that do-as-you're-told tour of American theatres and when I looked, bleary-eyed, around my featureless room there was nothing to convince me otherwise. The illusion was so real and my belief so strong that I even felt a tightness at the back of my throat: the half-remembered sensation of a nodule forming.

My euphoria on discovering the gas station's independent ownership the night before had disguised a similar truth. It was independent in name but it resembled the chains in every other way. Did it matter? I *wanted* every Mom & Pop place to be distinct and different. I wanted them all to have been there for 50 years. I wanted them all to be survivors. I should have been delighted by evidence of new independent businesses being founded... but in truth, while they sat neatly within the rules of our journey, they seemed counter to its spirit.

Maybe that's why the car was throwing a tantrum this morning? Maybe it had taken offence at the bland modernity of its surroundings. I mean, if we were going to stay in five-year-old motels, why hadn't we just bought a five-year-old car as well?

Or maybe she was playing up because she carried the number of the beast? After all, if the 666 was ever going to mean something, surely Halloween was the day for it?

Or maybe it was simply an old car suffering in the cold. It was a real, bitter, feel-it-in-your-knuckles kind of cold. It had been sub-zero at night for a while now – even back in the Nevada desert – but this was the first time we'd woken up to find frost on the ground.

After making several attempts, we decided to leave her alone to think about her attitude. Five minutes later I tried again and got the same disappointing result. It was only after we'd popped into the hotel's reception, found a *Yellow Pages* and looked up local garages that she finally decided to start, albeit with an uncomfortable belch of worryingly dark and dense exhaust fumes.

I recognised the mentality. As a child, if I tried to convince my mum I was too sick for school I often found myself making a speedy recovery just before she called the doctor.

We drove into town in search of breakfast and soon found ourselves passing by Jimmy Z's Independence Gas. A couple of hundred yards later my eyes were drawn to a long, low, red-brick building with a green-and-white striped awning. According to the neon sign out front, this was The Taylor's Fountain.

'That looks nice,' I said, pleased to see something authentically old.

I'm not sure if there was ever a British equivalent of the old-fashioned American soda fountains but maybe the milk bars that flourished in the 1950s come pretty close. The fountain itself is the machine used to make fizzy drinks, combining carbonated water with syrups – much as they do in fast food joints to this day, although naturally the ornate pewter and brass contraptions of yesteryear are rather more attractive than the stainless steel serve-yourself drink-dispensers of today.

In the early twentieth century these were all the rage in the States. They were installed in department stores, train stations, ice-cream parlours and the like, becoming an important social hub to many communities.

There was a time when every American town had an ice-cream parlour where skilled soda-jerks worked behind long marble counters dispensing sweets, candies, milkshakes and sundaes to local children and adults alike. You don't see many of them these days, and seeing one now was a sweet relief following the bland, twenty-first-century hotel of the night before.

In a country that takes its Halloween fun extremely seriously almost every business opts for a Halloween-themed window display – especially on the day itself. Not Taylor's. Not this Halloween anyway. They had something far more important to commemorate.

Their window was full of 'Happy Retirement' signs, photos of the store from years gone by and a couple of local newspaper articles with a distinctly end-of-an-era tone. Taylor's was closing. October 31 was their last day.

We walked through the neatly painted red doors and found ourselves in the middle of some beautiful, cheerful disorganisation. Directly in front of us was a collection of mix and match tables and chairs while on the right, running almost half the length of the building, was a beautiful long counter illuminated by a row of hanging lights with stained-glass, faux-Tiffany lampshades. Behind the counter was a huge mirror and a vibrant pink-and-green neon sign spelling out the message, 'we serve deluxe ice cream'. There was a buzzy atmosphere, food was sizzling on the grill and the musical *ker-ching* of an old-fashioned till rang out as someone's strong fingers depressed one of its huge clunky buttons. At the far end of the room it looked like a garage sale with old furniture, ornaments, plastic toys and 20-year-old Christmas decorations amongst the feast of delights on an everything-must-go display. Coca Cola[3] memorabilia was everywhere, with dozens of their old tin trays mounted on the wood-panelled walls, most of them depicting Renoir-esque paintings of pale ladies with coy smiles, floaty dresses, bonnets and parasols.

[3] Coca Cola might appear to be the very epitome of The Man™ so perhaps it's worth me explaining a little about the self-imposed rules of our journey.

We were concerned only with who owned the businesses we actually dealt with.

Not one of the people we'd bought gasoline from had dug the oil out of the ground themselves and manufactured their own fuel. They'd obviously had to buy it from one of the major oil companies just like everyone else, but that didn't mean they weren't independent businesses.

They weren't tied to one company and more importantly, they weren't part of a brand. They forged their business's own identity.

We had no way of knowing if our independent diners had bought their eggs from Costco or if our independent hotels had bought their laundry detergent from Walmart. We only knew that *they* were independent.

And the same goes for Taylor's. It was a one-off, chain-free, independent business that just happened to sell Coke.

If we were to exclude businesses on the grounds that they sold Coke, we'd also have to refuse to eat anywhere that didn't make its own ketchup, and if you followed that particular train of thought, I'm pretty sure you'd end up using cuckoo spit to knit your own trousers.

Along the length of the counter was a neat row of tall bar stools, their shiny chrome pedestals all attached to the floor. Two of their shiny red vinyl seats were soon attached to our arses.

'Hi, what can I get you?' asked the young girl behind the counter, which was just a little disappointing because it would have been perfect if she'd chewed gum and called me Toots.

I ordered the only vegetarian breakfast option I could see on the menu – just as I had done every day so far. While we ate we soaked up the atmosphere, watching as a steady trickle of people came and went, all seemingly determined to buy at least a small souvenir of some kind; a memento to remember the place by. The mood was largely jolly but it was inevitably tinged with sadness as each person delivered their eulogy to the soda fountain, explaining quite why they loved it so and how much they'd miss it.

This strange brew of emotions felt eerily familiar but it took me a while to identify quite why. Then, suddenly, the penny dropped and I realised it was exactly the same mixture of maudlin jollity that you get at a wake when the funereal tears have dried and you've moved on to humorous reminiscences.

The ringmaster for this circus of emotions was a woman in her early sixties, her shortish hair framing a jolly face with a mile-wide smile. She had a voice so shrill and piercing it was amazing any of the glassware was still intact and she deployed it with amazing frequency, displaying an incredible ability to handle three or four conversations at the same time without appearing to draw breath. Listening in – and it was difficult not to – was like spinning a radio dial back and forth, changing channels every two or three seconds.

'Oh, well, that's very nice of you to say that and we're gonna – *Marley, are you eating?* – miss you too. *Kinsey, there's some chocolate syrup that needs to go back* – that'll be $3 – *in the refrigerator* – Don't eat behind the counter, Marley – *well, we let people know 90 days ago that we were gonna close* – there's a lady here wants serving – *and they've been telling us not to, but y'know, it's time...*'

All in all, Taylor's was ticking a lot of boxes. It slotted in to the vision of America conjured up by a childhood of watching *The Waltons, Little House on the Prairie, Happy Days* and *The Littlest Hobo*. It was perhaps the perfect embodiment of the kind of businesses I'd imagined before the journey had begun.

Of course, the fact that it was closing for good only served to underline the fact that this side of American life was diminishing – and here I found my emotions in conflict. I was sad to see the place closing but I was excited to have found a place that so brilliantly summed up the reason for making the journey in the first place. I could sense Stef's excitement too.

Imagine you'd set out to make a natural-history film about an endangered species and that you happened to have the camera rolling as you turned the corner and found one of these rare beasts being savaged by a pack of lions. As horrific as it might be to witness such a thing you have to admit that some small part of you would be thinking, 'Brilliant! I can't believe we managed to film a species getting even closer to extinction… what a result!'

I was loving Taylor's for being what it was but I was also hating the part of me that was happy to see it closing. You see: television really is a corrupting influence.

'We *have* to film this place,' said Stef under her breath. 'It's amazing!'

'I'll have a word with the owner,' I said, sliding off my stool, 'see if she'll let us film.'

No sooner had my feet hit the floor than I found my path blocked by a sudden influx of customers as a group of 30 teenagers flooded in.

The owner greeted this injection of youthful bodies with a warm smile and a playful holler; 'I don't know what you want but you're too old for trick or treating!'

The kids didn't approach the counter. Instead they gathered in the centre of the room facing the lady of the fountain with benign, playful mischief in their eyes. She surveyed them all individually, trying to work out what game it was they were playing. It was only when she spotted a middle-aged man at the back of the pack that she suddenly grasped what was going on.

'Oh, it's you! I might have known! I might have known!' she cackled. 'This had to be your doing!'

'I've brought some people to see you, Billie Kay,' he smirked.

From the neck down he was a vision of middle-class normality, a country club refugee wearing neatly pressed chinos and a polo shirt but he'd topped the outfit off with a construction worker's hard hat eccentrically decorated with a variety of badges, stickers and tiny stuffed toys. He had a Pied Piper-like control over his young charges and he rallied them in an instant with a theatrical cough and 'A one, a two, a one two, three, four...'

Thirty hearty young voices filled the room:

You'd better not shriek,
You'd better not groan,
You'd better not howl,
You'd better not moan,
Great Pumpkin is coming to town.

The dozen customers who had been here when the kids arrived were all clapping along now.

He's gonna find out, 'bout the folks that he meets,
Who deserves tricks and who deserves treats,
Great Pumpkin is coming to town.
He'll search in every pumpkin patch,
And houses far and near,
He'll see if you've been spreading gloom,
Or bringing lots of cheer...

The Christmas carol/Halloween song hybrid didn't really end so much as disintegrate at the end but nobody really noticed or cared as it devolved into a rowdy round of applause and much chuckling. Nobody enjoyed it more than our hostess, Billie Kay.

'Oh my! That was just wonderful!' She wiped a joyful tear from her eye. 'Vanilla Cokes all round! They're on the house! Who wants a vanilla Coke?'

A forest of hands went up in the air and behind the counter the girls went to work on preparing the sugary drinks.

'Okay kids, now don't forget the cards,' said the hard-hatted song-master, and his choir obediently crowded around Billie Kay, taking it in turn to give her their own hand-made Halloween greeting cards.

I joined the back of the line and filed through waiting for my opportunity to speak to her – after all, I had been on my way to do just that when this musical interlude had arrived.

I'm glad to say Billie Kay was happy to let us film. I'm not sure but it's entirely possible that this most talkative of women became even more loquacious in the presence of a camera. Some people talk at 19 to the dozen. I think Billie Kay starts to cruise at 20.

'I've never heard of Halloween carolling before,' I said.

'No, nor have I!' Her words dripped with enthusiasm. 'But aren't these kids just great? This is what a small town is all about, I tell ya. They come from a little school out in the country called Perrydale.'

'We have 115 kids in high school,' said Teach, his chest swelling with pride. 'But half of 'em come from another school district to come to us because...'

'Because they love the school,' said Billie Kay. 'People *want* their kids to go there.'

'They're obviously good kids,' I said, 'but... shouldn't they be in school right now?'

'Nah... it's a little tradition to come in for a vanilla Coke after events. We've just been Halloween carolling for the Senior Citizens' Center. We had a huge party with 150 senior citizens coming to the school...'

'*He invited me!*' squawked Billie Kay, her jaw dropping in mock offence at the idea. 'Me! Because I'm a senior now! Now I'm retired! I'm *officially*, senior!'

'Aw, come here,' I said, putting my arm around her, joining in with the play-acting, offering the pretend comfort to match her pretend offence.

Billie Kay squeezed me back. She'd granted us permission to film but it was that squeeze that told me we were truly welcome and with that squeeze, I knew we had been welcomed into the fold. And I knew that meant we were going to stay far beyond breakfast.

I hadn't seen Stef as enthused by the project as this since we'd first discussed the idea in a London caff – and I knew why. So many factors had fallen into alignment. Taylor's *was* the perfect location, their final day of business was the perfect time to film and Billie Kay *was* the perfect hostess. I'm pretty sure a complete documentary could have been hewn out of this occasion alone and Stef's film-making instincts were kicking in.

I'd got used to her blending into the background. She'd film me filling up the car or ordering my food and somehow everyone involved would forget she was there. This was different. In Taylor's she could see the opportunity to capture a whole story as it unfolded and it wasn't a story that had anything to do with me. It was the story of Billie Kay and the fountain's last day and Stef went to work on it, dashing about the place, asking questions and filming everything and everyone she could.

In this environment I became her assistant. I attached microphones to people's lapels, replaced batteries, dated and labelled used tapes and loaded the camera with new ones. I was happy to do it too, impressed by the sight of Stef seizing control of a situation. While we only ever talked about the film as *ours* I could see now that, prior to this, she hadn't felt very much like it was *hers*.

Nothing we'd done so far had been particularly challenging for her. The filming required technical know-how for sure but it's not like there had been any great artistic choices to be made and for someone who was used to authoring her own work she must have been feeling pretty underused. You add a seriously bad back into the mix and it doubtless makes for a difficult and frustrating time. But now, after a day of treehouse-rest and a healing deep-tissue massage, she had an opportunity to express herself and she was revelling in it.

And there was a seemingly endless supply of stories for her to work with... most of them seeming to involve couples who told us how important the place had been to their courtship. Couples had met there, had first dates there and who had got engaged there. The only thing we didn't find was anyone telling us about conceiving a child there but I wouldn't have been surprised if they had.

A couple of eighty-somethings told us about their first date at Taylor's over 60 years ago. Well actually, she told us about it. He didn't. She pointed out the very seats they'd sat in, told us what they'd worn that day and how good the food and drink had tasted. He just sat there, eating his ice-cream sundae and staring out at the world through glassy eyes, saying nothing and yet everything at the same time.

Two of the girls working behind the counter that day – Marley and Kinsey – were amongst Billie Kay's grandkids. She beamed with pride as she flicked through a photo album and showed me various pictures of them growing up. There was one photograph in particular that made us pause as we both realised simultaneously that the picture was exactly 13 years old. In it, a two–year-old girl was all dressed up for Halloween.

It was possibly the first time I was aware of Billie Kay falling silent as she stared at the baby in the picture and watched as the same girl, now 15 years of age, served customers. It must have brought back memories of watching her daughters do the same and indeed of being a 15-year-old working for her own parents, too.

Of course Billie Kay's silence didn't last long. The front door opened and she let out an almighty squeal of excited delight and rushed to greet the new arrivals.

'Oh! It's my daughter, Tasha! From Portland!'

Tasha's long dark hair flowed down her back from beneath a fancy-dress witch's hat. At her feet, arm outstretched to hold on to her hand, was a toddling toddler dressed up as a Halloween cheerleader. Billie Kay lowered to her knees to meet her youngest granddaughter's eye level.

'And it's Sonia Bella!' she chirruped. 'Are you a cheerleader? Are *you* a cheerleader? Yes you are. Are you trick or treating? Are you? Do you want some candy? Yes you do. Can you say "trick or treat" to Nana? Come with me, let's get you some candy…'

Sonia can't have been more than two years of age and the resemblance to the girl in the 13-year-old photo was remarkable. Wearing a similar costume and standing in the very same spot, surrounded by the same fixtures and fittings, it was as if, by studying the picture, we'd brought it to life in some truly spooky Halloween magic.

When Billie Kay had finished clucking and cooing over her entirely cluck-worthy granddaughter she introduced me to Tasha.

'You must be proud of this place,' I said and she nodded. 'Independence might be a small town but I get the impression it would have been a lot smaller if it hadn't been for Taylor's.'

'What do you mean?'

'I keep meeting people who tell me they met their husband or wife here.'

Tasha's cheeks tightened as a broad grin took over her face.

'You're meeting another one right now,' she said. 'And it's not just me… one of my sisters met her husband here too.'

'Really?'

'Oh yeah!'

It took me a moment to work out how Tasha answered my question without moving her lips before I realised it wasn't her at all. It was a fast moving Billie Kay approaching from the left. Her radar had alerted her to the fact that a family story was about to be told and she had to be a part of it.

'Yeah, two of my three daughters met their husbands in

here,' she grinned. 'This must have been about 16 years ago, right, Tasha?'

Tasha nodded, happy to concede storytelling duties to her Mom. Sixteen years ago the man who would become her husband had been part of a large group of vintage motorbike enthusiasts who had come through town on a ride one day and stopped at the store. Billie Kay had been outside chatting to the young chap as he fiddled with the engine in his oil-stained shirt just as Tasha returned from a shopping trip and sashayed past on her way inside.

'Well, he took one look at her in this beautiful sundress, looking really cute and his eyes got real big and his mouth just dropped and I thought, "uh oh", isn't that right, Tasha?'

'Uh huh.'

So the oil-stained vintage biker and his pals had come into the store and Billie Kay introduced them all to her daughter. They sat along the counter and he'd made a bee-line for the seat next to Tasha.

'Well after 10 minutes, she just excused herself and left. She came back after a couple of hours and said, "I'm sorry Mom, I'd have helped you out with those customers but that gentleman was just too familiar", isn't that right, Tasha?'

'Uh huh.'

In spite of her daughter's cool reaction, Billie Kay's motherly instincts knew something was up and that night when a young man phoned the family home and asked for Tasha, she knew it was him.

Only it wasn't him, it was just one of Tasha's friends.

'I thought, "Gee... I was so sure he was smitten!"'

But, just as Billie Kay was coming to doubt her female intuition, she was proved right after all when a letter arrived in the mail.

'It was an introduction letter from him saying that he'd been on this wonderful ride through the countryside and that he'd found this wonderful store and that he'd really love to ask if he could possibly have her phone number to call her.

'So she passed the letter to me and her sisters and we all said it sounded wonderful and she sent a note back saying yes, he could call her. He had a ring made for her after the first date and they were married a year later. Isn't that right, Tasha?'

'Uh huh.'

It all seemed so impossibly romantic. A man sending a formal letter of introduction sounds so charming and old-fashioned, it surely belonged in the pages of a Charlotte Brontë novel, not real life. And bear in mind, this was *only* 16 years ago. *I* was dating 16 years ago! Not very successfully, I have to admit, but I know for a fact that letters of introduction were not part of the standard wooing procedure of the day. As far as I can remember it largely involved blushing profusely, looking at your own shoes and grunting unintelligibly. Now I know where I was going wrong.

'This place is match-making central!' I said with a chuckle.

'Yes it is,' grinned Billie Kay. 'My youngest daughter, Susie; same thing. This wrestling team from the college kept coming in and I knew one of them had eyes for her. Isn't that right, Tasha?'

'Uh huh.'

'Well,' I said, 'We're definitely going to hang around for a bit. This might be my best chance yet of meeting the woman of my dreams.'

'What, *you?*'

Billie Kay clearly didn't rate my chances. She looked me up and down and wrinkled her nose as if to suggest that I wasn't a good enough specimen for the womenfolk of Independence before adopting a miracles-can-happen tone of voice and shrugging a playful, 'ahhh… you never know.'

'Well, thank you very much!'

It was my turn to take mock offence now and Billie Kay responded by offering me an *only-kidding* hug before scurrying off to attend to someone who needed serving.

I sat back and watched Marley, Kinsey, Tasha and Billie Kay working like clockwork together; three generations of one family in cheerful harmony. For a moment it seemed like a vision of perfection but it can't have been because moments later it got even better when a fourth generation showed up in the shape of Billie Kay's 83-year-old mother, Marge.

Marge walked with the slow, precise steps you might expect for someone of her years but she wasn't just there to observe, she was there to work like everyone else.

'Mom's been making egg salad two or three times a week for, ooh, 50-something years now,' said Billie Kay with a wry smile. 'I called her this morning and said we need some egg salad and she said, "Oh, not again!" I said, "Mom... it's the last time you'll ever have to make egg salad. The last time." And she's made it. She won't let anyone else do it. She does the egg salad, she washes the aprons and the towels, she goes to the grocery store. She gets mad if we try to go out and unload the car for her. She carries everything in. Says it's good for her. And I s'pose it is.'

They really were a remarkable family. I watched in amazement as this 83-year-old great-grandma scooped a two-year-old cheerleader up into her arms with ease. Maybe, I thought, I'd discovered their secret. Maybe the soda fountain was just a decoy. Maybe the *fountain* their neon sign was referring to was the fountain of eternal youth they obviously kept out the back. Or maybe it was simpler than that and these estimable ladies had simple stumbled upon the recipe for a happy and healthy life: work hard and eat a lot of ice cream.

Billie Kay certainly saw the value of work to young people.

'The one thing that really upsets me about closing,' she confessed with misty eyes, 'is that Sonia won't get the chance to work here. All of the others have. I hope there'll be somewhere that will give her this kind of experience.'

Not only had all but one of her grandchildren and all of her children worked there it seemed that all of this mother hen's unofficial kids had worked there too.

'My son set up an advertising office for his company in Japan,' she told me. 'He lived there for five years and I thought, well, if the people of Japan are being nice to my son, I ought to do something nice for them... so I answered an ad in the paper asking people to take in foreign students.'

I couldn't fault her logic.

'So I took in these four Japanese high-school girls and they were delightful. When they'd gone I got a phone call from the English Language School asking if I would take in another student. So I did. And Yarakuni has become like an adopted son to me now. He's been back and forth for the last eight years, y'know? He's in Japan right now, trying to raise the money to put himself through school here.'

'Do you think he'll be sad when he comes back and this place is gone?'

'Sure. I've explained that we're not the norm anymore. That America's changed, that this store and this town are no longer the average. If you close your eyes for 10 minutes, when you open them up you're not going to know you're in the same place. Because there's going to be a Taco Bell and a McDonald's and a Walmart and so on. Everything's going to look the same. Everything.'

As the day unfolded I started to wonder why the place was closing. The main players might well have reached retirement age but they appeared to have boundless energy.

I guess I'd expected to find places going out of business because of competition from the chains but there wasn't a cookie-cutter Dairy Queen across the road competing for their customers – and if there had been, I dare say it would have lost.

Then, while watching Billie Kay replace a roll of paper in the till, I think I worked it out.

Instead of just slotting a new roll into the machine she was going through the laborious process of rolling the paper on to its cardboard spool first.

'Nobody makes paper the right size anymore,' she explained. 'So we take old rolls that we've already used and wind them backwards so we can print on the other side of the paper. It's the same with the ribbon. You can't get the right size anymore but I got one out of an old calculator and tied it on. We like to keep the old till going. These old machines are so reliable. They never break down, they just stop making the parts.'

And surely that was it in a nutshell. Wasn't that the reason Taylor's was closing? The days when children were expected to follow their parents into the business are gone. We enjoy more mobility now than ever before. These days children grow up and do things like move to Japan for five years to set up advertising offices. While Billie Kay's granddaughters were getting their work experience at the family store none of her children worked there full-time. They all had careers of their own.

It didn't matter how long Billie Kay and Marge kept the place going, there was no one to replace them. Billie Kay was the till-roll for this old machine and Marge was its ribbon. The place wasn't broken. It was perfect. It could keep on going for ever. But they've stopped making the parts.

Chapter 13
And when I say, 'knife', I mean 'machete'

It might have taken us seven days to get from one Independence to the other but at this point I was feeling pretty damn good about the whole thing. Our unchained journey was still intact – we hadn't yet given a red cent to The Man™ – and I reckon our Taylor's experience had made the whole stupid detour worthwhile.

There was something thrillingly perfect about the bittersweet occasion of their last day. Seeing 62 years of trading coming to such a sad but graceful end was undeniably special. If we'd been there the day before it wouldn't have been anywhere near as meaningful. A day later and we'd have missed out completely.

It was tempting to believe that the fates were on our side. Maybe the cars burnt-out brakes and Stef's burnt-out back had happened for a reason. Maybe someone somewhere was looking after us after all.

That feeling of being looked after didn't last long. When you see the route we took you'll understand why.

As you can see our drive from one Independence to the other is pretty similar in terms of distance to our drive from the second Independence to Moab. But while the first of those journeys took us a week, the second of them would take us a full fortnight. Our progress was getting ever slower and there was nothing I could do about it.

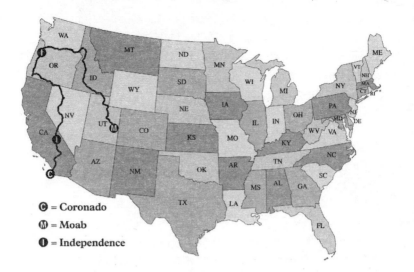

C = Coronado
M = Moab
I = Independence

I knew we were in for a rough ride when I knocked on Stef's door the next morning.

'Yeah?'

Her voice sounded muffled and distant.

'Come on, Badger,' I said, trying to buoy her up, 'it's me, Dave.'

'All right. I'm on my way.'

I was left standing in the cold carpark for an inordinately long time. I knew her room was small – it was a mirror image of my own – so my first thought was that she must be in the middle of getting dressed. I was wrong. She was just walking very, very slowly. When the door eventually swung open, the Stef that greeted me was not a happy one.

'Why did you call me Badger?' she asked, her eyes narrowing.

'Have you ever seen *Bodger and Badger*?'

She studied me to see if I was making things up.

'No.'

'It's a kids' TV show,' I ploughed on. 'There's a bloke called Bodger and he's got a friend called Badger, who's a badger. Well, he's a glove puppet really but you know what I mean.'

'So why am I being named after a glove puppet of a badger?'

'You really haven't seen it, have you?'

'No.'

'It's the theme music, isn't it?' One look at her blank expression and I knew I was going to have to sing it. 'Everybody knows, Badger loves... mashed potato!' Stef's face remained unmoved. How could this fail to cheer her up? How could this fail to cheer anyone up? 'I don't really know the rest of the words,' I confessed.

Stef said nothing.

What the hell, I thought, I might as well give it a go.

'Everybody knows, Badger loves... mashed potato!'

Nothing.

'Something and something else, something and oojaflip...'

Not even a smile.

'Bodger and Badger, Bodger and Badger, La, la, la, la-lah, la, la, la, la-lah...'

'I'm not in the mood.'

'Are you all right?'

It was obvious that Stef was far from all right.

'No,' she said. 'I'm in agony.'

Now that I looked at her again, I could see that she was standing awkwardly. It was as if she was scared to move, as if her body was held together by a thin layer of tissue paper and spit and she was worried she'd fall apart at the seams if the delicate balance was disturbed.

'I can't bend,' she said. 'At all. I can't move.' There was a pause. 'Dave... I'm worried.'

'Okay,' I'd started talking before I knew what I was going to actually say, 'so we're obviously not filming today and that's okay...'

'I need a chiropractor.'

'Exactly what I was going to suggest. Now, don't move... whereabouts is it hurting?'

I don't know why I asked. It's not as though furnishing me with the information was going to leave me better placed to deal with the problem. Stef tried to gesture towards whichever combination of muscles and tendons it was that she'd damaged but even that slight movement seemed to send her into spasms of agony.

It was Taylor's that had done it. Stef had worked like a trooper filming their last day. At the time I'd taken this as evidence that she was back to normal and that the combination of a day off and a massage had worked some magical health-restoring magic. I was wrong. With the heavy camera in her hands every minute that passed did a little more damage to her back. She was oblivious to it at the time because she was too consumed with enthusiasm for the task in hand. She'd got through the day on a burst of adrenaline. Adrenaline drives you on. Adrenaline masks pain. Overnight, that adrenaline had been washed away by the tide of sleep, leaving the pain very much exposed.

'Look, just take it easy,' I said, 'I'll get the *Yellow Pages*, we'll find a local chiropractor and we'll take another day off. I'm pretty sure we can stay another night here…'

'No,' said Stef. 'Not here.'

It was an entirely understandable reaction. 'Here' wasn't the most salubrious of locations.

Having left Taylor's neither of us had been keen on heading back to the motel we'd stayed in the night before so instead we'd decided to make the 15-mile drive into Oregon's capital city, Salem. (I know it's not *the* Salem of seventeenth-century witch trials fame – that was thousands of miles away in Massachusetts – but even so, there was something satisfying about driving our 666 into a Salem on Halloween. *Mwah ha ha ha ha.*)

When we got there, finding a bed for the night had proved trickier than we'd expected. We found a city centre motel quite quickly and everything seemed to be in order but when the elderly owner spotted our camera equipment he swiftly withdrew our rooms.

'What do you mean you're fully booked?' I protested. 'You just said you had two rooms! You've got the keys right there! I just saw you take those two keys off those two hooks there!'

'Not for you! Not with your camera! We don't want your sort!'

'We're not any type of sort! We just want a couple of rooms.'

'We're fully booked.'

'But…'

'No.'

We'd driven on to the outskirts of the city where we were taunted by a plethora of chain hotels. Eventually, on the outskirts of the outskirts we'd found a small homely-looking place with whitewashed wooden walls and neatly painted bright red windowsills.

We'd just pulled into the parking lot when a door to one of the rooms opened and a man came out to stand and stare at us. While I could see past him and into his room I didn't need to see the photographs on the wall and the ornaments on a sideboard to know that he was a permanent resident, his body language was territorial enough.

He stood with his feet apart and his hands on his hips, staring us down. He wore tight black jeans and a tiny white vest over his muscular and heavily tattooed frame. His hair was scraped back into a jet black ponytail which dripped down his back. He had a knife in his right hand. And when I say, 'knife', I mean 'machete'.

A man stepped from behind him and stood by his side. They looked so similar – blue jeans, white vest, a blanket of tattoos and a black ponytail – that for a moment it looked like he was some kind of computer game villain, regenerating himself at will. If it wasn't for the fact that only one of them held a knife I'd have suspected it was one man using mirrors.

The first guy looked at the blade. Then he looked at us. I looked at him. He looked at the blade. I didn't look at him. I looked at the gearstick. I slipped her into reverse and we left.

I have no idea how real the threat was or whether we'd inadvertently done anything to invite such behaviour but I wasn't in the mood to find out. Maybe they'd just returned from a fancy-dress Halloween party where they'd gone as two *Miami Vice* cocaine dealers? Maybe they'd had a particularly bad night being harassed by trick-or-treaters and had decided to fight back against anyone who came anywhere near their front door? Or maybe they were a pair of knife-wielding psychopaths?

We drove around aimlessly for almost an hour before eventually stumbling upon the faded glory of the Tiki Lodge. Plastic palms and fake 'wood' carvings vainly tried to evoke the pacific island spirit but the background hum of traffic noise won out. A dual carriageway separated us from a large retail park while a hundred yards west the gargantuan north–south I-5 interstate thundered overhead.

The rooms of the Tiki Lodge can best be described as, well, brown. A 1970s brown that, had it been well maintained, might have had some kitsch appeal but in reality just felt a bit seedy. The seediness of the place was nicely topped off by the novelty 'massaging bed'. By inserting a quarter and turning a switch the bed would vibrate for 15 minutes of what the sign described as 'relaxing tingling comfort'. I had a go. It delivered 15 minutes of wishing I hadn't wasted a quarter.

So I understood why Stef didn't want to stay at the hotel and, in light of our hotel-hunting adventures of the night before we decided to pass on Salem in its entirety.

'Look,' I said, 'you know I want to avoid the big cities and stuff… but it's not like we're in a normal situation here, so why don't we head to Portland? It's about an hour away, and there's got to be a chiropractor in Portland…'

'Sounds great,' said Stef smiling, and then wincing as the muscles in her face set off a chain reaction that seemed to make the muscles in her back do something they weren't supposed to do.

I started to load the car up while Stef tried out various ways of standing to see which was the least painful. We weren't the only ones checking out. Seven men traipsed out of the room two doors down from mine. Their ragged clothes were tattered and torn. Their faces were almost varnished with layers of dirt buried deep in their pores. They had hollow cheeks and hollow stares to match. They were, quite obviously, homeless. It made sense. With rooms at $39 plus tax they could have a roof over their heads, hot water, a TV and most importantly, safety, for a little over $6 each. And for only 25 cents extra they could all have a go on the vibra-bed too.

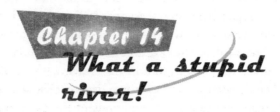

Chapter 14

What a stupid river!

Our first day post-Independence turned into a bit of a non-event as far as I was concerned. It was certainly a day when we failed to hit our targets. We were supposed to be on a road trip and I don't think anyone would suggest that driving only 50 miles really qualifies. We were supposed to be avoiding the big cities but Portland is the biggest city in Oregon and Salem is its capital. We were supposed to be avoiding the interstate and yet our day's drive was conducted solely on I-5.

It wasn't the first time we'd transgressed on these points but it was the first time when we screwed up all three in one day. The only saving grace was that our headline goal was still intact. At least we were still successfully unchained.

But unfortunately it was a sign of things to come. Over the next week Stef would see two more chiropractors, one in Boise – the largest city and capital of Idaho – and the

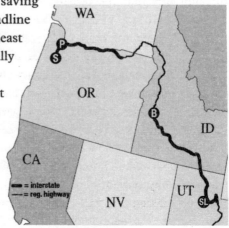

other in Salt Lake City – the largest city and capital of Utah, and getting there involved more interstate than anything else.

It became clear that Stef was experiencing a law of diminishing returns when it came to her time on the chiropractor's table. She emerged from every session feeling better but on each occasion the sense of well-being she took from it lasted for a shorter duration than the last. She felt okay for a day after Portland but was in agony within hours of leaving Boise. In Salt Lake City we decided to stay for three days so that she could have more than one session at the hands of the same practitioner but even so the next time she picked up the camera she lasted 40 minutes before she was once again forced to call a halt to proceedings. Three days off, 40 minutes on. The odds weren't looking good.

While this was clearly a horrible situation for Stef I can't pretend that I was happy about it either. I know it's selfish of me but deep down I was resenting the fact that *my* journey was being ruined by *her* back.

You've got to remember, this trip was planned long before the film was on the cards. I didn't turn down work, clear my diary, save up my money and sell my car so that I could be the driver on a film about Stef's back, did I? I wasn't doing this in order to make a film at all! My one condition for agreeing to the film was that the journey didn't change. The film was meant to be a document of what happened. It didn't matter that we'd gone off course. It didn't really matter that I'd driven in the wrong direction for hundreds of miles just to visit a town called Independence because if *that's what happened, that's what the film was about.* But the film wasn't supposed to be dictating where we went and when we stopped... and yet, via the medium of Stef's bad back that's exactly what it was now doing.

Now, obviously I know that it wasn't Stef's fault. But in a way that only served to make the situation worse. I'd set my heart on making this trip. It was a once-in-a-lifetime opportunity and it was being royally screwed up by circumstances beyond my control. Coast to coast across America: that's the trip of a lifetime; slowly from clinic to fucking clinic just doesn't cut it. We weren't experiencing the joys of the open road, we were limping across America like a wounded animal, which, with only one and a half functioning backs between us, is pretty much what we were.

I *wanted* to have someone to blame. I *needed* to have someone to blame. I wish Stef had been bad at her job because then I'd have been able to say something about it. That would have cleared the air. That would have got it out of my system. But she wasn't. She was ace. What was I going to do... tell a girl who's in pain that her back's shit?

There was no one to be angry at. Except, of course, myself. I'd agreed to the film. I'd chosen Stef. It was my fault.

With no way of letting off steam, the anger continued to boil inside me. It festered away, feeding itself and slowly, bit by bit, it started to consume me.

I tried my best to keep on top of it. I tried my best to perk the experience up. If you look at the route we took from Portland to Salt Lake City you can see there is one sizeable diversion from the interstate where we looped up north, cut across the corner of Washington and then returned south through Idaho on smaller roads. It's as if the journey from Portland describes a perfect graph of my worsening mood and if that really is the case, well, that three-day diversion represents an uplifting blip of positivity on the moodometer because that's when we stayed in a Beagle.

Late one night in an Oregon motel, with rain pouring down outside and team morale at an all-time low, I decided to get online to see if I could repeat the treehouse trick. Booking somewhere different to stay had proved an effective morale booster once, so why not a second time? I scoured the web looking for a novel location, somewhere, anywhere, en route that would give us that much needed fillip. One glance at the website of Dog Bark Park, a B&B in the small town of Cottonwood, Idaho, and I was sure I'd nailed it. What a truly wondrous thing the internet is! I *love* the internet. (Trust me, I speak as a man who once sold a hot-air balloon on eBay.)

The only problem with the place was that it was some distance away. Two days had passed since we'd left Independence and in that time we'd barely travelled 120 miles. Getting to Dog Bark Park would involve a drive of roughly 350 miles. The place was only available on one night, after that they were shutting up shop for the winter, so if I made a reservation it meant we'd have to do the whole thing in one long drive. I made the reservation. I wanted to be doing long drives. I wanted to force our hand and give us a reason to push on.

Many obstacles stood between us and the B&B, not least the Cascade Mountains. The Cascades start in California and the range runs through the length of Oregon on through Washington and continues on into Canada.

We'd crossed the Cascades once already as we'd travelled east to west from Nevada into southern Oregon. The sun was shining at the time. We saw the signs warning us that some of the mountain roads would be closed in the winter and we passed the laybys specially set aside for motorists to put chains on their tyres and at the time they elicited nothing more than mild curiosity. But the mornings had grown noticeably colder since then and with the local TV news channels carrying severe weather warnings our curiosity had turned to trepidation.

I view tyre chains in much the same way as I do bullet-proof vests. If they're deemed necessary, I'd really rather not bother at all. Besides, if we were trying to keep our souls and our wallets chain-free I could see no reason why our tyres shouldn't join in.

Luckily for us there is one sea-level passage across the Cascade Mountains and we were perfectly placed to take it. It's called the Columbia River Gorge and Mother Nature crafted it many thousands of years ago with the help of some glacial floods.

The Columbia River starts in the Canadian Rockies and flows into the Pacific Ocean due west of Portland. As the crow flies it's a journey of around 400 miles but as the river flows it's more than 1,200. It passes through one Canadian territory and seven US states. A glance at a map will show you that five of those states are completely unnecessary.

What a stupid river! Imagine visiting states that aren't on your route and covering three times as many miles as you need to as a result! You wouldn't catch me doing anything like that.

For the last 100 miles of its journey the river acts as a natural border between Washington to the north and Oregon to the south and with eminent good sense I-84 hugs the riverbank and carries motorists through the mountains.

On the day we negotiated it, a violent wind was bouncing through the gorge whipping the water up from the river and throwing it sideways at the car, adding to the already torrential rain that thundered down from on high. This wasn't the best time to discover quite how ineffective our ancient windscreen wipers were. They'd lived most of their life in the California sun and the rubber had been baked into brittle uselessness, which meant that each swoop of the blade did little more than redistribute the water that obscured my view. It felt like I was looking at a magic-eye poster version of the road in front of me, I sort of knew it was there but I had to defocus my eyes to find it. And just when I felt sure of the path we were on, a gust of wind would buffet the car with unpredictable ferocity and knock us ever so slightly off course.

When the weather is friendly I don't doubt that the Columbia River Gorge is a place of stunning beauty but in these conditions, the craggy mountains that towered overhead to our right and the vast expanse of rough-and-tumble river that bubbled away to our left just gave the landscape an ever more threatening air.

As we left the gorge the road stayed with the river for a while as it dipped down and round the land's natural contours through bleak rolling moors. To my untrained eye the land here looked largely unmanaged – and unmanageable – but I must have been wrong because every 30 or 40 miles a huge cylindrical grain elevator would loom up: a rural skyscraper proving that communities existed and crops were grown nearby.

We stayed on I-84 as it waved goodbye to the Columbia and started to dip south-east towards Boise. The rain cleared and the wind died down. It felt good. I felt like a survivor.

We left the interstate at Pendleton, heading north on Highway 11. We'd already eaten up more miles than the last three days combined which is probably why, when I pulled off Highway 11 and crawled into the tiny community of Adams, Stef assumed I was on the lookout for a motel.

'Population 297,' she said, her voice dripping with cynicism, 'do you really think we'll find somewhere to stay around here?'

'It's highly unlikely,' I said, 'but then that's not what I'm looking for. I've already sorted out our accommodation for tonight. I'm afraid we've got a lot more driving to do yet. Right now, I'm looking for gas.'

'You've already sorted out tonight? Really? Where are we staying?'

'It's a surprise,' I said, trying to project an air of mystery. 'Don't worry, it's really special.'

'Hmm.'

Stef's tone was definitely more suspicious than excited.

'What d'you mean by that?' I asked. 'You can trust me.'

'Can I! We both know what happened the last time you booked somewhere "special"!'

'What?'

'It only had one bed! Come on, Dave,' she teased, 'we both know you were trying it on.'

'Give over.' I paused. 'Not with your back!'

'Ha. Not with your face.'

'Oi!'

I pulled up outside the Adams' general store; a pretty little red-brick building with green-and-white gingham drapes. It presented a nice old-fashioned shop front to the world with the words, 'Inland Mercantile and General Merchandise' neatly painted directly on to the masonry. They'd probably given it a fresh coat every year since the place was built in 1895.

There was no pump in evidence but I figured it was as good

a place as any to ask. The store was just as quaint on the inside although somehow the sum of its parts didn't quite add up. I think it was all just a bit too hokey. While the building was clearly authentic and old, the feel on the inside was a bit ersatz. It could just as well have been Ye Olde Tyme Store in a Disney theme park.

I'd loved the Holland General Store because it was a living, breathing, necessary part of its community; here in Adams it seemed that what they were really selling was nostalgia.

'An independent gas station? In Adams? I'm afraid not,' said the middle-aged lady behind the till with an endearingly apologetic frown. 'I'm afraid you'll have to go all the way to Athena for that.'

From her tone of voice I assumed that a trip from Adams to Athena was quite a serious undertaking. According to my calculations we had around 50 miles left in the tank. I hoped it would be enough.

'So how far is Athena?' I asked.

'Ooh... let me see... it's about five miles.'

We jinked across Washington's bottom right-hand corner taking in a hundred miles of twisty, turny country roads all the while aware that we were racing against the setting sun. The sun won. By the time we made it to the Washington/Idaho border it was pitch black.

All along this stretch of road signs kept reminding us that we were on the Lewis and Clark Trail. The story of Lewis and Clark[4] is taught to all American schoolkids but it seems to be one of those culturally specific bits of history that isn't particularly well known elsewhere.

Before this journey I'd only ever heard of them because they were mentioned in an episode of *The Simpsons* in which Marge tells Bart and Lisa a collection of historical tales.

[4] Not to be confused with the mid-'90s TV series, *Lois and Clark: The New Adventures of Superman* starring Dean Cain and Teri Hatcher.

Their story dates back to the start of the nineteenth century, a time when a map of North America looked very different to that which we see today.

Back then there were only 13 states in the Union. Texas was a republic while Britain, France, Spain and Mexico all owned parts of what would one day be the 50 states.

Roughly speaking, the original 13 states occupied the easternmost third of the modern-day USA while a huge swathe of territory, some 530 million acres running from Louisiana and the Gulf of Mexico up to modern-day Montana and the border with Canada, was owned by France.

In 1803, President Jefferson oversaw the purchase of this land from the French for around $15 million. It doesn't sound like much for an area three times the size of France itself but given that they'd obviously stolen it from the Native Americans in the first place, I suppose they couldn't grumble. Once some debts had been wiped out and the estate agents had taken their commission, Napoleon's France ended up pocketing a little more than $8 million. Which is about how much it cost Pepsi Cola to secure the services of Britney Spears. Times have changed.

Anyway, once the United States had bought this land they naturally started wondering about what could be found if they travelled even further west and so, at Jefferson's behest, an expedition was set up to do just that. It was led by Meriwether Lewis and William Clark and along with nearly 40 others and a Newfoundland dog called Seaman, they spent a couple of years exploring and mapping the American west. Which makes me feel a bit pathetic for moaning about my windscreen wipers.

They clearly made their mark on this part of the world because straddling the Washington/Idaho border sit two towns that take their names. On the Washington side sits Clarkston and on the Idaho side, Lewiston. If I was in charge of these things there'd also be a little village called Seamanville snapping at the towns' heels. But I'm not and there isn't. It's just the two towns sitting side by side with no discernible gap between them. If they're twin towns, they must be Siamese twins.

We made our way through these two industrial, paper-mill towns just as another bad storm struck and we got bogged down in what might well have been our first proper traffic jam. Suddenly, I was driving in dense urban traffic with the world's most ineffective windscreen wipers and no real clue as to where I was going. It seemed like a thousand cars were honking their horns and it's entirely feasible they were all honking them at me as I was making turns at random and trusting to luck. If you were driving home in the Lewiston/Clarkston area on the evening of 4 November 2006 and you were cut up by a 1970 Ford Torino estate please accept this rather belated apology.

If memory serves I think we crossed the same river five times in the confusion and pinged back and forth across the state line even more often than that.

Eventually, spying a sign for a route heading south on Highway 95 I put my foot down and span us out of the congested heart of Lewiston and off into rural Idaho powering on into the pitch black and driving rain.

We were still some 60 miles away from our destination. Another hour. Longer in these conditions. Now that it was dark the poor performance of our windscreen wipers was even more of a factor. The piercing glare of headlights refracted in each drop of water that remained, creating hundreds of tiny, confusing, kaleidoscopic versions of the road ahead. My eyelids grew heavy.

It was only as we finally approached Cottonwood that the rain finally gave up.

'You must be knackered,' said Stef. 'Are you sure we're okay? Are we getting close?'

'Yeah I'm fine,' I said, rapidly blinking my eyes to check. 'And don't worry, we're very nearly there… oh my God… look at that!'

I flicked our headlights on to full beam and they did their feeble best to illuminate the scene. Standing in a small triangular plot of land created by two diverging roads was a huge wooden dog. Its snout must have been 30 feet in the air yet it was, unmistakeably, a beagle. Relief hit me. We were there. This giant dog was going to be our home for the night. But there was no need to tell Stef just yet.

'That is amazing!' I said. 'Look at that... a giant beagle!'

'That's brilliant,' said Stef.

'Do you want to take a closer look?'

'I dunno,' she shrugged. 'It's up to you. We could always come and have a look at it in the morning when it's light.'

'Nah, let's have a shufti now.'

'All right... but if we are, I think I ought to film it...'

The camera had been sitting in the back seat for most of the day but now Stef was twisting awkwardly, reaching into the back of the car to pick it up as I pulled off the road and into the grounds.

A hundred yards from the giant dog was a small outbuilding the size of a village scout hut. There was a family saloon car parked up outside it so I guided us in alongside that. As I did so, the door to the building opened up and light spilled out as two figures emerged.

'I think we're on somebody's property,' said Stef nervously.

'We'll be all right,' I said, trying to hide my inner smile. I was enjoying the soon-to-be-revealed secret. 'You wouldn't build a giant beagle and not expect people to stop and look at it, would you?'

The two people who had stepped out to greet us were the owners of Dog Bark Park, the world's only beagle-shaped B&B. Dennis had straggly grey hair falling out the back of his sawdust-stained baseball cap and his weathered face was decorated with a cheeky grin. Frances had short dark hair, a patterned waistcoat and a look of motherly concern.

'You made it!' she said. 'We were getting worried about you, what with the bad weather.'

'It's taken longer than I expected,' I said. 'I'm sorry... we should have called.'

'Well at least you're here now,' said Dennis, his voice as soothing as treacle. 'Are you hungry?'

I wasn't hungry until he asked the question, at which point I suddenly realised I was starving. I'd been so focused on making progress that meal times had passed by unnoticed.

'A little,' I said. 'Can you recommend anywhere nearby?'

'Actually, we were wondering if you'd like to come to dinner with us,' said Frances sweetly. 'We like to get to know the people who stay here. Only if you'd like to, that is.'

'We'd love to,' I said. 'Wouldn't we, Stef?'

I turned to see that Stef was on duty with the camera at her shoulder. The half a face that poked out from behind it carried a wry smile.

'Absolutely,' she said. 'Of course we would.'

She'd obviously worked out that we'd reached our destination, but I wasn't sure that she'd worked out exactly where we'd be staying. The beagle was huge, but would anyone assume that it was a building?

'Why don't you get your bags inside?' Frances handed me a set of keys. 'Take 10 minutes to sort yourselves out and then we can all go to dinner?'

I opened up the trunk of the car, hoiked out the first of our many bags and strode off towards the giant beagle. Stef wasn't far behind.

'What the hell's going on?' she whispered when we were far enough from Dennis and Frances to get away with it.

'This is where we're staying,' I explained in my best isn't-it-obvious voice.

'Here? What? With them? Where? Who are they?'

'Well not exactly *with* them,' I said. 'But here… in their dog.'

'What?'

'Inside the dog,' I continued. 'It's a B&B.'

'What? Really?'

'Yeah.'

A wooden staircase started by the dog's rear right leg, climbed up underneath the tail and round the other flank, entering the body near his left shoulder. Or should I say 'her shoulder?' Yes. I think I should.

As we climbed those stairs we both started to laugh, low, unfocused, gurgling laughs.

'I'll give you this one,' said Stef. 'This is amazing!'

'And how *nice* are they?' I added. 'It's not every B&B owner who offers to take you out for dinner!'

'It's not every B&B that's shaped like a giant dog either!'

I opened the door and we stepped inside. It was warm. It was cosy. It had small touches that make a big difference. Rarely has a bowl of fruit made me quite so excited. Vitamins!

Unsurprisingly, the room was decorated with a decidedly doggy theme. There was a bookshelf of dog-related books and doggy ornaments were perching on every spare bit of shelf.

I walked through the door to my right where, inside the dog's rear end, I found a nice, modern bathroom. I walked back into his belly. At the other end was a staircase, taking you up his neck and into the head. I climbed a couple of stairs and poked my head around inside his... Oh dear.

'Stef?'

'Yeah.'

'Um...'

'What?'

'It's not what you think...'

'What do you mean?'

'I mean... um... I've done it again...'

I gulped.

'What do you mean?'

'I promise you I *didn't* know but... well, there's only one bed.'

'What?'

'It's *not* what you think.'

Chapter 15
Buzzzzzzawhirrrrrrr

However impressive the B&Beagle had looked when we arrived it still had the power to surprise when I saw it again by daylight. I stood back on a small knoll to take in the scene and found myself chuckling at the ridiculous vision. The dog was as big as a three-storey building. It was standing in rolling prairie land, surrounded by fields of wispy, yellow grass waving gently in the breeze. But no matter how enormous it was, it was still dwarfed by the biggest of skies; a delicious deep blue canvas filled with candyfloss clouds. Yes, I know I've just resorted to a tired and lazy cliché... but I didn't start it, Idaho did. Honestly, its skyscapes were so perfect they *were* clichés... so how else am I supposed to describe them?

The giant beagle wasn't alone. There was also a 12-foot tall 'puppy' and, in case either dog needed to mark their territory, a supersized bright-red fire hydrant too. In cartoonland a fire hydrant might represent the classic doggy toilet but in a cute twist this hydrant was actually a human loo in disguise; a convenient convenience placed there to assist any curious travellers who might stop to take a look at the place.

People who spend large chunks of their time in hotel rooms often grumble about the impersonal nature of their surroundings. Hotels always claim to be your home-away-from-home but the nature of their business means they almost always fail to meet that lofty aim. Somehow, when the TV remote control is attached to the bedside table on a retractable wire and the picture frames are screwed to the wall things, just don't feel very homely.

I understand why hotels – especially the low-cost variety – do this sort of thing. They simply can't afford to trust people. But you can't provide homeliness without trust.

I think this might be the best feature of Dog Bark Park. Even though the accommodation is so strangely housed inside the belly of a large wooden dog it is undeniably homely. There are *things* in the room. Ornaments, books, magazines, photographs, toys and board games are all there and you know where they came from. You know *who* put them there. You *could* steal them. But you don't. And you don't because in leaving them there, Dennis and Frances have trusted you not to.

I know that all theft is wrong. At the same time we all have an instinctive, emotional sense that there is a greater wrong in stealing from a person than there is in stealing from a business. If someone was to break into my neighbour's house and steal their CDs I know I would feel worse about it than if they broke into HMV and did the same.

This is why a chain hotel can't afford to trust us. Because they know some people *will* happily steal from them. Why? Because people are more comfortable stealing from a business that has no real personality, where the person who suffers the loss is – we assume – a faceless millionaire with no emotional attachment to whatever it is you're stealing.

You could never say the same about a one-of-a-kind business like Dog Bark Park. There, you know the contents of the room are the personal effects of Dennis and Frances. You meet them when you check in, you look them in the eye and you know that this very special B&B is *theirs*. They designed, built and decorated it. And they love it.

Not that the B&B is their only business concern. Over dinner the night before they had explained how it came to exist.

Dennis used to be a building contractor. He was successful but unsatisfied with his lot. He wanted to change things. He wanted to be an artist.

'I felt inside me that I could do it,' he said. 'So I picked up a chainsaw and got a lump of wood and had a go at carving something.'

'What did you carve?'

'A pile of sawdust.' Dennis sipped at his beer. 'I couldn't do it. But I *wanted* to. So I didn't give up... I just kept on carving. I got better at it. And I've never regretted a day of it.'

Five years into his new life as a self-taught chainsaw carver, Dennis met Frances and the two of them have been together ever since. These days they carve dogs together and their two-person production line can cope with something like 125 different breeds.

The building our car was parked in front of is their studio and gift shop and the real base of their business. Of course there's quite a difference between carving small doggy sculptures and building a 30-foot-tall beagle that folks can live in.

'Originally it was just going to be a billboard,' explained Frances. 'It seemed like a good idea to build something which would attract more people; let them know that we were here carving our dogs.'

'Then one evening we got talking over dinner,' added Dennis, 'and we thought about making it a little larger and eventually we came up with a B&B. We thought that might attract even more attention... and it has.'

I loved the way they made it sound like the most rational of decisions. It can't be. It's a giant dog.

Dennis and Frances don't live on site but we hadn't been up for long when their car rolled into view. We exchanged cheery greetings and then the two of them set about opening the store. They fetched out half a dozen wooden sculptures representing various different breeds. A Welsh corgi, a Dalmatian, a Schnauzer and, of course, a few beagles were all arranged on the front porch.

Stef decided this was worth filming and so I stayed out of the way and out of shot and had a bit of rough and tumble play with a real dog, Dennis and Frances's energetic golden retriever, Luther.

'Hey, Dave!'

It was Stef calling me.

'What?'

'Come and have a look at this.'

With Luther leading the way, I headed inside.

'I thought you'd want to see this,' said Stef excitedly. 'I'm going to have a dog carved for me!'

Dennis picked up a slab of wood, about the size of two large encyclopaedias. Using a handmade template, he drew a 2-D beagle on the wood and then, using a bandsaw, he cut the block down to a very rough outline. Then came the fun part: the chainsaw. Dennis seemed lost in his thoughts as he wedged the wood in a vice, pulled the cord to set the engine in motion and, using a series of tiny little jabs, started etching out the dog's physique.

'You seem to really like people,' I said between bursts of the whirring, buzzing, whining engine. 'On the other hand, carving seems quite solitary. Did you have to adjust to the hospitality side of things?'

'Not really.' *Buzzzzuzzzzzurrr.* 'I think we've always been in hospitality. We've always invited people into the studio to watch us carve.' *Wazzzzirrrrrrrrkukka.* 'Obviously, when we put people up the hospitality side is bigger.'

'Do you ever think about expanding? Building another dog?'

'D'you know, we've given that a lot of thought.' *Buzzukuzzzzuzzzz.* 'Our first plan was to build five big dogs and rent them all out. Different breeds. But we've been so amazed by the relationship we can have with our guests.' *Buzzzzuzzz.* 'We can spend time with them. We didn't really anticipate that upside to the business. After we'd been open for a couple of years, we got to thinking about building more but then we realised... if we had four more we wouldn't be able to spend so much time with each guest. We're gonna ride with one dog for a while. We enjoy our lives the way they are.'

'It sounds like you've got things worked out.'

'Well,' *Buzzzzzzawhirrrrrrrrr,* 'the conventional view of business is that unless you grow you're not successful. But we don't feel that way at all. We live where we want to live, we do what we like and we have a lifestyle we enjoy. There are different kinds of success and we like ours just the way it is.'

He picked the part-formed dog out of the vice and held it up to the light, checking it from various angles. He seemed happy and passed it to Frances who also gave it the once-over before wedging it into her vice a little nearer the front of the building.

'So who stays in the dog?' asked Stef. 'Who are your customers?'

'We like to think of them as "light adventurers",' said Frances, still assessing the wooden hound. 'It's not an extreme sport, y'know... but it's different.'

'And it's not a chain motel either with its predictable – *exactly predictable* – features,' added Dennis with a visible sense of distaste.

'You're a man after my own heart, Dennis,' I said with delight. 'I toured the States last year and *those* motels drove me mad.'

'I don't know how it's become a part of American culture, this homogenisation of us.' He shook his head in disbelief. 'When we wake up in that motel room is that alarm clock immediately to our right? And is that television *immediately* to the left and the one picture immediately on the wall slightly left or right of the television? When you wake up, do you really know if you're in Istanbul or New York City? I don't know how society has moulded us to be comfortable with that.'

'Nor do I...' I started but Dennis was on a roll.

'And if you drive down the road and eat at a chain hamburger place in California or Massachussets, can you tell the difference between the two burgers? Probably not... and it seems to me we're becoming happy with that, that *that's* seen as good... and I just don't know why that is.'

'I think it's to do wi—'

'I know *I* don't think it's good. It just makes life blander. If you go to a mall in Seattle or Los Angeles or Chicago the same stores are there and you can buy the same shirt... there's no real choice.'

'Well, at least you're doing your bit,' I offered cheerfully.

'No. I'm not changing the world one iota,' said Dennis with a smile. 'I'm just living my life the way I want and I hope we appeal to enough people who want things different. Clearly not everyone does.'

If he hadn't been holding a chainsaw I think I might have hugged him.

Frances pulled at the cord and set her chainsaw in motion. It was slightly smaller and operated at a higher pitch. *Buzzzzuzzzeeezz.* With the blade at an oblique angle she smoothed out the edges and trimmed his wooden fur. There's something quite magical about watching such a macho piece of kit used for such a delicate job. And there's something quite extraordinary about seeing a couple work in such harmony too. That two so ridiculously compatible people can find each other in this vast world of ours is surely proof of something remarkable.

Using a blowtorch Frances singed the dog's splinters away. With a spray can of black hardware paint and a tin of white house paint he was soon utterly beaglified. We left him by the woodstove to dry and wandered outside.

'The thing is,' said Dennis, 'I have free choice. That's a very powerful thing. It feels to me that's what America is. I can stop being a building contractor because I want to stop. I can go into the arts because I want to.' He paused and stared out over the wide expanse of nothing. 'I suppose it may be more true in the west because... well, because we've got more space to do our own thing in...'

I gazed out at the prairie and confirmed for myself that they do indeed have more space. To put some context on quite how much space they've got, let me give you some figures.

Idaho is a little bigger than the whole of Great Britain. Great Britain has a population of approximately 60 million people. Idaho has only 1.3 million. But it gets even more ridiculous than that. Cottonwood sits in the largest county in the state of Idaho which, in order to help people with poor memories, is called Idaho County. At 8,500 square miles, Idaho County, Idaho is a little bit bigger than Wales. Population of Wales: 3 million. Population of Idaho County: 15,000. Imagine removing 99.5 per cent of the people in Wales (stop sniggering at the back of the class) and you have Idaho County.

'It's a really beautiful part of the world,' I said, as much to myself as anything. Turning to my hosts I asked, 'Do you think you could run a successful B&B here if it wasn't shaped like a beagle? If it was just a regular place?'

'It's an area that gets a lot of tourists,' said Frances. 'People want to explore Lewis and Clark country, there are lots of things to do nearby like white-water rafting, hiking, horseback tours... so maybe.'

'It's hard to know,' said Dennis. 'But take a look at the building just there.'

I looked across at the plot of land due south of theirs. It looked unoccupied but the architecture was unmistakable. It was a motel.

'What happened?'

'They "improved" the road.'

Dennis explained the lie of the land. Both Dog Bark Park and the former motel were squeezed between two roads. On the east was Highway 95, a major road carrying traffic that thundered past at high speed. On the west was the business loop, a road that carried cars through the town of Cottonwood and back on to Highway 95 further down its course.

'What is now the business loop used to be the main highway. All the traffic used to come through Cottonwood. But then they upgraded it. Even though it passes within a few metres of the motel they weren't allowed to have direct access from the highway. So when you're on the road it means that you've driven past the turn off before you even know the motel is there. If you're looking for a place to stay, well, by the time you see this place it's already too late. You can't get there.'

'No wonder they went out of business.'

'Don't get me wrong,' Dennis shrugged, 'it's not a conspiracy, it's just the way it is. The Highways Department builds roads. Intersections are more dangerous so they want fewer of them. People get from A to B quicker and safer and that means the Highways Department has done its job. At the same time it destroys the fabric of our small-business world. If the traveller can't get to you without a lot of work, you lose his business. Here on the prairie every small town is cut out by HIghway 95 and in every one the downtown business zone is all but destroyed. Unless your business can be sustained by the town alone, you're gone.'

When Stef's dog was dry I loaded up the car and we said our goodbyes.

Dennis lifted his cap and scratched at his head, trying to make his memory kick in.

'I'd love to help you on your way but I can't think of a single gas station that isn't badged,' he said. 'There's a Cenex, a Sinclair and a Shell nearby...'

'I'm afraid you probably are going to find gasoline tough here on the prairie,' said Frances.

'Oh!' Dennis's eyes lit up with a eureka moment. 'I know what you can do!'

Oh joy! He had remembered a gas station after all. I raised my eyebrows encouragingly, urging him to continue...

'How about I buy some gasoline from the Shell station and then sell it to you at a huge profit!'

My lips curled upwards but my heart dropped.

'I suppose that might be technically within our rules,' I chuckled, 'but I'm not sure it would really be in the spirit of things. I guess we'll just have to take our chances and see how far we get.'

Chapter 16
The numbers never lie

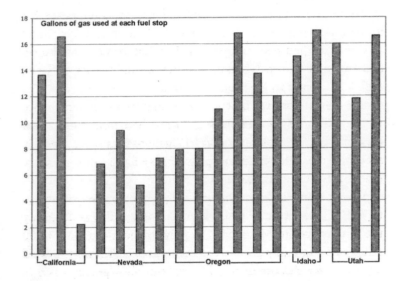

Gallons of gas used at each fuel stop

California   Nevada   Oregon   Idaho   Utah

Every night – or at least every night when it was practical – I would bring my little red notebook into my motel room, open up my laptop and add the information I'd collected about the car's performance to a selection of databases. It helped to pass the time.

I might not have been in complete control of the journey. But at least I was on top of the numbers game. I always knew what our average fuel consumption was and had a sense of how easy or difficult finding unbranded gas was.

The bar chart that I've used to open this chapter shows you

how much gas we pumped at each fuel stop we made on our journey prior to our arrival in Moab.

Our journey had taken us through six states, although we'd only refuelled in five of them, having only been in Washington for a couple of hours on our way to Idaho.

Simply put, where you see a series of tall bars that means we were putting in a lot of gas, which obviously means that gas was harder to find. Where you see shorter bars it means we were having to put in less gas, which means that finding the stuff must have been relatively easy.

With that in mind, Nevada clearly emerges as the best state in which to pursue an unchained life. The only other small amounts we pumped came at our last Californian gas station and our first two in Oregon; in other words, the gas stations that were closest to Nevada.

But the key thing to take in here is that we never came close to pumping the 22 gallons that Grant had told us was our capacity. The highest we got was 17 gallons and there are only six out of the eighteen fuel stops where we had to take on more than 14. Isn't that amazing?

Bear in mind also that the original plan – a journey from LA to NYC – should have taken around 2,800 miles and that by the time we got to Moab we'd already driven more than 3,000 miles and you really get the measure of our achievement. We'd driven *further* than coast to coast without once getting close to our 22-gallon threshold.

I hope you're impressed. I'd like you to imagine I'm sitting next to you. Now pat me on the back and say, *'well done, mate, I didn't think you'd get that far... I'm really bloody impressed.'*

Have you done it? Not out loud, you idiot... now everyone on the train is looking at you! Especially the person sitting next to you. What have you done? You fool. But the rest of you? Have you done it?

Good. Now read on.

★

It was the day we left Boise that Stef and I came closest to an argument. We hadn't got very far before we'd left the interstate in search of fuel and headed into the oddly named town of Mountain Home. I say 'oddly named' because it isn't on, by or even near to a mountain. Sadly for us, it wasn't just deficient in the mountain department; unbranded gas was nowhere to be seen.

Which was a problem because our fuel gauge said we were empty. I never got used to seeing the needle get that low. It didn't matter how many times it happened and how many times we worked out that we weren't *actually* empty, it was always a sight that brought a film of sweat to my palms and a worrisome flutter to my heart.

Now that Mountain Home had failed to nourish the Torino we had to work out where to go next. Stef wanted to rejoin the interstate and continue our journey south towards Salt Lake City. I wanted to change tack and head north-east on the far smaller Highway 20.

To me it was obvious that Highway 20 was the road most likely to provide us with an independent gas station. To Stef it was obvious that the interstate was the road least likely to see us run out of gas in the middle of nowhere.

'Look, if we're going to run out of gas,' she said, 'I want to make sure we're able to get help. If we're on the interstate we're going to be seen. We're going to be near people.'

'Yeah... but if we take the 20 we're more likely to find what we're looking for...'

'You don't *know* that.'

'Well, it's obvious, isn't it,' I said. 'We know that the interstate is the hardest place to find independent gas stations so it stands to reason that...'

'But you don't *know* that. And we don't want to run out in the middle of nowhere. What if there is an independent gas station in the next town off the 84?'

'Well look, neither of us know where the nearest independent gas station is... so we have to head in the direction that we think is most likely to have one...'

'Yeah… but only if it's safe.'

'But the 20 *is* safe. The needle has only just got to empty. And we know that means that we only need around 16 gallons. Which means we've still got 6 gallons left… which means we've got miles left in the tank…'

'So why leave the interstate?'

'Because the needle *says* empty and if we leave it till we really *are* empty it'll be too late! If we take the 20 it's only 50 miles to Hill City – which incidentally looks like it is in the hills but isn't what you or I would call a city – so we're not going to get stranded. We'll get *somewhere*. There'll be *something*.'

I wanted to put my foot down. I wanted to insist that this was *my* journey; that we should go where *I* wanted and then deal with the consequences. But I couldn't. Because it was no longer true. The truth was that we were in this together and I had no right to insist on anything else.

In the end we settled the stand-off in the maturest of ways. We tossed a coin. Stef – and the interstate – won. I sulked. We headed back to I-84.

As if to underline the fact that all was not well our route was decorated with a ridiculous amount of roadkill. I've never seen so many dead animals before. You'd think that in a state with quite so much wide-open space the wildlife would learn to avoid the tarmac but obviously not. They adorned the hard shoulder with such regularity that it felt like the people of Idaho had used them deliberately as some kind of macabre road-markers; perhaps each cadaver signalled that a mile had elapsed?

It wasn't just critters either. At one point we passed three quarters of a deer, blood still pouring from the gaping wound where its head and shoulders used to be. If that wasn't gruesome enough, three hundred yards later we passed its flattened head. Its dead stare followed us as we drove on by.

I was silent. Stef was silent. But the car wasn't. Like a child unaware that its parents were mid-row, it chattered away as normal. The engine was purring and the familiar creaks and rattles were all there.

And then, quite suddenly, they weren't.

With a few embarrassed coughs and splutters the purr became a gurgle, then a jolting clunk, then another and then nothing as the Torino joined us in our sulky void. I squeezed the pedal but the car did nothing. If she'd had arms I'm sure she'd have folded them. Nothing.

Hadn't Stef said the interstate would be a safe place to run out of gas? It didn't feel like it now that it was happening. We were doing 65 but slowing fast and the large truck in the rearview mirror was getting larger by the second.

Shit. I didn't want to join the roadkill. Shit. I flashed our emergency lights. The truck didn't get any slower. I yanked at the wheel and we careened across two lanes and on to the hard shoulder. The truck roared past, honking its horn in pointless frustration. Silence.

I lowered my head to the steering wheel and sighed a heavy, defeated sigh. I raised my eyes and glanced at the milometer. It didn't make sense. There was simply no way we could have run out of fuel so soon. No way. And yet nothing else made sense either. It didn't matter how much I wanted it not to be true... it was.

'Shit!'

Silence.

Another gargantuan truck blasted past us, rocking the car from side to side like a ship in rough seas.

'I think we should get out,' said Stef.

'I must have miscalculated,' I gabbled. 'We've only done around 260 miles since we last filled up. It doesn't make sense.'

I looked round. Stef was already out of the car and on the phone.

I had to wait for a clear road before I could open the driver side door in safety. I skipped out, slammed the door behind me and scooted round to the paddock of long, dry grass beyond.

Every time a cluster of traffic passed by I did my best to look needy at them, hoping that someone would take pity on us and offer assistance. Every time a vehicle cruised past I cursed the driver silently... conveniently forgetting the number of times I've driven down a British motorway and done exactly the same thing.

'I've got a number for a gas station in Glenns Ferry,' said Stef, handing me her phone. 'D'you want to give them a call?'

'Are they independent?'

Stef rolled her eyes.

'I don't know, but under the circumstances I don't really think we can afford to be picky. We've got no gas. We've run out. We need some gas. This is the only place nearby that I can find a number for. What else are we gonna do?'

I took the phone from Stef. The number was already punched in. I pressed the green button.

'Hello, Corner Market?'

'Hi... I was just wondering if you were inde—' I could feel Stef's eyes burning into me. I stopped. 'Sorry, I, er... we're um... on I-84 and we've um... run out of gas. I think we're about eight or nine miles north of Glenns Ferry and we were wondering if...'

'Sure thing, we can help y'out. Tell me which side of the road y're on and I'll send Mike.'

Half an hour later Mike and I were standing with our bellies pressed up against the side of the car while he glug-glug-glugged a few gallons of fuel into the bone-dry tank and cars whizzed uncomfortably close behind us.

'You've got about three gallons here,' he said. 'That'll get you going. Just come on down to Glenns Ferry and we can fill you up properly.'

'How much do we owe you?'

'Oh, we can sort that out back at the store.'

'Okay!' I was surprised. 'But... what about the call-out charge?'

'The what?'

'The call-out charge. Y'know... a charge for... calling you out?'

Mike stared blankly at me as if I was talking a foreign language.

'No... there's nothing like that,' he said as he strolled back towards his car.

I was expecting him to put the jerry can in the trunk and then return to see that all was well and our engine was running. Instead, he opened the door, hopped in, placed the jerry can on the passenger seat, gave us a cheery wave and went on his way.

'That was very trusting,' I said. 'How does he know we're going to turn up and pay? We could be Bonny and Clyde for all he knows. We could just drive off. We could go anywhere.'

'Yeah,' said Stef drily, 'anywhere that three gallons will take us.'

'Y'know what,' a thought had just hit me, 'I reckon this might work out perfectly!' I was feeling suddenly upbeat and energised. 'I reckon the Corner Market might be an independent!'

'What makes you say that?'

'Well, there's no call-out charge for a start,' I said. 'Think about it... it was just a guy and a car and he trusts us to just make our own way to the gas station to pay. It just doesn't feel like we're in the hands of an evil corporation, does it? I reckon a chain would have swiped my credit card before we even got a sniff of gas. We'd be down a hundred bucks, wouldn't we? Besides, I've never heard of the Corner Market, have you?'

'No. So the dream is still alive,' said Stef, perhaps just a little bit convinced by the notion. 'And there's only one way to find out. Come on,' she clapped her hands together, 'let's go.'

As we made our way to Glenns Ferry my mind was occupied, trying to unravel the mystery of how we'd come to run out of gas so prematurely. The numbers span through my mind while I tried to make sense of it all. We'd been averaging nearly 16 miles per gallon so a 22-gallon tank should have carried us nearly 350 miles... and yet we'd run out at around 260. What had I done wrong? What hadn't I added up properly? Had someone siphoned off some fuel the night before? Surely not!

'Keep your eyes peeled for the Corner Market,' I said as we came off the interstate and headed into Glenns Ferry.

'Is that it there?' asked Stef pointing ahead.

I looked ahead. It was like a punch to the solar plexus. The air fell out of me. The game was up. The dream was dead. The fuel that was swilling around inside our beautiful car's belly had come from a Sinclair gas station. Shit. You might not know the name. It's not a global brand to rival the Essos, BPs and Shells of this world but it's a chain all the same.[5]

'Arse!'

'I'm sorry,' said Stef. 'I really am.'

'That's it… we've fucked up!' I said, slamming my hand on the steering wheel. 'We've failed.'

Stef waited a moment.

'To be fair, Dave…' she spoke quietly, '…we always thought this would happen…'

'No.' I snapped. 'Not *always*. At the start? Yeah, maybe. I thought we'd end up filling up at a chain on day one. But we didn't. And every day we didn't gave me confidence. Every day we managed to get away with it, the more I believed we could do it.'

'Well, we've done more miles than anyone else thought possible,' said Stef. 'It's an achievement.'

'But we've failed,' I said. 'We've failed.'

The staff at the Sinclair were intensely annoying. And when I say 'annoying' what I mean is that they were charming, lovely and effortlessly polite and that *I* was annoyed. How dare they? I know the world isn't black and white but in the thousand miles we'd driven so far my view of things had simplified.

On this trip, playing by these rules, it was inevitable. For every unbranded gas station we saw we must have passed hundreds of gas stations we couldn't use. Each unbranded gas station appeared to us like an oasis in the desert and they

---

[5] At time of writing there are currently more than 2,600 stores in 22 states trading under this quintessentially American brand.

always elicited little yelps of joy. The flipside of that is that every branded gas station had started to annoy us. We'd curse them silently and sometimes not so silently. By this stage of the journey they weren't just *sitting there*, they were *taunting us* with their *forbidden fruits*. They were, in my mind at least, the enemy. They were the bad guys.

It's one thing characterising them as the bad guys when you're driving straight past them on the highway. It's quite another thing when they've come to your rescue. But I wasn't ready to have my simplistic world view shaken. I wanted them to behave like the bad guys. I wanted them to charge the earth for helping us out so that I could continue to curse them while lauding their badgeless rivals. I wanted them to twiddle wax moustaches and smile oleaginous smiles while gleefully taking advantage of our misfortune because I wanted them to reinforce my prejudice about them and their kind. If I was going to fail, I wanted the world to tell me that I'd at least failed in some noble endeavour. If the chains turned out to be nice surely we were just tilting at windmills.

But no... they had to go and ruin everything by being sweet natured, polite and concerned for our well-being. They just came to our rescue and didn't even think about charging us a cent for their time and their kindness! Typical!

I held the pump in the car and squeezed the trigger. I stared hypnotically as the dials on the front of the pump span round and round, ratcheting up the dollars, cents and even the tenths of cents we were about to give to The Man™.

Every spin of the dial hurt a little more. But I forced myself to watch it all. I knew where it was heading. Mike had added just over 3 gallons. We can't have used more than half a gallon getting here. So it was obviously going to thirstily swallow some 19 or 20 gallons and I was determined to watch every last drop of it.

Clunk. The automatic shut-off sounded and the flow of fuel ceased.

That didn't make sense. Just over 13 gallons? It must have

been a mistake. It can't have been the pump shutting down, I must have relaxed my finger. I pumped a bit more.

Clunk. The cut-off kicked in immediately.

I squeezed my trigger finger once more but again the pump made it clear that I wasn't in charge of this exchange and snapped off immediately.

Clunk.

There was no mistaking it… the tank was now full.

I stared at the dials on the front of the pump: 13.2 gallons. It might have been staring me in the face but it took me quite a while before I could make any sense out of the situation.

Oh my God. It was obvious. We didn't have a 22-gallon tank at all! We had 17 gallons at most! What? Grant had definitely told us it was 22!

I felt the blood drain from my face and a cold sweat enveloped me. My brain was running through a dozen thoughts at the same time. Like a television set to auto-tune it was picking up channels of thought, storing them and them continuing to scroll through looking for more.

The fuel gauge hadn't been lying after all. Grant was wrong. The needle told the truth. Every time it had said we were down to a quarter… we were. Every time it had said we were empty… we were.

I don't know that I'd ever experienced retrospective fear before now but that's what was happening to me as my head span through the past two weeks. How many times had we been running on fumes without knowing it? How many times had I been travelling at speed and in traffic and in very real danger of running dry?

There is no way on this earth I would have driven into the desert if I'd known that our car had only had 10 more miles of life in it! But, in the mistaken belief that we had another *90* miles worth of fuel that's precisely what I'd done. There were at least two occasions when we'd limped into gas stations and pumped more than 16 gallons. If any one of those fuel stops had been just a little further down the road we'd have been in trouble long before now. I thought back through the drives we'd done and the places we could so easily have been stranded. The potential consequences didn't bear thinking about. But I *was* thinking about them. And the thoughts were making me shudder. Shit.

It was nice of you to congratulate me back there. I appreciate it, I really do. But you were wrong to do so. It turns out you were right in the first place. Everyone was. The whole thing was impossible. I was mad for thinking it could be done. It couldn't. It was too hard. We'd run out of gas and only a chain had been able to help us.

This was the straw that broke this camel's back. This journey had already deviated from my dreams. I didn't want to be on the interstate. I didn't want to be visiting the major cities. I didn't want to be doing these stupid, piddly distances each day and I didn't want to have my route dictated by anyone else, least of all Stef's chiropractors. But while all of that had become the truth of this journey, the one thing that had kept me going was the simple fact that we'd somehow been able to cling to our main goal. I could tolerate anything so long as we continued to avoid the chains. But now we'd failed to do that. We'd given $40 to The Man™. Our beautiful car was soiled with the dirty chain gas that was sloshing around inside her. That was it. Now the whole thing had turned to shit. Now *nothing* was right. Now *everything* was wrong.

My grip was loosening. My mood had been standing on a precipice and this was just the nudge it didn't need.

We didn't get much further down the road that night. We put our hopes of reaching Salt Lake City on ice for another day. Instead we spent the night in the inappropriately named Bliss. I asked Stef if I could take possession of the camera for the night. While she slept in the room next door I went through some of our used tapes, slipping them into the camera and viewing the contents on the tiny screen. I was scrolling through them, looking for one particular moment. I found it; there we were in Coronado and there was Grant telling me that the car had a 22-gallon tank. I watched it through. Then I hit rewind and watched it again. And again and again and again. And again. Every time those pixels animated before my eyes I reassured myself. He had said it. I had remembered it right. It wasn't my fault. He had said it. I had remembered it right. It wasn't my fault. He had said it. I had remembered it right. It wasn't my fault. I was definitely loosing my grip.

I watched it again. I stared into Grant's eyes. One thing was clear. He wasn't lying. He might have been incorrect but he was no liar. It's just that the fuel gauge had a better memory. The numbers never lie.

Chapter 17
Any doubts about Smithy

You know when a new shopping centre is planned and the architects provide an artist's impression of what the finished development will look like? Well if you ask me they cheat. Because as well as their no doubt accurate rendering of what the bricks and mortar will look like they always paint in some suspiciously happy-looking people too.

These people are never laden down with too many grotty carrier bags. There are never any hoodie-wearing youths smoking at the bus shelter and there's not a Burberry patterned pushchair in sight. Instead their vision of the future is full of pencil-skirt wearing young women chatting to lantern-jawed men with pastel pullovers draped over broad shoulders. People sip cappuccinos and their children carry balloons on strings.

Well, the next time I see a drawing like that I'll have to look twice before I scoff at the developer's partisan vision. Because if it's being built anywhere near Salt Lake City then the happy, smiling, prim and proper people described will probably turn out to be pretty much on the money.

I wasn't in the best of moods when we got to Salt Lake City. In my mind, my wind-in-the-hair trip of a lifetime had most definitely been taken out of my control and transformed into a slow plod. Surely, I told myself, it was only a matter of time before failure would embrace us once more. The fact that we were even in Salt Lake City was symptomatic of how little sway

I had on events and the fact that we were staying there for three nights was just rubbing it in.

Not only was I not in a good way when we got there... I'm afraid SLC did little to lift my spirits. In fact, I can't think of many places worse to spend three days when you have nothing much to do but contemplate the mess you're in.

I didn't need thinking time; I needed forgetting time. A rowdy bar would have been good for me. In a bad way. Some energetic outdoor pursuits would have been good for me. In a good way.

Salt Lake City isn't blessed with many rowdy bars. It is, however, surrounded by quite beautiful scenery. It would have been interesting to drive out to the Great Salt Lake that gives the city its name. It would have been invigorating to head off into the snow-capped peaks to the north and east of the city too. But I didn't feel able to make that kind of jaunt.

That would have used up valuable petrol and now that I knew exactly how large – or indeed small – our fuel tank was, that wasn't a risk I was prepared to take. Finding gas had become more challenging in Idaho and Utah than at any other time and seeing as we'd only got away with it by the skin of our teeth in Oregon, I knew our margin for error was minimal.

When we'd filled up in Independence, Oregon we'd had no idea how close to empty we really were. We took on 16.82 gallons on that occasion. Surely that meant it was fumes alone that had carried us on to the forecourt. Every fuel stop since had involved more than 10 gallons and the two times either side of our I-84 empty-tank-disaster had involved over 15 and 16 gallons respectively.

As much as I needed to get out of the city – and out of my headspace – I knew that a five-mile trip was only going to make another empty tank five miles more likely. It had happened once already. I was determined not to let it happen again. It sure as hell wasn't going to be my fault if it did. There was no way we were going to run out simply because I'd wasted fuel on unnecessary nonsense like enjoying myself.

So for three days I did nothing much but walk the city streets in pursuit of something to stimulate me. My first impression of the place was positive. It's a large, modern city with nice, wide, open streets and a cared-for, scrubbed-up appearance. It feels affluent, youthful and, well, just a little bit soulless.

It wasn't long before the primness of the place started to grate. No doubt this says more about my state of mind that it does about the city but wherever I looked I saw beatific smiles hanging like masks in front of people's faces and in my head they didn't look happy, they looked… *programmed.* The happy shoppers I saw around me looked like *Stepford Wives.* And husbands. And children.

Of course one of the things that defines Salt Lake City is the Church of Jesus Christ of Latter-day Saints. The city was founded in the middle of the nineteenth century by Mormons fleeing persecution in the Midwest and it's remained their base ever since.

Everything in SLC centres on the temple, figuratively and literally. Like all sensible modern cities it is laid out in a grid system. At the centre of the grid sits Temple Square and every other address is then given as a set of coordinates relative to this point. So the first street to the east is called 100 East and the second street to the south is 200 South and so on.

The temple itself is a strikingly ornate and beautiful piece of gothic architecture with a gleaming granite exterior and six spires. It's stunning by daylight but lit up at night it comes into its own; as glorious a calling card for the faithful Mormon as it was for this amateur photographer.

Before this visit to SLC I confess to a huge dollop of igno-rance when it comes to Mormonism. The only Mormons I could name were the Osmonds. They may be best known as bubblegum pop merchants but with a song as rocking as 'Crazy Horses' in their back catalogue I reckon the toothsome cheese-mongers have to be admired.

But the Osmonds really were the beginning and end of my Mormon knowledge. I didn't have the first idea about the

Mormon's belief system or what set them apart from other Christian faiths. I just assumed Mormonism was another variation on a theme; a faith that shared the same core beliefs held by Anglicans, Baptists, Catholics, Methodists and all the other branches on the Christian family tree.

Now if I'm going to discuss these things it's only fair that I lay my cards on the table. I'm an atheist. That said, I've been raised in a country whose traditions are tightly bound up with those of the Christian Church and I grew up in a family where as children we said the Lord's Prayer before bed and Grace before Sunday lunch.

I count two and a half vicars amongst my friends and I like to think I'm tolerant of other people's beliefs. Unfortunately, the more I found out about Mormonism, the more I found my tolerance stretched.

I have a man called Jim to thank for my first Mormon lesson. I was on one of my many walks around the city when the skies opened and torrential rain started bucketing down. I made a dash for the nearest doorway and found sanctuary in the lobby of the Salt Lake City Convention Center.

'Hello there, can I help you?'

I turned to find a kindly old man with a thick head of white hair smiling at me. This was Jim.

'To be honest, I'm just sheltering from the rain...'

'Well, would you like to take a tour of the building while you're here?' he asked. 'It's a magnificent place...'

He was right about that. As we strolled together Jim told me what wood the doors were made of and what stone the floors. He told me which parts of the structure were load-bearing and how many pounds of pressure they were able to withstand. He told me how many cables were wired into the media centre and how many countries they could broadcast to at any one time. There was too much to take in and while each detail might have been dry and inconsequential, Jim sure imparted them with avuncular charm and there was no denying that they added up to make a truly spectacular building. I've been in many theatres in my time but the central auditorium here took my breath away.

An enormous church organ with a huge, ornate fan of lustrous pipes decorated the back wall. In front of it, beyond a wide expanse of stage was a circular sweep of seats, some 21,000 in number. The scale alone is mind-blowing and the clever pillar-free design means that you're constantly aware of just how cavernous the arena is.

'I think it's the biggest auditorium in the world used for worship,' said Jim.

'It looks amazing, Jim,' I smiled. 'And this is empty. What must it be like when it's full?'

'It's magical...' Jim was misty eyed at the memory. 'It's something else, it really is.'

I stood and gawped at the colossal space for a good while. By the time I was ready to move on, Jim's right leg had gone to sleep. Like a self-operating marionette he took a hold of his trousers and lifted his leg, gently shaking the dozing limb from its slumber. I liked Jim. It was impossible not to.

'Have you ever heard of an artist called Arnold Friberg?' he asked.

'I can't say that I have.'

'Well then, let's head upstairs and I'll show you some of his work. He's getting on in years now... he's even older than me and that's saying something ha ha ha... ahhhh.'

There were 12 of Friberg's paintings upstairs, each depicting a scene from The Book of Mormon. To me, they looked like typical examples of how the West likes to represent Biblical images; full of bare-chested Aryan hunks protecting their vulnerable womenfolk beneath thunderous skies. Perhaps one of the reasons they appeared so typical is that Friberg, in his capacity as the chief artist and designer on Cecil B. de Mille's cinematic epic *The Ten Commandments,* is responsible for setting the sugary standard by which such art is judged.

Jim told me the names of the paintings but didn't explain the stories that went with them. So while I looked at *Lehi Discovers* the *Liahoma* or *Alma Baptises in the Waters of Mormon,* I was none the wiser as to who Lehi or Alma were. I knew that one picture contained a lot of beards and Arabic robes, a camel and some tents and the other featured an unlikely blonde woman who was stood in a lake looking like an actress between takes on a Timotei commercial but that was it.

In my ignorance I genuinely assumed that Alma, Lehi, the Liahoma and the rest of the characters that populated Friberg's paintings were all characters in Biblical stories that I was hitherto unfamiliar with. After all there are plenty of those to choose from and the names – others included the Nephites, Moroni, Samuel and the Lamanites – all sounded nice and Bibley.

It was only when Jim showed me a painting by a different artist – John Scott – that I started to suspect there was more to this Mormon lark than I'd previously imagined. The painting was huge; almost floor to ceiling in height and as wide as a bus is long, and it was called *Jesus Christ Visits the Americas.*

Even with my obvious lack of Bible scholarship I was pretty sure that if Jesus had visited the Americas I'd have heard about it before now. Surely it couldn't be possible for me to reach the age of 36 without someone somewhere mentioning such an important historical fact? Was it?

'Well, it's not necessarily in what we would these days call the United States,' said Jim when I asked the obvious question, 'it's more likely that he was in South America or possibly Mexico… that part of the world.'

I looked around the walls, taking in the very European faces in the frames around me.

'Really?'

Oh. My. Life. There was so much I didn't know. So much I was about to be told. So much that Jim was only too happy to tell me.

Let me tell you a little of what I now know about The Book of Mormon. The most pertinent fact is that the full title, according to the copy I picked up that day, is *The Book of Mormon – Another Testament of Jesus Christ.* That's right; 'another'.

It's a sequel! Imagine that!

The book tells about an Israelite population that moved to the American continent somewhere where they were lucky enough to witness the second coming of Christ, who used his airmiles to pop up in those parts 400 years after His resurrection. Criminy! That's a lot to take in from a standing start.

So where on earth did these stories come from and how come I'd never heard any of them before?

If you believe the story, Mormon himself was a prophet and historian who belonged to one of these early American, Israelite civilisations. (I haven't worked out how they got there yet, but I'll run with it.) Along with his son Moroni, he engraved their people's stories on a collection of golden plates using a language that they called 'reformed Egyptian'. The plates were bound together in the form of a book, and some time round about AD 400, the whole thing was placed in a box and buried on a hill in what would one day be upstate New York. You'd think the plates were pretty safe buried underground in a box like that but it obviously wasn't secure enough for Moroni, who decided to hang around after his death to watch over them in angel form.

Now let's jump forward 1,400 years and meet a young man called Joseph Smith. As a teenager in the early 1800s Smith wasn't sure which religion to join and so he headed into the woods near his New York home to pray. It must have been quite a prayer because he was visited by both God and Jesus, who explained that none of the established religions were doing things right and that he should therefore not join any of them.

This wasn't the only vision Smith experienced in his life. A few years later the angel Moroni dropped in to see him as well. Unfortunately, the record doesn't show whether Moroni was especially bony, only that he told Smith about the buried book.

It took a few years of proving his worth to Moroni but in 1827, Smith was able to get hold of the book along with a few other artefacts that were buried along with it. There was a breastplate and some mysterious objects known to biblical scholars as *Urim and Thummin* (and known to at least one non-biblical scholar[6] as Gobbledy and Gook). Later, Smith was able to use the *Urim and Thummin* to magically translate the manuscript.

Signed statements were taken from 11 or 12 witnesses saying that they'd seen the plates but that's as much proof as the world has for their existence because once Smith's translation was complete he then returned them to the angel Moroni. Which is only fair when you think about it. Imagine the late fees on a library book that's 1,400 years overdue and made of gold?

The first English edition of The Book of Mormon was published in 1830. In April of the same year a church based on Smith's views of Christian theology – and originally called the Church of Christ – was formally organised. They believed that Smith was an infallible prophet who received direct revelation from God. To help him run things he appointed 12 apostles. On Smith's death, one of the 12 moved into the top job and a new apostle was appointed to keep up the numbers. They've continued to work in the same way ever since with the church president always having 12 apostles and God on speed dial. And my, how they've succeeded! Membership now stands at something like 12 million people worldwide.

And that's just the living members. They have a controversial habit of baptising dead people in their absence, regardless of the faith they had when they were alive.

Now there are lots of arguments that can be had here. I could point out that gold of the quantity Smith described would be impossible for one man to lift. I could point out quite how unlikely it is that the people described in the book could live in the Americas without leaving any evidence for archaeologists to discover. I could but it would be pointless because where spirituality is concerned there's no point offering prosaic arguments. Once a story involves an angel surely any debate about how much gold a man can carry is largely irrelevant.

[6] me.

I could question the merits of a church that used to promote polygamy but changed its mind when it became politically expedient to do so or about a church that expects its members to tithe 10 per cent of their income but again that would be pointless because while neither idea appeals to me, what you do in your personal life and with your money is no concern of mine.

But I will say this. Take a conventional Bible story about Jesus's life. Now, here's a remarkable thing about that story: the person who first told it to you was told it by someone who was told it by someone who was told it by someone who – if you follow the chain far enough – was told the story by someone who was *actually there*.

Now I'm not assuming that everyone in that chain of storytellers was telling the truth. I don't doubt that some of them exaggerated, some of them dramatised and some of them simply misremembered, but even so, these stories date back roughly 2,000 years and for the whole of that time there has been an unbroken chain of people telling them. How insanely amazing is that? How much you want to take literally and what conclusions you want to draw from it all... well, that's for each individual to decide but only the most blinkered amongst us could argue that there is absolutely *nothing* in it. An atheist I may be but I'd be a fool to argue against the Bible's importance as a piece of folk-history.

Now compare that with a story from The Book of Mormon. If you know a story from The Book of Mormon you know it because you were told it by someone who was told it by someone who was told it by someone who – if you follow *that* chain far enough – was told it by Joseph Smith. It can't be traced back any further than that.

What do you put more trust in? The 2,000-year-old story that's been told for 2,000 years or the 1,600-year-old story that's only been told for the last 180? Whether you want to believe in The Book of Mormon depends entirely on how much faith you have in the word of Joseph Smith. If you think he was divine – a real latter-day prophet – then the story holds water...

but if you have any doubts about Smithy… well then the whole thing falls apart rather quickly because there's simply nothing else to it. There isn't an option where you dismiss Joseph Smith as a liar or a fantasist but still accept the Mormon faith.

'When you get to the end of the book,' said Jim, 'there's a way of knowing that what you've read is true.'

'Really?' I asked. 'There's proof?'

'Absolutely.'

It probably won't surprise you to learn that it's the kind of proof that will only satisfy the faithful.

Moroni, Chapter 10, Verse 4:

'And when ye receive these things, I would exhort you that ye would ask God the Eternal Father in the name of Christ, if these things are not true; and if ye shall ask with a sincere heart, with real intent, having faith in Christ, he will manifest the truth of it unto you by the power of the Holy Ghost.'

D'you get that? You know it's true because it tells you it's true. If you *really* want to find out just pray and, assuming you're a good person with faith in the Lord, you'll soon know with absolute certainty that it's all true. Which I think means that if you don't believe it, you're obviously not a good person. A proof, if ever there was one.

I think there's probably room for one more snippet of Joseph Smith information, albeit something I didn't discover until long after I'd left Salt Lake City and was back in the UK. In 1835 he bought some papyrus rolls from an Irishman named Michael Chandler. The rolls had Egyptian hieroglyphics on them and so Smith used his magical *Urim and Thummin* to translate them. What he claimed to have translated – and what he then presented to the world – was the Book of Abraham.

At the time *no one* was able to translate hieroglyphics and so nobody was able to confirm – or indeed discredit – Smith's account. These days however we know rather more about such things and experts on the subject are queuing up to dismiss his translation as a load of baloney. Honestly, it's tosh. Not even close. The papyrus rolls had nothing to do with Abraham and were in fact just some kind of commonplace funeral record.

How anyone continues to believe in his teachings after that, I really don't know. If there's one thing more calculated to disprove the old infallible-prophet routine it surely has to be such demonstrable fallibility. Doesn't it become obvious that he was just, y'know, making stuff up?

By the time I left the Convention Center I was somewhat confused. I genuinely liked Jim but I was fairly convinced that his beliefs marked him out as a nutjob. A harmless nutjob but a nutjob nonetheless. And of course it wasn't just Jim... in Salt Lake City roughly 50 per cent of the population is Mormon and the idea that I was surrounded by so much insanity was truly unsettling. My confusion had a companion in the form of guilt... I didn't like myself for thinking such intolerant thoughts.

As I scurried back to the motel I avoided making eye contact with any passers-by. I didn't want to meet the gaze of any nutjob Mormons. I could feel myself coming slightly unhinged and I needed something to give me a jolt, a slap across the cheek to bring me to my senses and shake me out of this paranoid reverie.

As I entered the motel courtyard I passed Stef who was on her way out into the city.

'Hi, where're you heading?'

'The chiro,' said Stef, with a who-would-have-thought-it flip of the eyebrows. 'Where've you been?'

'I've just been on a tour of the convention centre... I didn't know anything about Mormons before... but now I'm thinking they're a bit...'

'Mental?'

'Yeah!'

'Of course. They're nuts... didn't you know?'

'I had no idea...' I said, definitely not feeling like I'd been brought to my senses. 'Oh well... hope the chiro's good, see you later.'

'See ya.'

Hmm. Well, if Stef hadn't supplied the slap I needed there was only one thing left to do. I did what any atheist would do under the circumstances. I emailed a vicar.

Hi Simon.

I'm spending a few days in Salt Lake City. It's fair to say the road trip isn't quite going to plan... it was meant to be nearly over by now and we're not even halfway across... it's a bit complicated but I'll explain more when I see you.

Just thought I'd say hello and see how you are.

By the way... is there anything I should know about the Mormons?

Dave

Simon is a University Chaplain. He's an Anglican but his work often involves working alongside representatives of other faiths. I don't really know what I was expecting him to say but whatever he came back with was bound to puncture the rather cartoonish view of Mormonism that had built up at the back of my mind.

I don't think I've ever heard Simon say a bad word about anyone so it seemed most likely that he'd tell me they were a decent bunch really. On the other hand, maybe he'd just confirm that they were, ahem, *eccentric*, while still finding some nice, friendly vicar way of reminding me not to be so judgemental.

I hit send and then made myself a cup of tea. Mormons don't drink tea. No booze. No coffee. No tea. Mental! Fifty minutes later I checked my email. Simon had already replied.

Hi Dave,

Salt Lake City? Never been there. Sounds... um... salty.

Obviously we've all got to respect one another's beliefs and try to get along. We all believe things that we feel are true but let's reach out to those of different opinions and treat them with love and tolerance.

You see? How much more vicarly could he be? A quick read of stuff like this and I'd be able to walk the streets of SLC with confidence again.

I long for the day when the Catholics, the Anglicans, the Methodists, URC and Baptists are all one big happy Church. I want to learn from others outside my faith as well. I've had many long conversations on spiritual matters with the Hindu family that live next door. I am deeply respectful of the Jewish religion recognising the roots of my own faith. There have been many times in my life when I have read the Koran and nodded to myself at the insights that book contains...

Did I ask how much more vicarly he could be? Clearly the answer was, 'a lot more'. Lovely stuff. Just what I needed.

... but where the chuff do you start with the Mormons?!?

Hang on a minute. Suddenly, he's not quite so clerical. Apart from the use of the word 'chuff', of course. That's got to be straight out of some vicar handbook. Bless him and his non-swearing ways. Chuff! It's almost cute.

Don't get me wrong, when seeking common ground with Mormons I find I have loads in common with them. It's just the stuff we don't agree on that makes things difficult. It includes: Jesus flying to America to find it populated by displaced Israelis, polygamy, making dead people part of your religion (Shakespeare, Elgar and victims of the Holocaust are all made posthumous Mormons whether they like it or not. You will be too one day), special hand-shakes, special underwear, a bloke who found Gold Plates and magic glasses which helped him to read them and the inherent evilness of tea.

Dave, you and I disagree about things. You know that I believe that if they kill really special people, three days later they completely come back to life but even I struggle with this stuff.

Oh. He really had surprised me now. I mean... this isn't him saying they're eccentric... I think he's pretty close to calling them nutjobs, isn't he? And what's all this about special keks? Really. I skipped over to Google. Mormon. Underwear. Search. www.mormon-underwear.com. Crikey. Back to Simon's email. There was more...

Then there's the word 'cult'. I know it's an ugly word. But when you open the door to two identically dressed young men with identical badges and identical smiles it's hard not to have the word flash across your mind. The Salvation Army turn up with an entire brass band but somehow that is significantly less weird.

Ha ha.

They are no doubt good, sincere people. They have a right to believe and I'm not saying they're wrong.

I'm just saying that if they're right, God isn't a DJ, he's a fucking weirdo!

What the hell happened to 'chuff' all of a sudden? Mormons? Cult? You see... they're nutjobs!

Everything is great here by the way (thanks for asking).
Yours,
Simon.

Crikey, I couldn't wait to get out of Salt Lake City. Three days with nowhere to go, nothing to do and far too much time to think was bad... and the certain knowledge that I was surrounded by nutjobs wasn't helping.

I plugged my iPod in and listened to 'Crazy Horses'.

Cra-zy hor-ses, Wah! Wah!

What a fantastic song! I think I liked it even more than I'd previously imagined. But then, the horses were crazier than I'd previously imagined. I mean, if Mormons are as crazy as I *think* they are, then surely the horses *they* think are crazy have got to be absolutely fruit loop.

Which is pretty much what had become of me at this stage of the journey. I think staying in one town for three nights was always going to fracture my well-being one way or another, but by the time we left Salt Lake City I was really on the edge.

Cra-zy Gor-man, Wah! Wah!

Chapter 18

You must have stayed in some real hell holes

Things got off to a good start the day we left Salt Lake City. For a start, we left Salt Lake City. Stef's three days of rest seemed to have done her the world of good and after two lengthy sessions in the hands of a chiropractor she liked she was, for the first time in a while, feeling fine.

There was a real sense that maybe things were set to improve when we found a quaint little gas station in a picture postcard location called Echo to the north-east of the city.

The drive there had been a precarious one. As we passed the Park City ski resort – one of the venues from the 2002 Winter Olympics – it's no surprise that there was snow on the ground. When we were on the sheltered side of the mountain there was ice on the road too.

But when we turned a corner to find a café, a gas station and then a motel, all nestled up to the base of a sun-kissed mountain we knew the drive was worth it. The gas station was a small, pristine whitewashed box of a building. Neat red lettering spelled out *Echo Gas* on the brickwork. A lonely old pump stood outside. Either it had taken a few knocks in its time or the building had because one of them was definitely not vertical. As we pulled on to the forecourt the gas station's charm evaporated in a fug of bad news: it was closed and the pump was firmly padlocked to its holster.

A sign in the window directed customers to enquire at the café but that proved to be a cruel joke because the caff was closed too. We scratched our heads and wondered what to do. Was there a phone number we should call? Were the hours of business posted anywhere? I was starting to worry when a long, low Cadillac pulled in and an old toadlike man clambered out with a scowl. He had his jacket on inside out over the top of a lopsided shirt that had been buttoned up all wrong. His face was lopsided too. I don't know what bush telegraph system had told him he had customers but I got the impression he'd left the house in a hurry to come and serve us and he was far from happy about it. I couldn't blame him for that – we're all going to reach an age when hurrying becomes impossible and he'd got there long ago.

He wore a dirty baseball cap and a grimace. I'd love to pretend that he was the charming old duffer that I'd hoped for when I first saw such a dainty, picturesque gas station but the truth is he was an old man in ill health and foul temper.

'I only take cash,' he said before being consumed by a hacking cough. Something solid found its way into the back of his throat and he spat it viciously at the dusty floor. 'I don't know why I ate that *fucking* chilli,' he spat his words out too. 'I ain't a fucking Mexican.'

He must have been 80 years of age if he was a day. There was something heartbreaking about watching him go through the painstaking process of opening up the gas station. His shaky fingers struggled to keep a key steady as he tried to unlock the front door and there were a lot of keys on his fob that had to be tried and then rejected. He then repeated the routine, trying to find the right key for the padlock that was shackling the pump. All this for one $40 sale. God, it felt bleak. There's no way this place was making him rich. I can't imagine it was even putting food on his table. It felt like the only reason he was still running it was that nobody had told him he was allowed to stop. As much as we wanted, no, *needed*, to buy gas from him I wanted to tell him to stop.

But of course I didn't. I just handed over my two $20 bills and got back into the car. He started to lock up. For all I know, he's still trying to find the right keys.

'I've got bad news for you,' said Stef.

'Go on.'

'That's all the filming you're going to get out of me for today. I thought I was feeling better but I can feel it going already. The only way I'm going to get through this thing is if I stop myself before I do any serious damage.'

'Jesus, Stef,' I said, trying to get the playful, teasing tone right. 'My mobile phone battery is better than you. I charge that overnight and I get three days of work out of it. You spend three days recharging *your* batteries in Salt Lake City, 50 minutes of work and you're dead again!'

'I can't help it!' she said, taking it in the right spirit.

'I know, and seriously you should save yourself for when we really need you,' I said. I paused to let the sincerity sink in. 'Now... let's just hope the scenery is dull from here on in...'

It was a throwaway comment that I made so that the two of us could, in our own way, laugh in the face of adversity. It wasn't long before I was wishing I'd never said it because the scenery we drove through was amongst the most beautiful I've ever seen.

Heading south from Echo, the rugged, inhospitable mountains soon yielded and we found ourselves descending into a beautiful, verdant valley. A patchwork quilt of lush green fields was spread before us and we could pick out small communities dotted around the streams and rivers that flowed there.

It was an incredible view. Hundreds of years before us people had travelled this way by wagon, by horse or worse, on foot. The idea of looking down on this green and pleasant land for the first time was almost unimaginable. They must have thought they'd found the Promised Land... how could it be anything but?

Despite Stef's ailing back it felt good to be finally on the road again. Especially as we'd finally shaken off the interstate and were no longer heading towards a major city. Mind you, as we came through Soldier Summit I was struck with a pang of embarrassment when I looked up at a sign and realised which road we were on. US Highway 6. That's the same road that had carried us from California into Nevada nearly two weeks earlier. How different our journey would have been if we'd stayed on Highway 6 and kept on heading east that day. In the last couple of weeks we'd travelled over 2,000 miles to get us to this point in the middle of Utah. If we'd stayed on Highway 6, it would have taken us 600 miles. What price, my stubborn stupidity?

By the time we passed through the town of Helper it was pitch black outside and the temperature had started to drop rapidly. I turned the car's heating system on. It blew cold air at us.

'It probably needs to warm up,' I said. 'Shall we leave it for a while?'

'Yeah, sure.'

Twenty minutes later it was still blowing cold air.

Stef pulled her coat up around her neck and pointed at the sliding control on the heater. 'Are you sure this is in the right position?' she asked. 'Shall I try pushing it the other way?'

'I'm pretty sure it's in the right place,' I shivered. 'But it's definitely not working at the minute so you might as well give it a go.'

Stef moved the control across with a creak. I couldn't tell if the noise came from her or the car.

Another 20 minutes later and the freezing cold air was still blowing. I was starting to get worried. Through the windscreen there was nothing but blackness and the road ahead. There was nowhere for us to stop and in these sub-zero temperatures we definitely didn't want circumstances to force a stop upon us.

The next building we saw did nothing to lighten the mood or lower the tension. We turned a corner and found ourselves suddenly confronted by a nightmarish vision. Piercing through the dark was a brutal structure, lit up by harsh lights there to warn the world of its dangerous presence. Smoke billowed out of chimneys and beneath the stark floodlights men with hard hats and high-visibility overalls toiled away in the inhuman cold. I've no idea what industry it was a part of but the bent and freezing men looked like worker drones preparing a nuclear warhead for launch on behalf of some dastardly Bond villain. Either that or Hieronymus Bosch had returned from beyond the grave to paint a dystopian, twenty-first century hell on earth. A shiver of fear ran down my spine.

There was a digital display by the side of the road telling us – and anyone else who braved this road – the temperature. Its flashing digits were two feet tall and blinked on and off, alternately displaying the result in Fahrenheit and then Celsius as it did so. I have no idea why it was there but it certainly did a very good job of ramming home quite how inhospitable this place was: 21°F, -6°C, 21°F, -6°C.

I did a quick calculation. If the temperature outside was minus six that meant that the temperature inside was… ooh… minus six. We. Had. No. Heating. By this time I was wearing a jumper, two coats, a woolly hat and gloves and still I could feel the cold in my bones. Stef had a coat, a body warmer, another coat and some earmuffs. It was horrific.

'There's a town up ahead called Price,' she said. She was hunching over the atlas and her warm breath hung in the cold air long after the words had evaporated. 'We're definitely stopping there.'

'T-t-t-too r-r-r-r-right we ar-r-r-r-re,' I s-s-s-s-said, unable to stop my t-t-t-teeth from clattering.

We didn't stop in Price. We tried. We looked. We saw a lot of hotels. We didn't see any that were independent. Not by our definition anyway. We stared at the Budget Host for a while. It had a suspiciously chain-like name but not one that either of us had seen before.

'I'm g-g-g-g-going t-t-t-to a-a-a-ask-k-k-k-k,' I said, jumping out of the car and racing into the quaintly tatty lobby and some oh-so-welcome warmth.

A married couple – presumably the owners – popped out of nowhere to greet me and so as soon as I was warm enough to be understood I went through the painstaking explanation of our chain-free hotel needs. At every step of my explanation the owners nodded.

'So will that be one room or two?' he asked.

'Two,' I said, relief flooding through me.

I turned to give Stef a thumbs-up gesture through the window but as I did so I found myself looking at a small cardboard stand containing copies of the *Budget Host Travel Directory*. I picked up the scrawny pamphlet and flipped it open. The front cover folded out to reveal a map of the United States. It was dotted from coast to coast with stars, each representing the location of a Budget Host Inn. There were nearly 200 of them. My heart sank as I turned back to the owners.

'I thought you said it was independent?'

'It is.'

'Right. But I asked you if it was part of a chain. I asked you if there were other Budget Hosts out there and you said no.'

'Oh... *I see,*' he said, the penny dropping, '*a chain...*'

I looked in his eyes, trying to work out quite how he'd only just realised what I meant by the word 'chain' even though I'd given him a very full explanation. It was clear he wasn't being disingenuous. He wasn't just saying whatever he felt was necessary to rent his rooms... from his point of view, the hotel *wasn't* part of a chain, he owned it and he'd just happened to affiliate it with the Budget Host organisation.

If you own a motel in the States I've no doubt that you too can put up the yellow-and-brown Budget Host sign and appear in their directory and on their website, just so long as your accommodation and your room rates meet their standards and you fill in the right paperwork.

But none of this mattered. According to our rules Budget Host was a chain and that was that. We had to apply the same rules to hotels as we did to gas stations and diners after all. Loads of branded gas stations are technically independent. They're owned and operated by individuals who just happen to have done deals with this or that brand. The largest hotel chain in the world – Best Western – is really just a network of independently owned venues and we'd already ruled them out for the same reasons. If we stayed one night in a Budget Host we might as well fill up at the Shell station down the road and that wasn't about to happen. It wasn't just about who owned the business, it was about not giving in to the homogenous world. If every branch of a chain offers an identical product in near enough identical premises then it doesn't matter that they are all owned by different individuals, what matters is that life gets more standardised and the world feels less different.

The driving seat of what was now a mobile freezer wasn't a very pleasant place to be. The warmth of the hotel was so incredibly tempting but I couldn't bring myself to do it. To be honest, if I'd been travelling alone I might well have cracked. What would it really matter if I'd stayed there? You, dear reader, would know nothing about it; you only know about the things I choose to tell you after all.

I might have been able to persuade myself that *one* night in *one* hotel that's affiliated with *one not-very-well-known* chain could be brushed under the carpet but I could never say it to anyone else. But I wasn't travelling alone. Stef was waiting in the car outside. Having a low opinion of myself is one thing – but I don't want other people to think badly of me. Sometimes it's only the presence of another person that keeps us honest. I steeled myself and returned to the cold with the bad news.

'Shit,' said Stef through gritted teeth.

'I know. We've got no choice… we're moving on, let's have a look at the map.'

There were no gas stations we could use in Price. We'd done roughly 150 miles since filling up in Echo which meant we couldn't rely on having more than 110 miles left in the tank. The next town, Green River, was 65 miles away. Beyond that, we had Crescent Junction and then, if no gas could be found, right on the edge of our limits was Moab.

'There'd better be somewhere in Green River,' I said. 'I don't think I can stand more than an hour of this.'

'Absolutely. At least Green River sounds like a nice place. I vote we stay there tonight and then get the heating system looked at first thing in the morning. We can't live like this.'

'You look freezing! Come in, come in!'

After another hour of driving through the precarious can't-feel-my-fingers cold, we'd finally reached Green River and had leapt on the first motel we saw. The warm welcome from our host was certainly an encouraging start. The sounds creeping under the door to his private quarters told me that he had friends over and that a nice social evening was in full swing and he seemed to carry the warmth of the occasion into the way he dealt with us. Instead of just going through the businesslike process of letting two rooms he chatted amiably, asking us about the camera, our accents, where we were coming from and heading to and so on.

'You are *so* brave!' he exclaimed, when we told him about our journey. 'That's insane... you *must* have run out of gas by now!'

'Once,' I said, and for the first time I managed to find a glimmer of pride in the fact that it was *only* the one time.

'And,' he swept his mop of blond hair back out of his eyes, 'you must have stayed in some *real hell holes*!'

'They haven't all been great,' I smiled.

'Go on,' he leaned forward with a big, gossipy grin plastered across his youthful features, 'tell me about the worst one.'

'A lot of them have been pretty good,' I said.

'What about Lovelock?' suggested Stef. 'Lovelock, Nevada, remember...'

'Oh God, yeah... that was terrible,' I concurred.

'Go on...what was it like?'

'It was just... *dirty*,' I said. 'I don't think the couple who ran it were really cut out for the hospitality game. I'm not making this up... the guy who owned it said he'd won it in a card game. In the morning when I opened the curtains there were over 50 dead flies on the windowsill. I counted them.'

'Ugh, that's *disgusting*,' squealed our host. 'You've got to keep

The only car I've ever loved.

The Torino, me and Obi Grant Kenobi. Coronado, California.

One of Lone Pine's many motels.

Robo-Stef.

Independence #1.

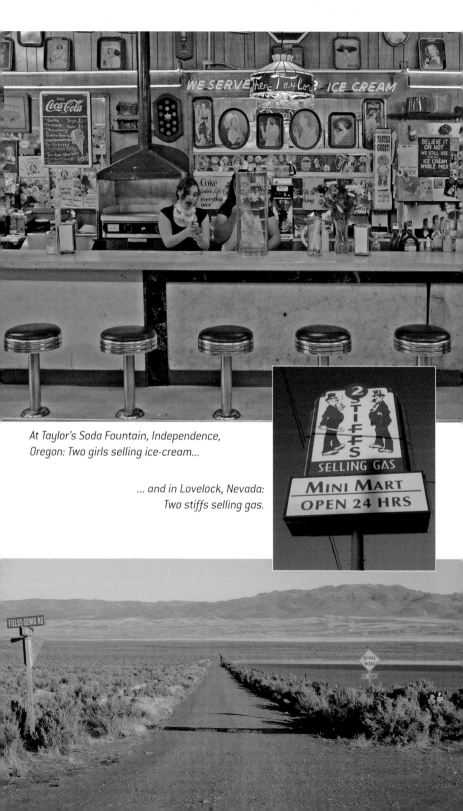

At Taylor's Soda Fountain, Independence,
Oregon: Two girls selling ice-cream...

... and in Lovelock, Nevada:
Two stiffs selling gas.

The treehouse resort in Takilma, Oregon. Perhaps the most unconventional place we stayed...

... or maybe not. Frances, Dennis and the giant Beagle in Cottonwood, Idaho.

Arches National Park. Near Moab, Utah.

Nutjob statues outside
a nutjob office building.
Salt Lake City, Utah.

Bedrock, Colorado. A gas
station with a beautiful view...

... and it's beautiful inside too.
Shame about the microwave.

This sight still
makes me sweat...

... and this one still makes me smile.
Non-Amoco-Joe in La Veta, Colorado.

500   350

a place clean, that's rule number one! Okay... let's get you two sorted out. Here you go,' he handed me two keys, 'and if you have *any* questions, don't hesitate to come back and ask...'

In the warmth of his conversation I'd forgotten how bitingly cold it was outside.

'Pick a key,' I said, offering Stef both fobs. She took one of them from my hand. 'Right... you make us a cup of tea, I'll move the car and unload the bags. Deal?'

'Deal.'

I pulled the car up outside the two adjacent rooms, then lowered the tailgate and yanked the first of our large bags out. I turned and entered the open door to Stef's room and my heart sank.

'Oh. My. God.'

'It's not good, is it?' said Stef glumly. 'What are we gonna do?'

I looked around the room. It didn't take long. It was truly revolting. There appeared to be some greasy film on the scratched and twisted wood panelled walls. A pair of tatty and torn nets hung in the window... but there were no actual curtains.

'Did we just have *that* conversation?' I asked. 'How the hell does a man who runs *this* place have the gall to ask us about the worst places we've stayed?! He must know how bad this is...'

'I know. This is... horrible. Look at this...'

I looked. Stef was holding up the bed covers. They were stained with God knows what and they were so thin I could see Stef's hand right through them.

'You're joking? There's got to be something more substantial than that?'

'This isn't the worst of it. Take a look in the bathroom.'

It took me three paces. I wish I hadn't bothered.

The walls were fake-tiled. In that they were covered with a sheet of vinyl that had been designed to look like tiles. Water had got behind the surface, rotting the wall and making the vinyl bulge in a huge, foot-wide blister. Parts of it were held in place with some crudely applied gaffer tape. The floor was rotten too and the bath was collapsing into a hole that had opened up in the corner nearest the taps.

'Oh. My. God.'

'At least there aren't any dead flies on the windowsill,' said Stef with a let's-look-on-the-bright-side chuckle.

'No,' I said and then, mimicking Blondie, 'that would be *disgusting*!'

'I'm going to have a look at the other room,' said Stef. 'Give us the key…'

I tossed it her way and followed her out. The other room was pretty much the same but had one advantage: curtains.

'I've never seen anywhere as disgusting as this,' I sighed, 'but I don't think we have much choice. We're going to have to stay here for one night. There's no way I can ask you to take the room without curtains so that'll be me…'

'Thanks.'

'But there's no way we're leaving several thousand pounds worth of camera equipment in a room without curtains either, so that'll all have to come in here with you… is that okay?'

'Fine. Do you still want a cup of tea?'

'Yeah. Why?'

'I could really do with a stiff drink? Fancy a walk?'

Green River sounds like such a nice place. It isn't. It's not remotely green for a start. It's just that the Green River flows through it.

We found a bar. It wasn't much bigger than a couple of Portakabins. There were no windows but loud music was leaking out of it from somewhere. A sign on the door said, 'Members Only'.

Nervously, I nudged the door open and craned my neck inside. There must have been 30 or 40 people there. The building was divided into two halves not by any physical structure but through social convention. At the near end there was a pokey bar and two or three tables but the crowd – if you could call them that – were all at the far end dancing away to some bland Bon Jovi rock. They didn't stop dancing but it felt like they were all craning their necks to look my way.

'What's it like?' asked Stef, nudging her head around the door to take a look.

A gnarly face with a dense five o'clock shadow and deep, dirt-filled creases in his sun-blasted face clocked Stef's feminine features and immediately turned to the barmaid and hollered.

'Hey... these guys are my guests, okay?'

The girl behind the bar shrugged. 'Sure.'

'Come in,' he yelled, 'close the door. Welcome to Green River. Where y'from? You can buy me a drink if you like?'

It seemed churlish to refuse. And quite possibly dangerous, too. I bought a rum and coke for myself, a whiskey for Stef and a tequila for our new friend, John, and a beer for his friend, Brad. Oh, and because I didn't want to look cheap, I got a tequila chaser for Brad as well. And that reminds me... I also got a tequila chaser for John because, hey, what's a tequila without another tequila to follow it up? And besides they asked. Nicely.

And when I say nicely, I mean two parts nicely to five parts threat.

I studied John's features. His face was lived in. Actually I think it might have had squatters. By contrast, Brad had a young, round face and eyes the size of saucers. He was chewing on a wad of tobacco, which in between chews, he kept stuffed behind his lower lip. When his features were at rest the bulge was so prominent it looked like he was very bad at hiding a golf ball. Either that or his face was doing a surprisingly good impression of the water damaged, vinyl wallcovering in my rotten, stinking bathroom.

The two men were clearly only interested in me because I represented a new supply of alcohol but it was obvious that they were interested in Stef for other reasons entirely. Stef and I had taken a table (wisely, the nearest one to the door), and without needing to be asked – and certainly without asking, Brad and

John had joined us. But they weren't the only men who buzzed around our table. I think every man in the place came by to, well, to take a closer look at Stef.

They were miners, truck drivers, oil prospectors and others of no fixed abode. I got the impression this was a town that men drifted through. I was certain that fresh females were not so common. Stef and I exchanged glances. She gave me a reassuring look as if to say, 'It's all right, I can handle myself.'

At the bar a man with a scar running from his left eye to the edge of his mouth was brandishing a small, handheld video camera. It was clearly his new toy and so far he had come up with just two uses for it. One was filming down girls' tops. The other was filming up girls' tops. I don't think there was a skirt in the place or I'm pretty sure he'd have come up with a third game.

We watched in silent amazement while he played his 'game' four times in a row. He'd film a girl dancing and then beckon her over as if to show her the footage of herself. From the look of these people you'd think they'd never seen a mirror so the prospect of watching moving pictures of themselves must have sounded like witchcraft which would explain why they'd skip over quite so eagerly. At which point, the camera would be shoved under their top through whichever route seemed easiest.

Each time the girl in question would react with a cheeky cackle and an 'Oi!', perhaps a playful slap on the arm but there was evidently no genuine offence. It was like watching some kind of malignly twisted *Carry On* film in which a spiteful Sid James half-heartedly abuses a procession of bored Babs Windsors and nobody can be quite be bothered with the bad jokes.

'If he comes near me with that thing I'll break his fucking face,' whispered Stef.

'Okay... but please bear in mind that, while I support you in principle, it's a course of action that might mean he ends up trying to break my face in retaliation. Nobody likes breaking lady-faces… but man-faces belonging to men who are with the lady-face you don't like are sometimes seen as very breakable.'

'Understood. So if he comes near me with that thing, you get the hell out of here because I'm going to break his face.'

Stef raised her glass to mine and we clinked.

John turned out to be an oil prospector.

'I spend a lot of time away from home,' he said. 'It's dangerous, dirty work. But it's well paid. I'm missing my daughter.' For a split second I felt sorry for him but then he leaned in a little too close to Stef, saying, 'Y'know, you remind me of my daughter…' and my sympathy turned to dust in an instant.

'Really?' She asked with disdainful sarcasm.

'Yeah. Kind of.' He leaned back to better scrutinise her face. 'Nah… maybe not.'

'What about you, Brad?' I asked. 'Are you in oil?'

'Not me!' came the oddly eager response. 'Ain't no way. I'll tell you what I wanna do… I wanna visit a third-world country!'

I shook my brain around trying to work out how we'd made this particular conversational leap but it didn't get any clearer.

'People will shoot you in a third-world country! You might not get out of there alive! Man… *that's* what I want to do!'

It wasn't entirely clear that Brad knew what a third-world country was, let alone why he wanted to go there and why the thought of possibly not surviving was so attractive.

'You want to be careful on the Indian reservations,' he continued, briskly changing tack once more. 'Them people will shoot you sooner than look at you! There ain't no law out there!'

'Is that right?' said Stef, her liberal hackles rising. Mine were too… but my cowardice was beating my hackles hands down.

'Oh, I mean it!' Brad's eyes stared with a new intensity. He inhaled deeply and his previously moon-like features were transformed as if his skull was suddenly being shrink-wrapped in skin. A vein bulged in the centre of his forehead, cheekbones appeared from nowhere and the golf ball-shaped bulge in his lower lip shone as the skin tightened around it. I got the idea that Brad didn't enjoy Stef's droll tone. 'Them Indians don't give a shit about shit all,' he said cryptically.

'Well... they *were* here first,' said Stef calmly. I couldn't decide whether she was displaying admirable dignity or sheer please-shut-up-now stupidity. This man clearly had issues. Couldn't she see the vein in his forehead?

The vein glowed redder than before and his stare challenged anyone that dared to meet it. Behind those scary eyes cogs were turning as he processed Stef's words. Nobody dared speak. John chuckled inwardly and downed a shot of tequila. Eventually, Brad spoke.

'D'y'know what?' he said, his knuckles white as he gripped either side of the table. 'You're right. They were here first. You got a point.'

And then, as if by magic, veiny, tense Hyde disappeared and moonfaced Dr Jekyll returned.

'Y'know, I like you,' he said to Stef with a bulbous smile, 'and if you get into any trouble I want you to remember my name. I'm a Floyd. You get into trouble you call for me. The Utah Floyds will help you out. You got that?'

'Thanks,' said Stef.

'And you?' Brad turned his attention to me. 'You got that?'

'Um. Yes,' I said. 'Thanks.'

Neither of us asked him how we were supposed to go about calling for his help if we needed it and he didn't offer up any contact details. Everyone involved knew that it was a nonsensical 'offer', but none of that mattered, all that mattered was that he'd staked his honour on it and we'd accepted. We were three drinks away from becoming blood brothers.

We had two more drinks and then made a hasty exit.

Chapter 19
Press the red button

I slept fully clothed that night. Partly because of the cold and partly because I felt very exposed being naked with only a thin pair of nets and even thinner bedlinen to protect my modesty. I didn't sleep well. If I hadn't had a few rums I don't think I'd have slept at all.

'You look shit!' said Stef the next morning.

'I feel shit,' I said. 'That bathroom looks disease-ridden. I haven't showered. I've hardly slept. We've got to get out of here.'

'Do you want to get some breakfast and go?'

'I'd rather just go.'

'What are we gonna do about the car?'

'What about it?'

'The heater. It's screwed, remember.'

I'd completely forgotten. The sun was shining outside and if Stef hadn't mentioned it I think it would have taken another night of cold torture to remind me.

'Shall we head to Crescent Junction then?'

As far as I can work out, Crescent Junction no longer exists. I don't know how substantial it had ever been but it was definitely marked on our map in bold enough type to suggest it was once a place of some size. And yet when we got there we found nothing but an abandoned Sinclair gas station, some burnt tyres, a burnt-out mobile home and some discoloured earth where other mobile homes had presumably once stood.

'Shall we head to Moab then?'

With my eye keenly trained on the gas needle we rolled our way south to Moab. And what a blessed relief it was when we got there... not just because we managed it but also because, unlike the skanky Green River, Moab was a place worth getting to.

With red-rock mountains all around us we crossed over a tumbling stretch of the Colorado River and into town. There were bars and restaurants and lots of signs advertising white-water rafting, jeep treks, mountain bike hire and any other kind of adventure tourism you could imagine, which of course meant there were hotels.

Moab was clearly some kind of small tourist Mecca. I imagine that in the height of the season it must be full to over-flowing with a young, mountain-biking party crowd but it was November now and finding a couple of rooms was easy. We chose The Virginian Motel – a large, two-storey affair sitting at the end of a small cul-de-sac. The rooms were huge, the furnishings were clean and basic but compared to our Green River experience it felt like we were wallowing in five-star luxury.

'I think we should get the car looked at as soon as possible,' said Stef. 'What are we going to do if they tell us they need to order parts?'

'I don't know. I don't want to be a nag but we've only just spent three days in Salt Lake City. I don't want to end up spending three days here as well.'

'You're going to be looking at the middle of next week.'

They were exactly the words I didn't want to hear.

We were in the front office of Arches Repair Center, speaking to Pat, a man with slicked-back hair, a square jaw and the bedside manner of a good physician. We'd left the car in his care for an hour and returned for the diagnosis. There were dark wooden venetian blinds in the floor-to-ceiling windows, a large pot plant, a wooden mantel clock and some small photos of family members dotted about the place but there was nothing fussy about the place.

I knew from the moment I stepped through the door that we were about to receive bad news. It might have been the way Pat furrowed his brow with concern, but it was probably more to do with the way he said, 'Ah… I'm afraid it's bad news.'

He then explained exactly how the heating system worked and why it had stopped doing so. Like a patient teacher he took the explanation slowly, checking that I'd understood each clause as he went. Of course, every time he stopped to see that I was on the ball I gave him an encouraging nod or an 'uh huh' of encouragement when in reality I didn't have a clue what he was on about.

The gist of it was that there were some pipes that were meant to carry water through the system and they were plugged with rust.

'I've tried blasting them out with compressed air and a high-pressure hose and it ain't shifting. You got a lot of rust in there. You need a new heater core and a heater control valve. Those parts are going to have to come from Salt Lake City.'

I looked at Stef, or rather at the camera she was now holding to her shoulder.

'We can't stay here for five days, can we?'

'Well, we obviously can't do any nighttime driving without heat… it's just impossible. But we don't need to stop completely. What if we keep going, doing short daytime drives and we look ahead and try and get someone three or four hundred miles away to order the parts for us?'

'That'd work,' Pat smiled. 'I can give you a list of the parts you need…'

'That would be amazing, Pat,' I said, surprised to see a mechanic so cheerfully losing work. 'I mean, obviously we'll pay you for today…'

'You want a heater core, yeah?'

'Uh huh.'

'And a heater control valve, okay?'

'Uh huh.'

'And they'll ask you what engine you've got under the hood there, and that's a 351, you got that?'

'Uh huh,' I said and this time I wasn't uh-huh-ing in vain. I had definitely got that. 'Okay... so how much do we owe you right now?'

'I've put down for a half-hour of labour,' said Pat, 'I probably spent around an hour on it but that's fine.'

As I dipped my fingers into my jeans' pocket and started to retrieve my wallet I was aware of a sudden movement behind me and to the right. I span round to see what it was. It was Stef.

If you've ever watched an Olympic weightlifter fail to hoist the dumbbells over his head you'll know it's an explosive moment. He doesn't just shrug and then gently lower them back down to the ground... he strains, pushes, tenses, *tries with all his might* and then, when his body finally refuses to lift the thing, he gives in and it all comes crashing down.

Well, that's what happened with Stef. Her body gave in. Her arms fell to her side in defeat. The camera clattered into her knee as it dropped and she did well to keep her grip on the handle and stop it from smashing to the floor. I jumped with shock at the suddenness of it all and then crouched down, first taking the weight of the camera and then encouraging her to loosen her grip and let me take it. She was clearly in some very real pain.

'Are you okay?' asked Pat, genuine concern written across his face.

'It's my back!'

The girl who'd been gamely prepared to challenge Brad the night before in Green River was challenging herself now. The look on her face defiantly spelt out a simple message. I. Am. Not. Going. To. Cry. I wished she'd stop being so bloody stoic about everything. It would have been so much easier to know what to do next if she'd just crumbled.

'I can't move.' The words fought their way past gritted teeth.

'Well then *don't* move,' I said pointlessly, 'Just relax.'

Stef stood there, crooked, awkward and in pain. Confusion was the dominant mood. Especially for poor Pat who must have been wondering quite what was going on. I looked outside at our poorly car and then I looked at Stef, my poorly director. I did the only sensible thing.

'Pat,' I said, 'I think we have a change of plan. Why don't you go ahead and order those parts… we're going to stay in Moab for a few days.'

Stef sat against the orthopaedic back support she'd bought from the chiropractor in Salt Lake City. On her bed was the spine-aligning orthopaedic pillow she'd bought from the chiropractor in Boise. Wrapped around her middle, holding her insides together was the girdle she'd bought from the chiropractor in Portland. The only thing tenser than the fabric in that girdle was the atmosphere in her motel room. The two of us sipped at our mugs of tea, stared into space and said nothing.

Neither of us acknowledged it but deep down we must have both known that our time together was coming to an end. After three days off in Salt Lake City and only two days driving we were now staring at a four- or five-day break. Yes, the car needed repairing but even so, if Stef had been fit and well, we'd have been continuing our journey first thing in the morning.

According to Plan A, we should have been rolling into New York around now. Stef would be home and I'd be heading for the airport. Of course we'd abandoned Plan A long ago, we must have been on Plan G by now, but it was becoming clear that we'd slowed to an unmanageable pace. If we carried on like this we'd still be on the road when Christmas and New Year rolled round. We might have taken a cavalier view of deadlines at the start of our journey but there was no way we could carry on through Christmas. Annoying the film people by handing in our footage late was one thing… upsetting our mums by missing Christmas quite another. (Deadlines can be missed, mum-and-dadlines can't.)

So something had to change. But what? Stef wasn't going to let go. She was too much of a fighter for that. I wasn't going to suggest she leave because, well, because she was too much of a fighter for *that*, too. Besides, I didn't want her to leave. I wanted her to be fit and well and happy. It's just I knew that wasn't an option.

The awkwardness that hung in the air between us was palpable. And strangely familiar. How many of my relationships have ended in this kind of attritional silence?[7] Great; all the pain of ending a relationship without any of the fun of having one!

Two days passed like this. Neither of us wanted to talk about what was going to happen next but there seemed to be nothing else to talk about and so for most of the time we said nothing.

With neither of us willing – or perhaps able – to say anything that would change the situation closure was going to have to come from another place altogether. The person who intervened was the film's accountant, Penny.

We'd been very bad at staying in touch with the film's producers back in London. But the one person we were inadvertently staying in touch with was the film's accountant, Penny.

Our producers had impressed upon us how important it was to keep a track of our expenditure. Which means we kept receipts for everything. Every now and then we dutifully bundled our receipts up, stuffed them in an envelope and posted them back to the UK so that Penny could keep tabs on things. 'Look after Penny,' we told ourselves, 'and she'll look after the pounds.' Ho ho.

I suppose the alarm bells might have gone off sooner if anyone had told Penny where we were meant to be going. But they didn't. So unless she suddenly found herself dealing with receipts from Hawaiian hotels our location was no concern of hers. To her, a receipt from an Idaho motel was just *another* receipt from *another* motel and nothing more.

[7] Four.

If she'd seen receipts for inappropriate things like, I don't know, a grand piano, a diamond necklace and a bulk order of Chinese DVD players I don't doubt she'd have been straight on the phone and we'd have found ourselves answering some difficult questions. But of course there was nothing suspicious like that to set her accountant's radar beeping. In the end, however, it was receipts of a different kind that raised a different, very un-accountant-like kind of concern.

It was the receipts from chiropractors that set Penny's spidey senses tingling. When an envelope arrived with three of them in she thought something must be up and so she called the producers to let them know.

There then followed a flurry of phone calls with two of the film's executive producers, Jon and Sally[8]. Both Stef and I took calls from both Jon and Sally as they first established which one of us had been receiving treatment and then worked out how serious the condition was. They asked for the phone numbers of the chiropractors and called them to find out more and then, two days later, Stef took the call that finally put the situation to bed.

The film's insurers weren't prepared to let her carry on. She was injured and there was simply no way anyone was going to risk her making her injury worse. The message came down from on high: put the camera down and don't pick it up again.

The first I knew about this new development was when Stef called me in my room and asked me to come through to hers.

As she opened the door and I stepped inside she handed me a freshly brewed cuppa.

'What's up?'

'You'd better film this,' she said. 'You just need to press the red button...'

---

[8] You might wonder what the difference is between a producer and an executive producer. What does an executive producer *actually* do, you might ask? Well the answer is that I haven't got a clue. As far as I can tell you, *this* is what executive producers do... they call you up when you're stuck in Moab, Utah.

It was obvious from her solemn expression that she wasn't asking me to film because she had a great party trick to show me. I picked up the camera and pressed the red button.

'I'm going to have to leave the film,' she said.

My brain struggled to cope as two separate threads of thought were released at the same time. Selfish and concerned thoughts tumbled over each other, fighting to get to the front of my head. I wasn't expecting this.

'Wha... what?'

'I'm going because my back's in a complete mess and I can no longer hold the camera.'

'Shit. Are you okay?'

'No,' she said. 'I'm not. I don't know what's going to happen. I don't know if they're going to get a new director or not. They said they'd call you about that.'

'Sod the film... what about you? What are you going to do? How are you supposed to get home? You can't just *go*!'

'Apparently, I can. Moab's got a tiny little airport just north of here. I can fly from there to Salt Lake City and then to New York. It's already booked. I'm leaving first thing tomorrow morning.'

'Shit. They don't hang around, do they?'

'No.'

There was a pause. I could tell from Stef's terse response and the cold matter-of-fact manner in which she'd told me the news that she was toeing a party line. She was telling me what she had been told to tell me and nothing more.

'So how are you feeling?'

'Not great,' she said. 'I don't want to stop.'

'So what will you do?'

'I don't know. *This* is what I do. I've been filming things for a living my whole life.' She pursed her lips and then took a sip of tea. 'Maybe this is it? Maybe I'll never film again? Maybe I'll have to find something else from here on in.' Another slurp of tea. 'It happens.'

'Are you gonna be okay?'

There was a silence. Stef stared impassively down the lens.

'Dave,' she said, 'are you trying to make me cry because you think it would make good footage?'

I wasn't looking at the real Stef. I was looking at the little pixellated Stef in the camera's viewfinder. She continued to stare me down via the lens, refusing to break my second-hand gaze. In my heart I knew I'd asked the question out of genuine concern. But then why was I feeling guilty? Somewhere at the back of my mind I knew the self-serving thought had occurred to me. I turned the camera off and placed it on the table to my right.

'Yes.' I picked up my tea. 'In a way, I guess I was.' I took a sip. 'Sorry.'

'Well, it's not going to happen, so don't.'

'I've turned it off now,' I said.

'I'm still not going to cry, y'know.'

'I know.'

There was another silence. This is what our time together had been reduced to: two normally chatty, outgoing people sharing stilted, awkward, emotionally stunted silences.

'I'm sorry,' said Stef.

'What for?'

'For what's happened to your trip. I know how much you wanted to do this thing.'

'It's not your fault.'

'I know. But I'm sorry.'

Pause.

'Do you need a hand packing?'

'No.'

Silence.

'Look, this is shit,' I sighed. 'Everything's shit. But it's our last night and there's no way we should let that be shit... so I think we should go out and have a really nice dinner somewhere. You've got to go out on a high.'

'I think you're right.' Stef smiled.

'Okay. So what kind of food do you fancy?'

'I think you know the answer to that one...'

And of course I did. Everybody knows Badger loves mashed potato.

At the airport the next morning Stef and I hugged each other goodbye. In the midst of that embrace we shared the briefest of exchanges but somehow, in that squeeze and with just two words, I think we summed up our entire relationship. This is how I will remember my time with Stef.

'Ow.'

'Sorry.'

From: Jake Lingwood (Ebury Publishing)
Subject: Chapters 12 to 19
To: Dave Gorman

Dave,

Thanks for the new chapters.

Have you miscalculated something? There was a four week gap in the narrative. It took you one week to get to Independence. Then another two weeks to get to Moab. That's just three weeks isn't it? Or have I misunderstood?

Only if this is right, the only way we're going to find you in that hotel room 'four weeks later' is if you spend a whole week in Moab. That can't be right can it?

Jake.

PS: Attached is some artwork we've had roughed up for the cover. Let me know what you think

From: Dave Gorman
Subject: Re: Chapters 12 to 19
To: Jake Lingwood (Ebury Publishing)

Jake,

You're right. A whole week.
See Chapter 20. (Attached)

Dave

PS: the artwork looks fine.

Chapter 20
63 eggs!

When I'd first decided to make this trip it was meant to be something I did alone. That was how I'd envisaged it. That was what it was meant to be. And yet now that I was alone it felt far from right. It felt very, very wrong.

I wanted to throw off the shackles of the film. I wanted to throw the whole thing away, get in the car and just drive. I wanted to reclaim control of the journey and make it *mine* once more. But I couldn't. For one, the car had been left in Pat's care at Arches Repair Center but beyond that I simply wasn't allowed. It was forbidden.

I'd done a deal for a film and the film company had invested. The various bags and crates of equipment that I lugged to and from the car each day belonged to them and in a series of phone calls they made it quite clear that my car was actually, in legal terms at least, theirs.

My instructions were to stay where I was. Various people promised me they were trying to find a new director to come and take over the filming but they were unable to tell me when, or even if, it would happen:

'What happens if you can't find someone?'

'Then we have to cut our losses.'

'What does that mean?'

'We sell the car, sell the gear and bring you home.'

Had it all been a waste of time? They might well have

invested financially in this thing but I'd invested more than that: I'd invested myself. The fact was, though, I had sold a piece of my dream. Why had I yielded control of something that meant so much to me? Why had I let them persuade me to make the film? Greed? Vanity? Probably a bit of both. But it didn't matter why. All that mattered was that I was deeply regretting it now. Was the whole thing about to be tossed aside? No one had the answer. Each day I was simply told to wait. What had I done?

I looked at myself in the mirror. My life, I'd put on weight. In three weeks! It shouldn't have been a surprise. In London my normal mode of transport is a bicycle. I regularly cover more than 100 miles a week on two wheels. I'd taken precisely no exercise so far on this trip and the running shoes I'd packed were languishing untouched at the bottom of my case. And I wasn't exactly eating a healthy, varied diet either. Roadside diners aren't overflowing with healthy options and meat-free options are rarer still. I'd been living almost exclusively on a diet of eggs, bread and potatoes. And caffeine. There were many times when my request for a vegetarian breakfast had seemed to completely bamboozle a waitress. On at least two occasions my only way of explaining it was to first order a ham omelette... and then ask them to leave the ham out. I must have eaten three eggs a day. For three weeks. That's 63 eggs! No wonder my little pot belly had appeared.

I decided to do something about it. I'd spent my time in Salt Lake City moping around and getting angry about the situation and I didn't want to repeat that pattern of behaviour here. I wanted to occupy myself. At least that was something I could take control of. The solution was easy. Moab does claim to be the Mountain Biking Capital of the World after all.

'How many days do you want it for?' asked the man in the bike hire shop.

I think every third business in Moab is a bike hire shop. Wherever you are in the world the staff in shops like this all seem to be of the same breed. It's a non-specific subgenus of the type you see in all 'extreme sports' related retail outlets so if you've ever been to a skate/surf/snowboard shop you'll know what I mean. It's what the guys who work in indie record stores would look like if they ever took exercise or saw the sun; a curious blend of high-school-geek and jock physique. It might just be the best of both worlds.

'I'm not sure how long I'm in town for,' I said. 'Can I take it a day at a time?'

I thought I was likely to spend three days burning off some energy and exploring the countryside. I didn't know it then but I was about to put myself through a week-long, mountain-biking boot camp.

The red rock landscape was amazing, with so many spectacular buttes, mesas, towers, stacks and arches around that at times it was cycling into a real world version of a *Roadrunner* cartoon.

The area's sandstone is so smooth its known as sliprock. When I first experienced it I thought the name curious, because the cycle tyres seemed to have plenty of traction. But that's because the rock was dry. When it's wet it's as slippy as ice.

'It can be dangerous out there,' warned the man-child in the bike hire shop. 'People get lost and end up dying of dehydration so it's probably best not to go alone.'

I didn't have much choice on that score but even so I wasn't going to be cocky. I knew that this rugged terrain was a very different proposition to the city streets I was familiar with so I asked for plenty of advice on which trails a novice could sensibly handle.

I'm not sure I managed to convey quite how new to it I was because the first route he recommended nearly killed me. He chose the Hurrah Pass Trail because the round trip is only 35 miles long and all of it is on either a paved road or a graded dirt track. If only I'd known quite how much of it was uphill. Still, the views of Kane Creek Canyon and the Colorado River were indisputably stunning. Not stunning enough to take away the burning sensation in my calves but stunning nonetheless.

Of course the real value in this ride – and all the others that

I made – was that it took me out of myself and meant that, for a few hours at least, I wasn't thinking about what a ridiculous mess this whole project had become.

Because I was staying put for a short while I decided to treat the Virginian a bit less like a pit stop and a bit more like a home. I had a small kitchenette and some basic crockery was provided so by doing a simple bit of shopping I was able to break free of the eggs, bread and potato breakfast tyranny.

I asked around for an independent grocer and everyone recommended the same place: Dave's. I liked Dave's. Dave's is to grocery shopping what *Cheers* is to bars. In Dave's everyone seemed to know everyone else's name. Every time a customer walked through the door I'd hear one of the staff greet them with a cheery 'Hey Tom', 'Hey Greg', 'Hey Jackie' or whatever.

It was one of those busy little stores that plays with your sense of space. You can see how small it is and you can see how few shelves they have and yet if you name a product, no matter how obscure, they appear to have it on display. You leave feeling confused as to why supermarkets are built as big as they are. Either supermarkets are 20 times the size they need to be or Dave's has found a way to break the laws of physics and bend space.

I put some fresh fruit, a box of cereal and a carton of milk in my basket and joined the back of the line. Over time the register had been decorated with all manner of ephemera. There were odd plastic toys Blu-tacked to the side of it along with a collage of stickers, some looking like they'd been there for ever and others looking good and fresh. The largest of the stickers brought an involuntary smile to my face. In bold green-and-white lettering it bore the legend: 'Friends don't let friends drink Starbucks'.

'Do you sell these?' I asked when my turn at the till arrived.

'I'm afraid not,' said Dave.

I knew he was Dave. For a start he was the only man working in a store called Dave's but if that wasn't proof enough there was a lifesize cartoon of him wearing a 'Dave' name badge propped up in the window. He had short white hair, small round wire-frame glasses and the kind of gently aged face you can only acquire if you're at peace with the world. Imagine the Dalai Lama as a white, Western shopkeeper and you're getting close.

'Never mind,' I shrugged. 'I'd have liked one of those...'

'It's just a bumper sticker that one of our customers brought in one time... if we had any more I'd let you have one. Sorry.'

'It doesn't matter,' I said. 'It just would have been kind of appropriate on my car.'

'Why's that?'

'It's kinda complicated. I guess I'm sort of making a film about things like that,' I said. 'Or at least I'm supposed to be.'

'You're making a film?' asked the woman waiting in line behind me.

'Kind of.'

'In Moab?'

'Well, at the moment...'

'I'll bet the mayor would like to talk to you. I can introduce you if you like...'

'Sure,' I said. 'That'd be nice.'

I was just being polite. It was easier. I had no great desire to meet the mayor. Not unless he was an out-of-work filmmaker who fancied a trip to the East Coast, anyway.

'Well,' she smiled a cheeky smile, 'there he is... he's right there.'

Confused, I turned back to the till where Dave was standing with an outstretched hand and a grin every bit as cheeky as hers.

'Pleased to meet you,' he said. We shook hands.

'You're the mayor?'

'That's me.'

'Mayor Dave?'

'Yup.'

I ran the words round in my head. Mayor Dave. It definitely had a nice ring to it.

With my groceries paid for, Mayor Dave and I went out and sat in the mid-morning sun for a chat and a cup of non-Starbucks coffee. He asked me about the film and I asked him about Moab.

Apparently the place had been a 1950s boomtown when they'd discovered uranium somewhere beneath its red rock husk. While those days had long since gone the '80s saw the rise of mountain biking and the advent of a new boom. They've been riding the adventure tourism wave ever since. And it's not just tourists who come for the spectacular scenery. Moab has been the backdrop to a few movies too. When Dave proudly showed me a photo of him as a youngster standing next to John Wayne he sent a tiny splutter of déjà vu through my system before I realised it was just a memory of Lone Pine arcing from one part of my brain to another and causing a small short circuit.

By the time I'd shaken my head straight and tuned back into our conversation I discovered Dave had moved on.

'We don't have too many of the big chains here and I don't think people really want them. Sure we have a few, there's a McDonald's and so on... but Arby's, Dairy Queen and Taco Bell all tried and failed in Moab. That's gotta say something.'

'I think it says it's my kind of place...'

'You want to be careful...' Dave leaned in to make his play-warning a little bit more play-ominous. 'You might end up staying for good.' I chuckled but he immediately raised his hand to shush me. 'I mean it,' he continued. 'You'd be amazed at the number of people who were "just passing through" and then stayed for years. A lot of artists; those kind of people. I promise you, stay here long enough and Moab will suck you in...'

I'd seen three different cities in Utah and the contrast between them couldn't have been greater. The prim and proper Salt Lake City, the lawless Green River and now Moab, the liberal outpost, equal parts hip and hippie. If SLC is a new-build show home on a modern housing estate – empty, hollow and phoney – then Green River is the untaxed, beaten up motorhome that's parked in the driveway and is scaring the neighbours. And if I'm to continue with the metaphor that makes Moab the enchanted windmill at the bottom of a secret garden.

Of all the places I could have ended up stranded I guess I had to be thankful it was this one. It could have been so much worse.

'So when are you leaving town?' asked Dave. 'As soon as your car is fixed?'

'I should be so lucky,' I said, wincing. 'The garage called me this morning and said I could pick the car up this afternoon. But then the London office called as well and they still don't know what's going on. I'm stuck here until they tell me any different.'

Dave looked at his watch.

'Do you think your car will be ready?'

I shrugged. 'Dunno. Why?'

'Come on, let's find out. I'll give you a lift.'

Could Moab be any nicer? I only popped in to buy a box of cereal and the next thing I knew the mayor of Moab was offering his services as my personal chauffeur. Who knows, I thought, maybe I will just stay. You never know... in a few years' time there might be a vacancy for a new Mayor Dave?

Under normal circumstances, Moab would be an almost perfect holiday destination for me but these weren't normal circumstances. I was doing everything I could to enjoy my time there but somehow it wasn't quite enough. Taking away my road trip and replacing it with a mountain biking holiday wasn't good enough for the same reason that you can't console a child whose dog has just died by giving them a really nice hamster. It didn't matter how much I *liked* the holiday, I *loved* the road trip.

Moab mornings coincide with London afternoons so my bowl of breakfast cereal was normally accompanied by a phone call from one of the executive producers. Every call it seemed that all they could tell me was that they had nothing new to tell me.

'What about Andy?' I asked one morning. 'He's meant to be producing this thing. He helped me find Stef, he must have some ideas.'

'He's been through his phone book,' said Jon. 'There's not a lot more we can ask him to do. He's busy shooting something else. He's not meant to be working on this until you're back and we start the edit. It's not easy getting someone at this kind of notice. Everyone's working at this time of year, Dave, Christmas is just around the corner...'

With every day that passed I grew more convinced that they were about to pull the plug. There was certainly nothing in these terse transatlantic exchanges to convince me otherwise.

So this became my Moab routine. I'd start with breakfast and a phone call that would leave me feeling frustrated, angry and upset. Then I'd load up with bottles of water, get on my bike and take a lung-busting, muscle-burning ride into the middle of nowhere. With every rotation of the pedals helping to shine a little light on the darkness of my mood, eventually I'd success-fully forget about my woes, for a while at least. Then the evening would come, I'd be back down to earth with a bump and the melancholia would start to edge its way back in. I'd eat out, have a couple of drinks and then go back to the motel and sit in my room all alone where, unable to stop the good day from coming undone, I'd sink slowly into a why-me state of maudlin.

What a self-regarding, self-indulgent, wallowing prick I am at times. It's not a nice trait. Sorry.

Every day the pendulum of my mood seemed to swing a little further in both directions. The morning phone call would leave me angrier than the day before. I'd compensate by cycling harder and faster and working up a bigger rush of exercise-fuelled endorphins. The transition from the enjoyable solitude of the wide open country to the depressing solitude of a meal for one would bring me back down to earth with a bigger bump and so on and so on.

The routine was broken on the sixth day. There was no

phone call. I checked my emails. Nothing. I tried to call the office. Nothing. The regular no-news phone call was frustrating. The complete absence of a phone call was even worse. My pedalling that day was more aggressive than any before.

I was intending to do the Arches Loop that day, a trail that would take me through the amazing Arches National Park – an area some 100 square miles in size that contains some of the most dramatic scenery I've ever seen. Over countless millennia the sandstone has been compacted, shaped and eroded, leaving a myriad of dramatic natural features that leaves anyone with an ounce of wonder in their body completely dumbstruck. There are sandstone fins as tall as Big Ben but as thin as a knife, huge monoliths side by side like a Manhattan skyline as imagined through Flintstone eyes and, as the name would suggest, there are arches.

Tarmac roads spread like veins through the park, leading tourists to a network of footpaths around the headline attractions. In the park, cycling off-road is punishable with a $500 fine so I stuck to the roads and from time to time, locked up the bike and went off on foot to explore.

Wandering around these wonderful structures it's impossible not to be awed by the natural forces that have shaped them over the 300 million years since an ocean flowed there. How can so many fantastic natural sculptures survive? At around 100 feet tall, Balanced Rock stands like a double-decker-bus-sized golf ball on a tee. Quite how something so huge remains balanced so precariously on top of its delicate rocky pedestal is beyond me.

Two huge arches, both extending from the same cliff face, meet and combine to form the feature known as Double Arch. Sitting in the cathedral sized space that lies between them it feels like you're in a fantastical conservatory. The two huge elliptical windows reveal glorious fantasy landscape views to either side while overhead there is an amazing natural skylight. It makes for a contradictory set of sensations. At the same time as you feel like you're in the middle of a desolate, wide-open nothingness, there is also a feeling of sanctuary and containment.

But it was while sitting there that I realised how unhappy I was. I looked out across this most impressive of views and realised that I was still seething about the aborted road trip. For the first time my daily excursion had failed to take my mind off things. For the first time my mind had refused to let go.

As the sun moved through the day the landscape changed colour dramatically. What appeared to be salmon pink at midday glowed a deep, blood red before sunset.

It was against that blood-red backdrop that I pedalled back into town. The long, winding descent down the zigzag road out of the park being scarier than any of the more remote rides I'd made purely because there were two winnebagos right behind me.

I took a shower back at the motel but whilst I could wash the sheen of sweat from my body I couldn't scrub away the gnawing anger inside. That night instead of having a couple of drinks to accompany my lonely meal, I had a couple of drinks to accompany the couple of drinks that were already accompanying my first couple of drinks. I don't remember if I had a meal.

I felt it in the morning. My head throbbed. I looked at the box of cereal on the side but it wasn't very appealing. I wanted fried food. Suddenly that eggs, bread and potatoes combo seemed attractive once more. But I didn't want to leave the room in case I missed a phone call. I sat in and waited. The phone didn't ring. I checked my emails. Nothing. They'd gone silent on me. Surely that could mean only one thing.

I'd been out on long bike rides for six consecutive days. I knew it would be good for me today but with my hangover cramps I couldn't persuade myself to get on the saddle. No. On the seventh day, I rested.

And seethed.

By the middle of the afternoon I knew there wasn't going to be a phone call so I headed out for lunch. I walked into the centre of Moab, passing the two Best Western hotels that sat on either side of the main road. Like the rest of Moab they looked benign. Were they part of an evil empire? They didn't look so bad.

Oh, what was the point? Why was I bothering? Why was I clinging on to this thing while everyone else was giving up? Why didn't I just face up to the fact that I'd failed? It was a nice idea but it had gone awry, surely it was best to just throw the towel in and leave it at that. The journey I'd dreamed of making just hadn't happened. I hadn't stayed on the small roads, I hadn't avoided the big cities and I hadn't gone wherever I'd wanted. And of course, I'd already run out of gas and been rescued by one of the chains. So what was left to play for? Nothing. Absolutely fucking nothing.

Something had to give. Something had to snap. I knew what I had to do.

I would build a funeral pyre for my trip. If I was going down anyway, why not go down in flames? By breaking every rule I'd demonstrate how little I cared and if I could prove to myself that I didn't care... well, then there was nothing to be upset about, was there? You can't be upset about something you don't care about, can you? And I didn't care about it, did I? Did I? Shh.

I loaded the camera equipment into the Torino. She started easily enough – well done, Pat – but inevitably, the fuel gauge told me she was almost empty. Good. I was about to break all the rules after all, so I could start by filling her up. There were loads of gas stations in town and I didn't care which one I used. I was no longer playing that game. I went to the Shell station. Seventeen gallons of branded fuel were easily swallowed. Next stop? A hotel. How had checking in to a Best Western come to feel like an act of rebellion? How exciting it felt to be a rule-breaker. Before I could continue with the ceremony I had to set the cameras up and then... then I waited. I waited for the sun to set.

When darkness came I went out on my mission. Food. Food from a chain. But which one? Why not more than one? I *was* trying to show how little I cared after all. I drove from McDonald's to Burger King to Wendy's and at each one I bought a large burger and fries. If Arby's had succeeded in Moab I'd have gone there too. Then, back to the hotel.

Was I really going to do this? You bet I was. I wasn't going to let other people take this project from me. Not when I could torch it first. Fuelling the car, booking the room, buying the burgers... that was all preparation. That was just sprinkling petrol on the corpse. Now it was time to light the match. Now it was time to eat.

Four a.m. I don't know how long I'd been asleep, only that I had. I tried to lift my head from the sheet but it wouldn't move. Sweat, spit and vomit combined make a remarkably powerful adhesive. Slowly peeling my face away from the bed I was worried I might end up leaving some skin behind.

It took me a while for my eyes to adjust to the dark but as the surroundings started to make sense to me so the events of last night thudded home. I could see the cameras, the tripod and the detritus from three meals. Unhappy meals. I should never go into marketing.

My nostrils burned. The back of my throat burned. I was disgusting. I was disgusted. I needed to piss. I padded my way through to the bathroom where the foul stench of my own vomit nearly made me throw up all over again. Meat. I can't believe I did it. Meat!

I tried to clean myself up. I washed my hands and face but the smell had somehow worked itself into the pores of my skin and the follicles of my beard and I couldn't shift it from me. I had to get out of this place. I had to get back to my real room. I had to get back to the Virginian.

I tidied the room as best I could but to be honest, when you're trying to wash a puke-stained pillowcase in a hotel sink without detergents and all you can do is pick the solid bits off by hand you're probably better off admitting defeat and walking away.

The hefty tip I left for the chambermaid did nothing to ease my guilt as I slipped silently out of the hotel at five in the morning, leaving a room that looked like a bomb had hit it. Not a conventional bomb, I admit, but perhaps something chemical. Or then again, perhaps just a bomb full of sick.

I made the short drive back to the Virginian, showered and went to bed.

Part three
Beyond Moab

Chapter 21
The Bumper Sticker Elf

When I woke for the second time that morning I was still feeling rough. My stomach muscles ached like I'd been kicked in the guts a few times but at least no part of me was glued to the sheets.

I got myself a glass of water and crawled back to bed. My brain felt numbed by the whole thing but I tried to analyse how I was feeling. I knew I'd managed to get quite a lot of *something* out of my system – solids mainly – but what about the angst? Remarkably, it seemed as though the exorcism had worked. I didn't feel angry any more. I tried but it wasn't there. I no longer cared. I'd come to accept the journey was over and it felt fine. I didn't care about anything. Apart from my stomach muscles and my acid-burned throat.

Well, that was a turn up for the books! The spell had worked. Maybe I could forge a career as some kind of amateur voodoo guru. I'd taken everything that was wrong in my tiny, selfish microcosm of a world, consumed them and then rejected them and now they were no more. Now, my troubles were no more.

If the car was any kind of team player it should have thrown up the petrol too. I knew it was a ludicrous notion but for some reason I still felt myself drawn to the window to have a look. I pulled back the curtains. Needless to say, there was no regurgitated four star sloshing around the Torino's wheels. But *something* was different.

I was looking at the car's rear end and there was definitely something on the back bumper. A sticker. At this distance I couldn't make out the lettering, but then I didn't need to because I recognised the colours and shapes. I'd seen that sticker before: 'Friends Don't Let Friends Drink Starbucks'.

Mayor Dave! I threw some clothes on and rushed out to take a closer look. Kneeling on the gritty floor, I could see that the sticker had a few creases and tears. The kind of creases and tears that might appear if you peeled a sticker off of something, then tried real hard to keep it from sticking to itself while you drove round to a motel and surreptitiously stuck it on to someone else's car bumper while they were asleep. It was the only answer. Unless the Tooth Fairy has a Utah cousin called the Bumper Sticker Elf. I chuckled to myself and raised an imaginary glass to the mayor of Moab. What a super mayor! The photo of a boyish Dave stood next to John Wayne flashed through my mind. What a Western Super Mayor!

Oof! If my bad-pun gene was kicking in already I knew I must be on the mend.

Was it a sign? Was the sticker there to tell me that I *should* care, that I shouldn't have given up hope? Such thoughts were shaken from my brain by my Pavlovian response to a ringing telephone. I raced back inside and took the call.

'Dave?'

'Yeah.'

'It's Jon. I've got some news for you...'

My heart stopped.

'Really?'

'We've got a new director...'

My heart started again.

'You're joking!'

There I was, convinced that I no longer cared and now all of a sudden I immediately found myself caring a very great deal.

'It's all been a bit last minute but he's on his way.'

'Who is it? Where'd you get him?'

'You've got Andy to thank for it...'

Andy. I knew he'd think of someone.

'So who is it? Anyone I know?'

'It's Andy.'

'What?'

'Andy's taking over; he's on his way...'

'I thought he was working on something else...'

'He was. But it finished two days ago. I'll be honest with you, Dave, he's completely saving your arse here. He's been working 24 hours a day for a month, he's had one day to spend with his wife... if I were you, Dave, I'd be grateful, very, very grateful.'

'Oh man, I am. Believe me, I am. Thank you! Thank you, thank you, thank you.'

There was a short burst of staccato laughter on the other end of the line.

'Not to me, Dave... I mean to Andy.'

'Oh. Of course. Yeah. I knew that,' I lied. 'So should I book him a room?'

'That depends on how grateful you want to be.'

'What?'

'Yes, Dave. Book him a room. He's in the air already... he's flying in to New York. The he flies to Salt Lake City. Gets in around 10 p.m. your time. Then we've told him to get a cab to... where are you again?'

'Moab.'

'That's it.'

'Are you sure that's a good idea?'

'Why?'

My head tried to do the working out as my memory stretched back through our journey from Salt Lake City. In the end I just took a guess.

'That's gonna be at least seven hours in a cab.'

'Well, you'd better stay up late then, hadn't you?'

'I suppose so.'

'So how's it going? Are you enjoying... where is it?'

'Moab.'

'That's the place. What's it like?'

I thought about explaining the night before. But I didn't think about it for long.

'It's great,' I said. 'The mayor's ace!'

I'd drifted off to sleep still fully clothed on top of the bed with the telly on. I heard an engine and the opening and closing of car doors but it wasn't enough to rouse me. It was the rat-a-tat-tat rap of English knuckles on my bedroom door that did it. He was here! I leapt up and off the bed and rushed to the door. Just before I got there I remembered something. I turned on my heel, picked up the camera, pressed the red button, took a deep breath and then opened the door.

Given that he'd just completed a 24-hour journey, the full-beam smile on Andy's face was remarkable. It turned into a chuckle the minute he realised he was being filmed.

'You ordered an extra film-maker?' he said.

Our handshake turned into as much of a hug as was possible with a camera at my shoulder.

'I'm so glad you're here,' I said.

'I'm glad to be here.' Andy smiled. He looked at his watch. 'I can't believe it. I left my wife and child this morning...'

'Oh no... don't make me feel guilty already. I'm really sorry. And grateful.' I lowered the camera. 'Do you want a cup of tea? Coffee? A camera?'

'I don't know... I'm all over the place. I'm just glad to be out of that cab.'

'How long was it?'

'Five hours.'

'Is that all?'

'You're kidding me! It feels like for ever! I kept drifting asleep in the back. I opened my eyes one time, we were in the middle of nowhere and there was this huge chemical plant or something with smoke billowing out of it... it was like I was having a nightmare...'

'We saw that!' I said with childish excitement. 'It was near Helper...'

'Yes! God, it was scary. I kept thinking we were going to crash. The taxi driver was mad. Did you know Jesus went to America? What're you laughing at?'

'Yes, I did know,' I said, still chuckling. 'I'll tell you even more about it another time.'

We paused. I put the camera down and Andy dropped his luggage. It was time for a proper hug. And a cup of tea.

'You know I want to get going,' I said. 'I've been in Moab for too long already. But I know how knackered you must be and another day won't kill me so if you want to take a day or two to acclimatise that's obviously cool. I'm just glad you're here at all.'

'I guess I won't know for sure until I get up, but I reckon we should just get going. Lou's been brilliant letting me come and do this but I can't take the piss. The sooner we get going, the sooner we reach the coast. The sooner we reach the coast, the sooner we get home. The sooner we get home, the sooner Lou forgives me for cancelling our daughter's christening.'

'You what?'

'Didn't I say?'

'A christening?'

'Yeah... Anna was meant to be christened on the 26th ... but we've cancelled it.'

'Are you making that up? Are you just *trying* to make me feel guilty?'

'A: No. And B: Yes.'

'Shit. I'm *really* sorry. Okay... we'll head east in the morning just as soon as you're ready to go.'

As I brushed my teeth before bed that night my mind was spinning. The man who stared back at me in the mirror looked normal enough. Had he really put himself through last night's ordeal?

I tried to reassess what had happened. It still felt like voodoo. It's just it wasn't my woes that were being rejected... it was the taint of failure. All the bits of gristle and bile that had sandblasted that toilet bowl represented the miles of interstate we shouldn't have driven, the hours we'd spent visiting cities we shouldn't have gone to and most importantly, the gallons of chained gas that had been swallowed by our car. My body and soul had rejected it all, I'd purged myself and I'd purged the project. And I'd been rewarded for it.

Would that bumper sticker have appeared on my car otherwise? Would Andy have volunteered to come out at such short notice?

Of course the answers were 'yes' and 'yes' but I didn't want to think such prosaic thoughts. Why let the dull truth ruin an exciting feeling? It was magic and I'd made it happen with my burger-puking, project-purging voodoo.

And now it was time for a fresh start. America Unchained rides again.

It had taken us 22 days to get to Moab and in that time Stef and I had spent $2,555.26 on unchained accommodation, $519.67 on unchained gas and $396.47 on unchained car repairs. With unchained food added into the mix that must have been well over $4,000. And we'd *only* given $42.06 to The Man™.

That meant our journey to Moab was still 99 per cent unchained! But I could do better than that. I could make a case to suggest we were 100 per cent successful. The trip from coast to coast was supposed to be about 2,800 miles. In getting to Moab we'd already driven 3,153 miles... with a full tank taking us roughly 260 miles I reckon that means we'd successfully driven 2,800 unchained miles! It was a very successful journey... just with a big cock-up on the navigation front.

But none of that mattered, because in my mind the slate was now wiped clean. The tank of gas, the night's accommodation and the beef patties I'd bought from The Man™ in Moab didn't count. What was I going to do, give the gas back? They were sacrifices to the Unchained Gods and they'd served their purpose. They'd helped to summon a new director from nowhere and breathed life back into the journey.

If we could make it to the coast from here and keep the rest of our journey chain-free would I really look back on that one dry tank and feel like I'd failed? Not a chance.

Running out of gas and being rescued by a chain *was* undoubtedly a knock-out blow. I'd hit the canvas and the referee had begun the count.

One-ah, two-ah, three-ah. Three nights in Salt Lake City. Four-ah, five-ah, six-ah. A miserable night in Green River. Seven-ah, eight-ah. Moab. Nine-ah. Voodoo.

Whoosh. The smelling salts hit me. A sudden surge of fresh energy was pulsing through me. I was going to attack this thing like never before. I was going to get to that coast and I was going to do it without giving a single dime to any of the chains. If I did that... if I did that I'd be chalking this thing up to a win. On points.

Chapter 22
Stubborn, manly pride

I managed to get a couple of hours' sleep that night but not much more than that. By 9 a.m., I'd showered, brushed my teeth, breakfasted on a bowl of cereal, brushed my teeth again, had a coffee, brushed my teeth once more and now I wanted to get going.

I wanted to go and knock on Andy's door. I wanted to wake him up, pour coffee down his throat and then get in the car and go. I wanted to be heading east. I wanted to be driving into the glorious unknown. I wanted this leg of my coast-to-coast journey to have started. I wanted it now.

I tried to read but I couldn't focus on the page in front of me. I tried to watch TV but just felt assaulted by the multi-channel nothingness on offer. I tried listening to music but nothing my iPod shuffled to seemed to sit with my mood. Hmmm. I still hadn't programmed that special music-for-impatient-people playlist. Another day. Not now.

Given the day of hellish travel Andy had put himself through in order to join me I knew I couldn't be annoyed with him for not being ready and rearing to go. So instead I just sat and stared at my packed cases and told myself to sit tight. And because I'd packed my washbag I didn't even brush my teeth.

When Andy did appear – at a perfectly reasonable 10.15 – I smiled and offered him a cup of tea.

'No thanks,' he said, 'I've already had two cups of coffee this morning.'

'Have you? Oh. So you've been up for a while then?'

'Hours,' he said. 'I've done a complete inventory on the camera equipment, checked all the mics and repacked the camera bag so that I know where everything is. There's a clever fix on the tripod... did Stef buy a new part somewhere?'

'Um yeah,' I said, as the small part of me that had been consumed with impatience melted into guilt. 'Back in LA...'

'So,' said Andy, 'shall we pack the car and get going? I believe we've got an urgent appointment with a coast.'

On a crisp, clear, bright November morning I finally left Moab behind me. I might go back one day. I think I'd *really* like it if I went there on purpose.

The road was clear and we made good, steady progress heading south on the 191. To our right the land was dotted with higgledy-piggledy clusters of mobile homes, some of them grouped together in such density that they were almost a shanty town in appearance. As fascinating as it was to see these Utah favelas we weren't in the mood for dawdling. We were going to cover some ground; today's drive was a statement of intent.

As we sliced through some more red-rock country Andy pumped me with questions about the journey so far. All he knew was that it had taken me three weeks to reach Moab. It was obvious that even with Stef's bad back it shouldn't have taken us that long to get 800 miles from Coronado and Andy wanted to know why.

So I explained the curiously circuitous route we'd taken. As I did so, Andy placed a map on his lap and tried to trace our route with his finger. By the time his digit was crossing the border into Oregon he was looking worried. When it snuck into Washington he was positively aghast.

'Dave,' he said, 'look at this.'

I turned to my right where Andy was holding up his mobile phone to show me a photograph. It was an impossibly cute picture of Anna, his one-year-old, unchristened daughter taken

a few months earlier when she was a vision of bug-eyed loveli-
ness strapped to his belly in a papoose.

'She's cute,' I said.

'Yes she is,' said Andy. 'And I'm already missing her like
crazy. So we're not messing around anymore. We're heading
east from here on in, all right? None of this Independence lark,
all right?'

'Ah.'

'What do you mean, "ah"?'

'Well...' I paused, 'I've been meaning to speak to you about
this...'

'What?'

'You know I told you about Taylor's?'

'Uh huh.'

I reached into my pocket and pulled out a small shiny medal-
lion. I handed it to Andy.

'Billie Kay gave me this.'

Andy studied it briefly. If it came down to cuteness his show-
and-tell was definitely winning.

'What is it?'

'It's a special coin. It was made in 1959 to commemorate
the 100th anniversary of the wagon train that brought pioneers
from Independence, Missouri to Oregon. That's where
Independence, Oregon took its name from. In 1959 they celebrated the centenary by recreating the wagon train all over
again. And to celebrate their celebration, they struck these
commemorative coins.'

'And?'

'And I thought that as Independence, Oregon was so good
and it was named after Independence, Missouri... it kind of
made sense to go there.'

'To Missouri?'

'Yeah.'

There was a pause. Andy looked at his phone and smiled.

'Dave... you're not honestly suggesting another detour. I
mean, where the hell is Missouri anyway?'

'Well, that's the good thing. Take a look at the map. The next state east from Utah is Colorado… then Kansas, then Missouri. I mean, it's on the way.'

Andy looked at the map. He looked at me. He looked at Anna. He looked at me again. He was trying to work out if there was some kind of trick going on. There wasn't. How could there be once I'd seen that photo?

'All right,' he said cautiously. 'It's probably a good idea. If it gives you something that's actually east to aim for… let's do it.'

Whenever I look at a map of the US the straight-line borders that define so many of the States always strike me as being rather arbitrary. It just looks like someone's picked up a ruler and divided the place up at random. I mean, how else could Wyoming and Colorado end up as almost perfect rectangles? I suppose I'm just used to the squiggly lines of Europe where the borders trace mountains and rivers or have been drawn and redrawn through history as battles have been fought and won. In my mind nature and war should define borders, not neatness.

Yet within five minutes of crossing just such a border I was struck by how genuinely different Colorado seemed in comparison to Utah. There were trees for a start. The border might have been a man-made construct, but there definitely seemed to be some natural sense behind it.

We turned a corner and both our jaws dropped. The land just seemed to fall away beneath our wheels as if some enormous hand had just reached down and scooped out a huge section of it. The valley floor was green but in the far distance it reached an abrupt end against an enormous terracotta-coloured cliff face while above that the clear blue sky added a third bold stripe of colour; like a tricolor flag for a country that hasn't yet been invented.

We were looking out over the Paradox Valley, which is odd because I've always thought that would be a good name for a mountain. Apparently it has this peculiar name because of its peculiar formation. Most canyons follow the flow of a river's path but in Paradox Valley the Dolores River cuts through it at right angles. So now you know. I still think it's a better name for a mountain.

As we reached the valley floor we were met by a beautiful stone and timber building by the side of the road. It could have been the grand house of some wealthy landowner but the faded adverts adorning the walls gave away its commercial life. I slowed, hoping against hope that it would sell fuel and, yes, a few yards beyond the building there stood a solitary pump. Many years ago the sign by the pump had read Texaco but it had been painted over and nowadays it reads simply: 'Gas'.

We'd stumbled across the Bedrock Store. It was built over 120 years ago and apart from the weathering of its dark timbers I doubt its appearance has changed all that much over time. It wouldn't have been at all surprising if Grampa Walton had emerged from its doors with a sack of grain on his shoulder.

As I pumped the gas I looked around. Behind us was a mountain. In front was the valley floor stretching all the way to the horizon. There wasn't another building in sight. There wasn't another vehicle on the road either. It was just us and whoever owned the gas station. I breathed in the fresh country air and marvelled at how Andy's first day on board had got off to such a perfect start.

'This is stunning, Dave,' said Andy, his voice full of breathy amazement. 'I can't believe I was in London yesterday and I'm here now. I can't believe I was in the *twenty-first century* yesterday and I'm here now. This is amazing. I didn't realise these places still existed. If you've been doing this for three weeks I'm truly jealous.'

I thought he was joking to begin with and chuckled obligingly... then I looked up, saw his face and realised he wasn't.

'It's not always this easy, y'know!' I said, just dipping the conversation's toes in indignant waters. 'Gas doesn't normally just present itself like this... sometimes we have to go looking. Sometimes it isn't there!'

But Andy wasn't listening to me. He was listening to the world. I wanted him to understand how difficult this thing could be but the world wasn't backing me up. The world was too busy being marvellous to give Andy Devonshire a reality check.

In fact there was nothing that day to shake Andy from his idyllic view of the journey. It was perhaps the perfect day. We covered nearly 200 miles, ending in the Colorado town of Cortez where a giant axe-shaped neon sign drew us to the comfort of the Tomahawk Motel and it's delightfully dotty Polish owners. Better still, it was only a few doors away from another unbranded gas station, which, while devoid of rustic charm, was still a fantastic guarantee that we'd start the new day with a full tank.

'Are you up for an early start tomorrow?' asked Andy as we unloaded the car. He was brimming with confidence. It's one of the best things you can brim with. 'Let's really see how far we can get.'

'Absolutely,' I said. 'Let's go for it.'

I liked Andy's attitude and his confidence was infectious but I wondered if he really understood how challenging the task could be. On present evidence it did seem ridiculously easy. He must have been wondering what all the fuss was about. The poor chap didn't know what he'd let himself in for. Or maybe, just maybe, he was going to be my lucky charm. Maybe with him on board it *was* going to be easy from here on in? God, I hoped so.

'I was looking at your licence plate, with the three sixes,' said the mechanic as he used the car jack to lower the Torino back down to the ground with a bump. 'Y'know, Route 666 runs right through Cortez. Now *that's* a bad omen you got right there.'

I couldn't decide which part of this experience was telling me the most about our lack of good fortune. Was it really the impending union of a highway and a licence plate that both bore the number of the beast... or was it the fact that we hadn't yet left Cortez and our car was already jacked up outside a garage being attended to by a mechanic? I mean one of those things is really just superstitious guff while the other surely suggests that some actual bad fortune has already occurred.

Our day had started well enough with both Andy and myself rising bright and early. The confidence of the day before was still in us and we'd loaded the car up with an enjoyable *Hi-ho-hi-ho-it's-off-to-work-we-go* sense of industry.

While Andy went to make a final check on his room I took my stills camera out and snapped a few shots of the car with the huge neon tomahawk behind it. I didn't get the shot I was after because in trying to find an angle that emphasised the classic timber panel that stretched down the Torino's length I found my interest diverted elsewhere.

I was crouching down near one of her front corners and for perhaps the first time in my life I found myself studying a car's tyre. There appeared to be a little grey pebble lodged in the tread. I was pretty sure my father had once told me to dislodge such things or risk a blow out so I put my camera down and tried to flick it out using the car keys as a lever. It didn't move. I tried again and still it stayed where it was.

How odd. Maybe there was a lump of chewing gum gluing it in place? I lowered my shoulder for extra leverage and really tried to jemmy it out, but still nothing.

'What're you up to?'

The question came from Andy. I didn't look round, I just explained while taking yet another unsuccessful stab at it.

'Here. Try these.'

This time I turned. He was offering me a pair of pliers. I took the tool and gripped either side of the mysterious object and gave it a tug. It clung on. A beam of torchlight appeared from over my shoulder to help. Andy's ability to produce tools at will was impressive. Was I working with Inspector Gadget?

'Mate,' Andy sounded concerned, 'that's not a stone.'

'Isn't it?'

'Nah. That's the tyre.' He moved the torch into a better position, moving his hand directly into the wheel arch and shining straight down. 'Look.'

He was right. It wasn't a pebble and there was no chewing gum involved; it was just shredded rubber. It was as if a tiny tyre volcano had erupted and this was its frozen lava flow.

'I've never seen that before,' I said, trying to sound like a man who'd examined a lot of tyres. 'Have you?'

'No.'

'D'you think it's safe?'

'I dunno.'

Which is why we ended up at Dennis Rieb's Autoworks with a mechanic telling us about Route 666.

It turned out to be a fault in the tyre and once someone tells you that, your only real choice is to replace it. Discovering one faulty tyre placed enough doubt in our minds about the ageing rubber that was keeping us on the road to persuade us to change all four. After all we had at least 2,000 miles still to travel and you can't put a price on peace of mind. Or rather you can and it comes to about $300 for four new tyres.

'So much for our early start,' I said as I pulled back on to the highway.

'Yeah... but it was the right thing to do,' said Andy. 'Better safe than sorry. Besides... I reckon we can make up the time.'

From Dennis Rieb's we headed back towards the motel so that we could visit their near-neighbours the unbranded gas station where we filled the tank and bought ourselves a selection of sugary snacks in lieu of breakfast.

Finally, two hours later than planned we were ready to get out of town. We just weren't sure which was the right way to go.

'Is it right or left?' I asked Andy as we idled on the gas station forecourt.

'Not sure,' said Andy. 'The guy at Rieb's gave you directions... what did he say?'

'He said to take a right and then another right and then a left. I think. But that was before we came here. He didn't know we were coming here. We took a right and a left and a right in order to get *here*. Didn't we? So... um... no, sorry, I'm confused. What do you reckon?'

The car behind me honked its horn.

'I *think* you want to go... left,' said Andy, although it was obvious the cogs were still turning. 'Yep, yeah. Left.'

Forty miles later we found ourselves driving on a smooth tarmac ribbon through the golden sands of New Mexico, which was a pain in the arse because we weren't supposed to go to New Mexico. Andy consulted the maps quickly before declaring that we were idiots and that the only sensible way of correcting the mistake was to turn around and head back the way we'd come.

Maybe the tyre-fitting soothsayer of Cortez had cursed us with his double 666 talk. Maybe the omens were bad.

By the time we'd corrected our mistake and got back to square one the detour had cost us a full two hours. We stopped at the same gas station to fuel up a second time and bought some more sugary snacks, this time in lieu of lunch.

In four hours all we'd done was bounce back to the same point over and over again like a Ford-Torino-shaped yo-yo hanging from a Tomahawk-Motel-shaped finger but finally, we were ready to head east.

Finding our way was easier this time – we used a process of elimination and headed out on the one road we hadn't yet taken – and pretty soon we were cruising at speed down the 160 with the New Mexico border only 20 or 30 miles to the right and the San Juan Mountains almost immediately to our left.

Ridiculously, we made another wrong turn at a town called Durango and while this one only cost us 20 minutes it definitely served to underline the fact that this was a fractured kind of day where nothing was quite going right. Unless it was meant to go left.

With that in mind, we really should have weighed anchor and called it a day when we got to Pagosa Springs. At that point we'd somehow conspired to spend six hours on the road covering 200 miles of tarmac while only getting 100 miles from where we started. The night sky was overhead already so perhaps we should have chalked the day up to experience and started afresh in the morning. Perhaps we should have... but we had too much stubborn, manly pride for that.

'Stick or twist?' I asked.

'We've only travelled a hundred miles!' said Andy, not even prepared to countenance the idea of stopping. 'Twist.'

And so we pressed on. Had we looked at a map or done any basic research about where in the world we were we'd have surely waited until daybreak. Had anyone said, 'By the way, if you carry on from here you're about to go over the Rockies. You'll climb to nearly 11,000 feet. If you do it by day the views are spectacular but if you do it by night it's as scary as hell... oh, and by the way... the road is called... Wolf Creek Pass,' I think we might have waited. (Especially if they'd ended with a devilish, sinister laugh and a strike of lightning; *Wolf Creek Pass, mwah ha ha ha ha!*)

As we started our ascent under a pitch-black sky and a bright full moon it felt like nothing more than the start of a journey to Dracula's castle and the headlights we could see zigzagging their way slowly down the mountain looked like flaming torches in the hands of angry villagers.

Back in London, when I'd first explained my plans to Andy, I'd always said I didn't want to know where I was going, that I just wanted to get in the car and drive. That was what had excited me the most about this idea. It was also a huge part of what I felt had gone missing in my time with Stef. We'd definitely allowed caution to rule. But no longer. Not now my new copilot had a fully functioning back. Now we were driving into a truly frightening unknown and I was cacking myself. And loving every minute of it.

Wolf Creek Pass would take us from Pagosa Springs to South Fork. It's a distance of roughly 40 miles as the road defiantly slices its way through the rugged and threatening terrain. When the first pioneers used this route (travelling the other way, of course) it would take them between two and three weeks to get across. Imagine travelling at an average speed of 0.1mph... for two weeks! Even when the trail was well worn and the motorcar had arrived the journey time wasn't much improved with many still taking up to a week to get through.

Of course cars have improved since then, as has the road. Even in the last few years the highway has been widened and in 2005 a 900-foot-long section of tunnel was opened. Even so, with snow on the ground, frost in the air and the occasional deadly drop into oblivion just beyond the kerb, it remains a scary mother of a mountain to traverse.

'I'm not sure we should be doing this,' said Andy

We were part way up and we could both hear how hard the car was labouring to haul us up the unforgiving slope. We'd been heading up the side of this mountain for ages already but the summit never seemed to get any nearer.

'I know what you mean,' I said, willing the car to keep going. My palms were sweating. 'But we haven't got much choice now, have we? It's a Magnusson.'

'A what?'

'I've started so I'll finish.'

'Pfft.'

CLANK!

My foot went straight to the brake pedal. My heart went straight to my mouth. It probably bumped into the word 'fuck', which was just on its way out.

There are lots of sounds you don't want to hear when you're in a car. Andy had just heard two of them. You definitely don't want to hear the driver cursing like that and you definitely, definitely don't want to hear the clank of metal hitting road. Not when your car is made of metal... which most of them are. You don't need to know much about motors to know that when a bit of metal falls off your car it's rarely – if ever – a good thing. I know nothing about cars but I do know that most of the important bits that make them go forward are made of metal.

I didn't have a clue what had just happened. All I knew was that this was not a good place to break down. This was a terrible and terrifying place to break down.

'What the hell was that?' asked Andy. There was panic in his voice. He didn't know that I'd hit the brakes. He must have thought our sudden loss of speed had been caused not by me but by the bout of metal-thingy-falling-offiness we were currently experiencing.

I gave the car a quick test by moving my foot back to the gas. She responded okay but gurgled grumpily as if to say, 'All right... I'm going to speed up but in my own time. It's your own fault for slowing me down in the first place. This slope isn't easy, you know. It's all right for you, you're only 35... I'm 36... and that's 72 in car years.'

'The car's still driving,' I said, 'but that was definitely something falling off, wasn't it?'

Andy sighed heavily. 'Come on,' he said, 'let's pull over and take a quick look.'

As I steered us into the snow-covered verge I crossed my fingers and hoped I was driving on to solid ground. The reassuring sound of gravel beneath the wheels was a huge relief. We jumped out of the warm car into the freezing night air. Thanks to our recently repaired heating, I hadn't realised quite how cold it was outside.

I trudged a hundred yards down the slope trying to study every inch of the road as I did so, while at the same time completely clueless as to what I was actually looking for. My knuckles were already feeling the cold. Of course it was only a matter of seconds before Inspector Gadget produced another torch from nowhere. This was a much bigger device than before and with a beam brighter and fuller than anything our old headlamps could manage. He shone it in my direction, illuminating the ground in front of me. There was nothing there.

As the torchlight disappeared I span round to see what Andy was up to. Instead of shining the light where the part might be he'd decided to shine it where he knew it wasn't. He was circling the car with the flashlight, trying to see if he could work out what was now missing.

'Got it!' he yelled.

'What, you've found it?'

'No, I've found *not-it*. We've lost a hubcap. That's a relief.'

'Okay... well, at least I know what I'm looking for,' I said, turning to continue my search. I knew I should have been happy that it wasn't an important part of the engine that had been given to the mountain but I wasn't.

'Dave! Give up!' called Andy. 'It's probably still spinning back down to Pagosa Springs.'

'Give me a minute,' I said. 'It might still be here.'

'You'll catch your death, you idiot. It's freezing. It's only a hubcap. The car's fine.'

'I know... but I haven't looked over here yet.'

'Dave!'

'Yeah?'

'I just want you to know that I'm looking at a photo of Anna. She's very cute. She wants you to get back in the car and drive her dad over the big scary mountain in safety.'

'O-kayyyy,' I said sulkily.

I turned and huffed and puffed my way back up the mountain, my lungs working overtime to squeeze every bit of oxygen out of the thin air.

'I bet they didn't put it back right when they changed the tyres,' I said huffily. And puffily.

'Maybe,' said Andy. 'But it's *just* a hubcap. I was worried the exhaust had fallen off.'

'Yeah, I know...'

'By the way,' said Andy. 'Have you stopped to look around you? I don't mean looking at the ground, searching for a lump of metal... I mean, really looked around you?'

I did. It was amazing. There were more stars than there was sky and the way the mountain dropped away to nothing made it feel like we were looking down on some of them. We were floating. We were in outer space. I've never felt smaller. I've never felt more alive. I've never felt more stupid for caring about a hubcap. There are other things in the world. Millions and millions and millions and millions of them.

'Good, isn't it?' said Andy. 'Now come on, let's drive.

★

'It's been a strange day,' I said when Wolf Creek Pass had finally released us from its grip. 'Four new tyres, three old hubcaps, two wrong turns and one moment where we both thought we'd broken down halfway up a freezing cold horror-film-mountain... is that it or do you think there's a zero to round off the countdown?'

'There's definitely a zero,' said Andy. 'Zero worries. We're undefeatable. The day has tried its best and we've won. I say we keep going and we keep winning. You must have another hour in you.'

'Two.'

'Then let's do it.'

For the next two hours we snaked our way round mountain passes, through small towns and villages and on, eastwards all the way. For huge swathes of the drive we were the only car in sight and I was enjoying the way the bounce of our headlights revealed the next bend in the road just in time.

But this day of minor errors and tiny woes hadn't stopped messing with us yet. It had another fretful, fearful moment for us yet. And it was to do with a zero. The threat of zero fuel.

We hadn't seen an unchained gas station since leaving Cortez. Since we'd filled up there the second time we'd driven nearly 250 miles and bitter experience had taught me we weren't capable of getting much more than 260 out of her. Of course we'd seen plenty of chain gas stations and ignored them all. Perhaps we should have given in and taken one of them? We had less than 15 miles in the tank. Running out in the middle of the afternoon with a big bright sun burning in the vast Idaho sky was one thing. Running out at night in the freezing cold mountains of Colorado was quite another.

There was no point in turning round. The last gas station we'd seen was at least 30 miles away now. There was only one choice. Forwards. A sign pointed towards a town called La Veta. If it didn't lead us to gas we figured it would at least get us nearer to people.

Luckily, we made it into La Veta – and before the needle had firmly rooted itself at zero. We paused at a junction. Straight ahead there was an Amoco station on one side of the road and a Phillips 66 on the other. The Man™ or The Man™. Such a difficult choice. We started crawling towards them.

'Hang on,' I said. 'What does that sign say up ahead?'

Andy peered through the dark, his eyes taking their time to tune in.'

'Sammie's Motel,' he read, 'and RV Park.'

'You never know,' I said. 'They might sell gas. In Lakeview, Oregon we got gas from an RV park... what d'y'reckon?'

'It's got to be worth a try, hasn't it?'

'Of course... and if we run out between here and there, I reckon these gas stations are within pushing distance.'

With hope in our hearts we spurned Messrs Amoco and Phillips and turned in to see what Sammie had to offer.

You know where this is going, don't you? You know how these things work. We're nearly out of gas and then just at the last minute we decide to look at the local RV park? Obviously they're going to sell gas and the day will be saved? Right?

Wrong.

Not this time. Sammie's had no gas station. Sammie's didn't have much. There were plenty of parking spaces for RVs while the 'motel' turned out to be a few neat rows of permanently sited trailer homes.

'Nice try,' said Andy. 'But I guess we've got to bite the bullet. Let's turn around and choose your favourite chain.'

'No.'

I didn't want to give in. Not yet.

'We haven't got much choice, Dave.'

'Yes we have.' I turned the engine off. 'We can stay here.'

'What?'

'Who knows what tomorrow will bring? Why give up and

take the chain gas when we don't absolutely have to? We might as well take a couple of rooms for the night...'

'... in a trailer park?'

'Look... these are our choices. A) We get the chain gas now. B) We stay here for the night and get the chain gas first thing in the morning. C) We stay here for the night, ask around in the morning and discover that we're only two miles from an unchained gas station. If there's still a chance of getting away with it, we've got to take it no matter how slim.'

There was a pause.

'But... wouldn't brick walls be nice?'

'I'm telling you now, I'm not starting the car again tonight. We're not wasting another drop of fuel. If you want to stay somewhere else you're walking. Or prising the car keys out of my cold, dead hand.'

'My God, this thing's heavier than I thought,' said Andy through gritted teeth.

'Just keep pushing, will you,' I said, my left shoulder leaning into the frame and my right hand reaching through the open door to the steering wheel. 'We're nearly there.'

'It's 400 yards... we could drive... 400 *bloody* yards.'

'Yes we could,' I said, 'but we're probably saving a quarter pint of petrol doing this... it might be crucial... now push...'

At nine in the morning I took a stroll into the centre of La Veta to see what I could find. There was nobody about. I wasn't surprised. You have to find a good reason for leaving the house when it's minus five out. Of course, more important than the lack of people was the evident lack of unbranded gas. Damn. An unbranded gas station would have made that night in a trailer park worthwhile.

Plumbing is the one arena in which America definitely leads the world. I've stayed in some cheap hotels in my time, but no matter how cheap, the one thing you can count on Stateside is a strong, steady flow of hot water. Not here. For the first time on our trip I'd washed under a cold drizzle. Ugh. It was almost like being in England.

I suppose it wasn't as bad as the motel in Green River where the bathroom was so unpleasant even the bath itself was trying to escape. Mind you that place was so farcically bad it was almost unreal. They might just as well have put small bottles of scabies on the side instead of shampoo.

There was no jolly, Seven Dwarves style of hi-ho industry when we loaded the car up on that freezing cold La Veta morning. The mood was sombre. Like we were preparing for our own funeral.

'Well, it's about 17 miles to the next town,' I said. 'According to my calculations we did over 260 miles on a full tank yesterday. When we ran out of gas in Idaho we'd done 267.' I sighed heavily. 'As much as it pisses me off when you've only been on this trip for two days, I think we have to admit defeat again.'

'We *could* risk it,' said Andy, making a half-hearted stab at Blitz spirit defiance.

'But,' I told him, 'it's a risk based on the next five miles of country roads.'

Andy looked out of the window. The car hadn't warmed up yet and we were both wearing woolly hats and heavy coats.

'Five miles through mountains,' he said. 'And it's minus five out.'

There was a pause while we both pretended we were weighing up the options. We weren't. We both knew what we were going to do. But the pause helped us show each other how much we didn't want to do it.

'I know I've only been on this for two days,' said Andy, 'but I want to live.'

'Okay.'

I slipped the car into gear and slowly we turned towards the two chain gas stations. In the middle of the road lay the bloody remains of a cat. They say cats have nine lives. That would explain why this one looked like he'd been hit by 10 cars. His guts spilled out into the lane – there were more of them than you'd think his slender frame could contain – and fresh blood was still running through his fur, staining his ginger coat.

Was death always going to show itself when the car was on her last legs? Or was death always there and I was just more attuned to it at times like this?

I looked at the two gas stations on offer. How do you choose between them? They were both dressed up in their respective corporate uniform but the Amoco looked a little rough around the edges. If a gas station could loosen its tie, that's what it was doing. The backseat had been torn out of some minibus and placed beside the front door, pressed into service as some kind of improvised settee. I've no idea if anyone ever sits on its tatty, torn, tartan upholstery but I'd like to imagine they do. (And for some reason I'd like to imagine them whittling while they do it.)

That was enough for me. I pulled unhappily on to their fore-court and with a glum sense of resignation parked up besides the pump.

'We didn't keep the dream alive for long, did we?' I said. 'Two days. I can't believe you flew all the way from London for *this* and we only lasted two days. Sorry.'

'It could be worse,' said Andy. 'Think of the cat.'

As the gas glugged in and our dream of getting to the coast unchained died I tried to tell myself that the cat was having a worse time than us but somehow it didn't help much. I'd wanted this thing to be possible. But it wasn't, was it?

Andy knew this fuel stop was going to have to be docu-mented in the film so while I went in to pay, he stayed outside and took some arty shots of the Amoco sign and the red, white and blue company stripe that lined the canopy roof.

Inside, standing in front of a wood-panelled wall decorated with dozens of faded and yellowed business cards was Joe. He wore oily green overalls, a baseball cap and a quizzical expression.

Why, he wanted to know, was my friend filming something as ordinary as a gas station sign? It's a fair question and it deserved an answer so I adopted my best *we-don't-mean-any-offence* tone of voice and explained to Joe that we weren't the happiest of customers and that we really hadn't wanted to buy gas from Amoco.

'But I own this gas station,' said Joe.

His comfortable jowls softened his face as if he was blurred at the edges. Somehow his words seemed to be blurred at the edges too.

The fact that he owned the gas station didn't lift my mood. So what? I knew a lot of branded gas stations were individually owned but that wasn't good enough for our rules. Owning this station just meant he owned a link in the Amoco chain. I tried to explain this to Joe but he wasn't having any of it.

'The corporation *does not* own this business,' he repeated, puffing his chest out with pride. 'I *was* branded Amoco last year but that was before they pulled out of Colorado.'

Pulled out of Colorado? There *was* a glimmer of hope. I didn't dare to believe I'd heard it right. If Amoco had pulled out of the whole state then surely this wasn't really an Amoco station. Excitement was bubbling up inside me. I glanced out of the window at the Amoco sign. Hmmm. Why was that there? Why was he still branded if they'd pulled out of Colorado?

'But you've got the sign...'

'That isn't mean' a' be there.'

Before I could relax, before I could celebrate, I had to make sure.

'Sorry? The Amoco sign out front isn't meant to be there?'

'Nah huh,' said Joe with an emphatic shake of the head. 'That was meant to be gone three months ago but they still haven't come to take it down.'

Amazing! We were saved. I called Andy in and asked Joe to confirm for me on camera that the gas station was not just *owned* by him but, more importantly, that it was no longer an Amoco. He did just that, beaming a big broad smile as he showed me the company name on my receipt. We hadn't bought gas from Amoco, we'd bought it from La Veta Oil.

What a result! My mind raced as I tried to quantify our good fortune. What a way to snatch victory from the jaws of defeat! We'd done more than just teeter on the brink this time, we'd fallen head first into the abyss. But just when I was convinced we were about to land a superhero had swept down and scooped us up in his arms. And that superhero was Joe.

How many tiny events had conspired to bring us to this place? The various wrong turns and miniature crises of yesterday had somehow left us with just enough gas to get here but not enough to have confidently spurned La Veta. What luck! Thank God for the minibus seat cum sofa outside. Without it we might well have supped from The Man™'s Phillips-shaped teat.

As we floated on excitement to our car I swear a ginger cat danced beneath our feet and then disappeared round the back of the building. Andy and I both clocked it and immediately looked at each other in silent did-you-see-that amazement. The roadkill really was the perfect metaphor. So much so that this one had been reanimated to reflect our own back-from-the-dead salvation?

Either that or it was just another cat with the same colouring. But let's not spoil it, eh?

If you look at the map I think you can see why Andy was happy to make Independence, Missouri our new target. The idea was always to drive from coast to coast and Plan A had always been to drive from Los Angeles to New York. Draw a straight line between LA and NYC and you'll see for yourself that by getting to this third Independence we'd be putting ourselves right back on track.

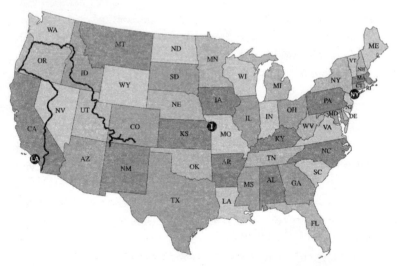

All we had to do was complete our trip across Colorado, whip through Kansas and, well, that was pretty much it. From there it was just Missouri, Illinois, Indiana, Ohio, Pennsylvania and New York left and, compared to the states we'd already crossed, they were tiny!

The border with Kansas was roughly 150 miles due east from La Veta so we planned to be out of Colorado in about three hours. Then we'd have a spot of lunch and then it was just a question of seeing how much further we could get in whatever daylight we had left. Surely we could eat up a fair chunk of Kansas on the same day.

As it was we were out of Colorado in under two hours. Sadly, it wasn't because we were speed freaks... it's because we were idiots. So excited were we by our La Veta reprieve that we'd paid very little attention to the signs and for the second day running we'd managed to accidentally head south and find New Mexico.

'Not again!' I wailed when I saw the sign. 'Welcome to New Mexico, Land of Enchantment. Land of en-pants-ment, more like.'

'Did you just say "en-pants-ment"?' Andy sniggered. 'As in *pants*?'

I had as well. How embarrassing.

'Um yeah. Don't tell anyone though, will you?'

'It's on camera.'

'I'll give you $10 to wipe the tape.'

'Make it 20.'

'Ten and I'll buy you lunch.'

'Deal.'

'Right,' I laughed, 'now that's sorted, can we actually sort out the important things as well? Like, what are we going to do and why do we keep coming to sodding New bloody Mexico? We don't want to come to New Mexico! We're meant to be going to Kansas! Have you secretly fitted the car with some kind of New Mexico homing device?'

'Are you ranting? Is this the land of en-rant-ment?'

'Oh sod off,' I said, more amused than abused. 'And get the map out? We need to work out what to do... do you think we should head back?'

Andy put the camera down at his feet and picked up the map. He wrestled with it for a while, having to wrestle it into submission, which seemed odd because I'm sure if he'd simply said the words, *'Go go gadget map'* it would have magically presented itself to him just as readily as if it was a pair of pliers or a torch. Maybe he was trying to keep his identity secret.

'Okay,' he said, 'was that Raton?'

'Yep.'

'In which case I say we keep going. Amazingly, we are now going east. We should reach Texas in about a hundred miles.'

'Texas! Bad things happen in Texas. The last time I went to Texas I got a tattoo I didn't want. Do we have to go to Texas? We don't want to go to Texas, do we?'

'Not if you're going to turn it into the Moan Star State, we don't.'

Andy rewarded himself with a smirk.

'Oh, it's like that, is it? Are you gonna keep this up for the whole trip?'

'I might do,' he replied. 'Does Kansas have a nickname?'

'The Sunflower State.'

'The Bum-flower State, more like!'

'Very good,' I said. 'Well done. I can tell this is going to be a fun day.'

'You know what,' said Andy, his head still buried in the map, 'I think it will be. I've got a plan for today... all you've got to do is trust my directions and put your foot down. If we can cover the miles this'll work out fine.'

'You're assuming we'll be able to get gas then, obviously...'

'Why are you worried about gas? After this morning? I think it's pretty obvious we're being looked after. Have faith, believe... and the gas will be there.'

About half an hour later I think Andy must have been doing some believing because I suddenly saw a gas station by the side of the road and I'm sure it wasn't there a moment before. It would have been easy to miss this one. The small, white, corrugated building was so anonymous it went beyond being unbranded... it was almost not there at all. The only sign was about three feet tall and divided into three panels. In relatively large letters the top panel said simply, STOP. The words, EATS GAS and DIESEL occupied the second panel and ICE COLD

DRINKS the third, but they'd been painted using the kind of lettering stencil that I used to carry in my school pencil case and were so small that no passing motorist had a chance in hell of reading them. They were only legible once you'd already stopped. Which I suppose explains the first panel.

There were four pumps lined up in a row but at least one and probably two of them were out of commission. The pump bodies were marked where stickers had been peeled off, leaving behind shadowy outlines. From the outlines of these sticker-ghosts I could see it had once been a Chevron station. Not any more.

It only took about six and a half gallons to top us off which felt good; gas hadn't been so readily found since we'd left Nevada behind a lifetime ago.

Cheerfully, I skipped towards the store to go and pay, pausing to read a handwritten notice on the front door: 'This station will be closed Thursday 11/23/06 – Thanksgiving Day. Sorry for any inconvenience.'

It took me a second to work it out. What day was today? It's so hard to keep track when you've got no schedule to stick to. It didn't matter to us what day of the week it was because our goal was the same: drive east. Well it mattered now because Thanksgiving was sure to throw a spanner in our works. It was tomorrow. Arse.

I really hadn't realised it was just around the corner. I wasn't watching TV or reading newspapers so nothing was connecting me to the pulse of the nation and, not being American, it just isn't on my internal calendar. When November starts my juices warn me about the impending arrival of Christmas and that's all.

I looked at the empty road running past the gas station. I could hear a light breeze and somewhere a bird cawed. The view didn't seem to tally with the date. Was it *really* the day before Thanksgiving? Movies have always given me the impression that the day before Thanksgiving is the most chaotic day imaginable. Isn't this the day when everyone tries to cross the country to spend Turkey Day with their loved ones? Aren't the flights supposed to be full and the roads jammed? There was no sign of that here.

As it happens, I really like the idea of Thanksgiving. I suppose it's really Harvest Festival's more successful American cousin, it's just that in Britain the only people who seem to know when Harvest Festival actually is are clergymen and primary schoolteachers and the only people who actually celebrate it are primary schoolchildren... that's if you call donating one of your mum's tins of marrowfat peas 'celebrating'. By contrast, Thanksgiving is celebrated by practically everyone.

That's because it's the most equal opportunities holiday on the American calendar; it's actually *relevant* to everyone. A country's traditions are normally only truly meaningful to those that are raised within them but, as Thanksgiving is a way of giving thanks for the bountiful land in which you live, I reckon it's just as relevant to the most newly arrived immigrant... indeed, quite possibly more so.

That said, I understand why any Native American might take offence at it. They definitely got the worst side of the arrangement. They yielded land and gave food and got genocide and smallpox in return. Hardly a fair trade. But aside from acknowledging that truth – which in itself is nothing more than a glib gesture – I don't really see what the average American is meant to do about that.

Of course none of this was running through my mind outside that New Mexico gas station. I was concerned with more selfish thoughts about how this particular Thanksgiving was going to affect us.

There was no way we'd be able to buy fuel on the day itself. Mom & Pop would be serving turkey to their children, not gas to strangers. Would restaurants or diners be open? I doubted it. We'd only just gathered momentum and now it seemed that 300 million people being thankful were going to force us to put the brakes on. They're so selfish, those 300 million people.

'Wherever we get to tonight,' I said, 'I think we should stay there tomorrow. If we can't buy gas, we can't really get very far, can we?'

'I guess not,' said Andy.

'In which case, let's make sure that wherever we get has at least got a microwave... and let's get some food.'

I opened the door, stepped inside, said hi to the bored girl behind the counter and started browsing the strangely sparse shelves.

The selection wasn't great. I think even Old Mother Hubbard would have been disappointed with the range. With many products, they appeared to have only one item in stock. But as if to emphasise how little was there each solitary item was spread out so that the full length of the shelf was employed. So one lonely tin of chicken soup would sit on a shelf occupying a space large enough for a slab of two dozen tins and then a foot or two further along would be another tin all on its ownsome, only this one would be oxtail. If I picked something up I felt guilty for disturbing the delicate balance of the display and making things look even bleaker than they already did.

Finding something meat-free was a challenge. In the end I settled on a small box of instant macaroni cheese. I'm not sure if it had a sell-by date to check but then I'm not sure if it needed one. Was it actually classed as food? Andy was not impressed.

'If I end up eating macaroni cheese,' he teased, 'I'm leaving and you can find yourself a new director.'

'If you don't like my choice you can always have a look yourself and buy something else,' I said. 'It's not like I *want* to eat it either. It's just an insurance policy, that's all. If there's nowhere open tomorrow you'll thank me for this.'

'There'll be something,' said Andy. 'We'll be all right. We'll find somewhere. Now come on, let's get back on the road, we've got some distance to cover yet.'

An hour later and we were nearing the border with Texas but lunch was calling so we stopped for a quick lunch in the sleepy railroad town of Clayton first. We ate at the Rabbit Ears Café, which I'm pleased to say was named for two nearby mountains and not a speciality of the house.

Back in the day, the town of Clayton was an important staging post on the Santa Fe Railroad and the Santa Fe Trail before it. Wagon trains first charted and used the Santa Fe Trail in the early 1820s, making it a vital international trade route between the United States and Mexico. During the Mexican–American War it inevitably became an invasion route and when the US had acquired the South West it naturally became one of the arteries by which the new land was populated.

The trail started in Missouri and one of the jumping off points was, you've guessed it, the city of Independence. Having never heard of the place before Billie Kay had mentioned it, I was surprised to find it cropping up again. Independence, Missouri was turning out to be a far more important town than I'd imagined; a starting point for the Oregon Trail, the Santa Fe Trail and the California Trail too. It was a tap – or perhaps a faucet – through which the population of America had poured west.

It made me even keener to visit the place. We didn't realise it at the time but when we crossed Wolf Creek Pass[9] we also crossed over the Continental Divide. Every river on one side of the line eventually makes its way to the Pacific Ocean while every river on the other side noodles a path to the Atlantic. Independence, Missouri seemed to represent a different kind of continental divide. One not for water, but for people. By reaching Independence, Missouri I thought we could really claim to have completed the American West.

Our deep-fried lunch took us an hour from our journey and probably three from our lives. As we entered Texas – at the imaginatively named border town of Texline – we lost another hour from the day simply by passing into a new time zone. Bye bye Mountain Time, hello Central. Progress. I put my foot down a little harder.

[9] *mwah ha ha ha ha ha.*

Every state in America has its quirks. There are little customs or strange laws that remain on the statute books as archaic oddities. Texas is no exception. For example, did you know that when driving south-east on Highway 87 towards Amarillo, all drivers *and* passengers must sing at least three choruses of Tony Christie's 'Is This the Way to Amarillo'? No? Andy didn't know either. I soon put him right. He's lucky I was there.

If, as the song predicted, Marie was waiting for us there she was going to be disappointed because on Andy's instructions we took a left turn at the town of Dalhart and started heading north-east on Highway 54 instead.

Here's another one of those quirktastic Texan bylaws: Did you know that when driving north-east on Highway 54, away from Amarillo, all drivers *and* passengers must sing at least three choruses of a made-up song called, 'Was That the Way to Amarillo'? No? Andy didn't believe me either. It's a good job we didn't get pulled over by the police or he'd have been in trouble. Still, I did my best to make up for it by doing extra duty and doing six choruses. Was he grateful? No.

'Was that the way to Amarillo? Stef is sleeping with an orthopaedic pillow, you see her back was too fragillo, so Andy flew to be with me.'

'No, Dave. Please stop.'

'Sha la la lala lalala hey! Sha la la lala lalala ha! Sha la la lala lalala oof! So Andy flew to be with me. Come on now, it's for your own good...'

'No.'

'Ah h-everybody... two, three, four... was that the way to...'

'No. N. O.'

Within an hour the countryside blended into town and we cruised through Stratford. It was a grittier and more urban town than anywhere we'd seen in a long while, yet the place was dominated by the largest grain elevators I'd seen yet; huge steel cylinders that glowed majestically with the setting sun. They looked like they'd been left standing in line at the rocket ship auditions and nobody had bothered to tell them that the Apollo missions had been abandoned and the part was no longer available. This was where agriculture and industry met. This was the kind of place that meant the rest of America got fed.

It was also the kind of place to have an unbranded gas station. I won't pretend there was anything especially charming about the building or its location but the man in charge, Po, had a singsong Southern accent that sounded like he was constantly on the verge of hiccups and a permanent shrug in his demeanour that meant he was precisely the kind of chap I'd like to imagine whittling outside Joe's La-Veta-No-Amoco.

The day was nearly done and Po was in the process of locking up when we rolled on to the uneven forecourt and I think it was only a combination of our exotic English accents and old Californian station wagon that persuaded him to serve us.

'Well ah was gittin' ready to go,' he drawled, three parts Uncle Jesse to one part Boss Hogg. 'You got cash?'

He asked us why we were filming so I explained our journey to him. He didn't bat an eyelid. In fact he just shrugged as if to say, *yeah… sounds easy enough.* I guess from his perspective chain-free gas stations probably don't seem that hard to find. He sees one every day after all.

We stepped inside the small office to pay. I handed Po a 20 and while waiting for the change, I made polite conversation by asking what he had planned for Thanksgiving.

'I'm gonna eat.' He paused, as if considering whether or not that was a full enough answer. He obviously decided it wasn't. 'Watch a little footba'. Drink a little beer.'

As he completed his holy trinity of Thanksgiving activities a smile crept across his face as if I'd asked him a quiz question and he was confident he'd got it right.

Po wasn't the only person with that plan in mind. All of America was planning the same. It only served to underscore how impossible a day it was going to be for us. Which meant we knew we had to squeeze everything we could out of what was left of today.

'This has been the best day so far for gas,' I said as I clambered back into the driving seat. 'La Veta, Colorado, Capulin, New Mexico and now Stratford, Texas.' I buckled up. 'Three different gas stations in three different states. That's amazing.'

'Well, that's the plan,' said Andy. 'Let's see if we can visit even more states.'

'What?' I'd just followed Andy's directions and had no idea whereabouts we were. 'Really? Are we close to getting out of Texas?'

'Not just that.' Andy smiled. 'I reckon we can get out of Texas and straight across Oklahoma.'

'What?'

'Take a look...'

Andy showed me the map.

As you can see, the far western edge of Oklahoma is a narrow strip of land about 170 miles long and only 40 miles deep. It's known as the Oklahoma Panhandle and I can't imagine anyone needs me to explain why.

Mind you, I did once manage to persuade a New York drunk that it had nothing to do with its shape and was in fact named after the man who'd brokered the land deal on behalf of the state, a made-up Mr Joshua Panhandle. It wasn't hard. I managed to persuade the same man that the state of Kentucky was named after the chain of fried chicken restaurants. It's a good game to play if you have the time.

Incidentally, Oklahoma isn't the only state to have a panhandle, it's a generic term used to describe any state's sticky-out bit. Florida, Nebraska, Alaska and Idaho all have panhandles. Even the little stubby bit of Texas we'd just driven across is called the panhandle and West Virginia has two of the damn things. But if you ask me only Oklahoma's is satisfyingly panhandlesque. I think someone must have come up with it one day to describe this part of Oklahoma and when it went down a storm everyone else started jumping on the panhandle bandwagon in an attempt to look as cool and inventive as the first guy.

The little bump on the western edge of Nebraska isn't a panhandle. I can't see any reason for it to need a special name but if it does it's quite clearly the lens on Nebraska's video camera. Idaho's panhandle is really the chimney on its factory and while I apologise for lowering the tone I doubt there's a man alive who looks at Florida's so-called Panhandle and thinks it resembles anything more than a shrivelled scrotum. (And it's in the sea so it *would* be shrivelled.)

Anyway, I appear to have digressed slightly and what I was trying to explain is that when Andy showed me the map we weren't far from the border with the Oklahoma Panhandle. It can't have been more than 20 minutes after leaving Stratford that we found ourselves entering Oklahoma.

Incidentally, if you thought the town of Texline was going to win the award for Best Quirky Town Name on the Texas Border, think again. Bordering Texas and Oklahoma, ladies and gentlemen, I give you Texhoma. How do they think of these things?

It took us just over an hour to get across the panhandle and into Kansas where, after a long, exhausting yet satisfying day's drive, we were content to stop at the first unchained motel in the first town we came to: Liberal, Kansas. Liberal? It's not a word you associate with Kansas these days. The motel was basic but clean and the guy who checked us in, a late-twenties Costa Rican Harry-Potter-alike by the name of Al, was as warm, welcoming and smiley as anyone we'd encountered thus far.

'And the rooms have microwaves, yeah?' I asked.

'Oh yeah, they've all got microwaves... but one of your rooms also has a full-size fridge and a stove... it's a one-bedroom apartment.'

'Oh great. Because I think we're going to be spending Thanksgiving in there...'

'Is that right? Well you know my family are going to be here tomorrow evening and you're more than welcome to stop by.'

'Really?'

'Oh yeah. We'd be delighted.'

'Well, that's really nice of you,' I tried but failed to make my smile as broad and full as his. 'You don't get that at a Holiday Inn.'

'No,' Al chuckled. 'And I hope you drink!' he said 'Because we drink!'

What a find! It was the perfect place to end the perfect day!

The only thing to take the shine off things was the smell. I don't mean the motel. I mean the whole city. The largest employer in Liberal is National Beef Packing. According to Al, they kill roughly 40,000 head of cattle a day. (I don't mean they kill them roughly, just that I doubt it happens in such neat, round numbers.) The plant was only a couple of miles away... but then Liberal is a small city and pretty much everywhere was less than a couple of miles away. I doubt there's a way of killing 40,000 cows a day without making a smell. You can't kill that many cows a day unless there are hundreds of thousands of the big dopey beasts hanging around nearby waiting for their turn on the choppy-knife machines and that's got to smell even before you've killed one of them.

The stench is difficult to describe. Unless you've smelled 40,000 dead cows there's not really anything I can compare it to. I can tell you that it doesn't smell like a farm; this isn't the fragrant smell of cow manure I'm talking about although obviously that must be playing its part. Nor does it smell like a really big butchers; it's not an odour that would make anyone think, *Ahhh, Bisto!* It smells of burnt fat and hair, mixed in with the most intense slurry imaginable and just to ensure that when the wind changes your eyes water, there's a delicate top note of ammonia.

And you can believe me when I tell you this isn't just some non-meat eater bleating about the poor little animals. I promise you that Andy, the committed carnivore that he is, was every bit as affected by it as I was and we were both gripping our noses and covering our mouths as we said goodnight at the end of the day.

There were so many ways of measuring a day like this. Five states; three gas stations; 330 miles. But I think there was a more abstract measure that somehow accurately summed up the extent of the journey. We'd travelled from one dead cat to 40,000 dead cows. How strange that a day of such triumph should have such macabre bookends.

Chapter 24
Magic macaroni

On Thanksgiving morning we didn't really know what to do with ourselves. We tried to watch some of the Macy's Thanksgiving Parade on TV but for some reason neither of us could get excited by watching giant inflatables hoiked down a street in New York. Across the country millions upon millions of Americans were watching this parade but it's difficult to imagine they were actually enjoying it. Surely it's one of those things people watch simply because they've always watched it? I'm similarly perplexed by the British obsession with the Queen's Christmas Speech. She's never going to throw any gags in, is she? No, when it became obvious that none of the big balloons were going to pop we gave up, jumped in the car and went for a quick tour of Liberal instead.

In normal circumstances we'd have conserved fuel and gone on foot but in all seriousness the smell of Liberal made that idea untenable. With two sweaty men sitting in the car for long stretches at a time it's true that the car's own bouquet left something to be desired, but at least it smelled of us and at least we were alive.

We were both hungry and Andy – surely thinking with his belly and not his head – was still confidently predicting that we'd be able to find a diner that was serving. The first signs weren't good. What chance is there of a Mom & Pop place being open when the local MacDonald's is closed for the day?

Not only was nothing open on Thanksgiving, depressingly it

looked as though quite a lot of Liberal was closed for good. The Great Western Drive-In Movie Theater was now just an overgrown bit of scrubland and too many shops had boarded up windows and empty spaces where their names used to be.

Despite the down-on-its-luck, ghost-town feel there *was* an admirable sense of civic pride to the place. We cruised down litter-free streets. The houses were all different – we'd see a humble bungalow standing next door to some huge, two-storey place with galleried balconies and a double garage – but they were all presented in the same neat and tidy, modestly buttoned down fashion. The message was: 'They can make our town smell of death and they can kill our downtown shopping... but damn it, we're still going to mow our lawns.'

One street we simply had to take was Yellow Brick Road. To be clear, it wasn't actually made of brick (although there were a couple of old Kansan brick roads still surviving elsewhere in Liberal) and it wasn't actually yellow... it was just a street that was named Yellow Brick Road. Even so, it obviously had to be follow-follow-follow-follow-followed. It led, perhaps inevitably, to some *Wizard of Oz*-themed tourist attractions: The World of Oz and Dorothy's House.

The World of Oz was contained inside the kind of large utility building you'd expect to find on a Swindon industrial estate but inside it promised 5,000 square feet of Oz-related entertainment. Dorothy's House however was, well, a house. It wasn't *the* house that was used in the film. I thought maybe they would lay claim to being some specific house that had helped inspire L. Frank Baum's creation... but no, it was just a house. It was a pretty little wooden cottage with a white picket fence and a small lawn where two-dimensional wooden cut-outs of Dorothy, the Tin Man, the Scarecrow and the Lion played.

Of course the attractions, such as they were, were closed for Thanksgiving so we didn't have the opportunity to spend a few bucks and have a local girl dressed as Dorothy give us the tour. Of course the circumstances in which we'd do that didn't exist. If it hadn't been Thanksgiving we wouldn't even have known that Dorothy's House existed because we'd have been on the road out of fetid Liberal at first light.

We did see a few businesses trading that day but of course they were out of bounds to us. About half of Liberal's chain gas stations seemed to have opened for the day and then there was the überchain itself: Walmart. Their parking lot was ticking over with a steady stream of cars coming and going. The presence of this behemoth on the edge of town can't have made it any easier for those small businesses that were still making a go of it downtown.

I'm glad we saw it though. It made for an interesting test of Andy's resolve. Technically, I was the one trying to get from coast to coast without the chains and he was there to make a film about it. If he'd really wanted to pop in and buy himself some food he was welcome to do so. But he didn't want to. We were brothers in arms. So we went back to the motel and lunched on our single portion of magic macaroni cheese.

I say 'magic' because it pulled off the remarkable trick of smelling terrible while tasting of nothing. I don't understand how that's possible. But as a measure of how bad it smelled, let me tell you we chose to eat outside so as not to contaminate the motel room.

'You know when Al invited us to spend some of Thanksgiving with his family?' I asked. 'Do you think he really meant it?'

'Yeah.'

'But do you think it's his *actual* family Thanksgiving?'

'What? Do you think he's got a pretend family that he spends it with?'

'No... but I mean... do you think it's like a small drinks reception for guests or something? Would you really ask two strangers to come and join your family for their Thanksgiving dinner? Your mum would kill you if you invited some strangers round for lunch on Christmas.'

'I see what you mean.' Andy mused for a while. 'Yeah. Probably some cocktail sausages, some lumps of cheese and pineapple and a glass of cheap warm wine with the other saddoes who've got nowhere to go... then they close the door and have a proper do. Why? Don't you want to go?'

'No. I think we should show our faces. I just kind of romanticised it a bit last night. But in the cold light of day that doesn't make any sense. It's still a nice thing to do. If we were Americans, being away from our families and stuck in this place would be terrible. We'd be bloody glad of a warm glass of wine in those circumstances.'

As the day wore on and the macaroni cheese wore off we started to think we'd be bloody glad of a warm glass of wine in our circumstances too. Andy looked like a man who might kill for a cocktail sausage and in my mind cheese and pineapple had never seemed more appealing. Oh, this hungry soldier couldn't wait for the twin cubes of yellow delight. Al came and knocked on our doors at around 7 p.m. and suggested we came over in about 30 minutes. We were there in 29.

Our plan was to be polite, chat to the other guests, mingle a little but mainly, to grab as much of the buffet as we could without appearing rude. And if that wasn't sufficient then Plan B involved appearing rude.

The do was happening in one of the motel complex's outbuildings, which, with its semicircular domed roof, looked more like a small aircraft hangar than anything else. Inside, the breezeblock walls had been painted white but remained otherwise undecorated. The tables and chairs arranged around the edge of the room looked like they belonged in a school classroom. The cups were polystyrene, the plates and cutlery were plastic and the whole thing was occurring beneath the unflattering glare of fluorescent strip lighting.

We stepped inside full of social trepidation and convinced that we were spare parts... but within a minute or two we'd had to find a whole new plan of action. Plan C: spend the evening there and have a bloody good night.

All the cynical assumptions we'd made that afternoon were unfounded. It wasn't an event being laid on for the benefit of the motel's guests. It really was Al's family Thanksgiving. Al was Costa Rican and his wife was Mexican and it was her side of the family that filled the room. We were introduced to brothers, sisters, aunts, uncles, nephews, nieces and Al's own children; a three-year-old boy and a one-year-old girl, whose presence inevitably tugged at Andy's heart strings and made him miss Anna all the more.

They'd cooked two enormous turkeys (which Andy tells me were done to perfection), the veg was piled high and the pecan pie was stunning. Far from scheming to squeeze as much sustenance as we could from a meagre buffet, the difficulty came in persuading people that we didn't want more. As soon as my plate was empty more food arrived from nowhere with everyone insisting I have a second, or third, helping... and it would have been rude not to have accepted. Honest.

Al had warned us that they liked to drink. He wasn't kidding. Bottles of Corona were being uncapped faster than we could handle them and it wasn't long before both Andy and I were cheerfully sozzled and doing the things we do when we get drunk. In Andy's case that meant getting maudlin and showing portly, moustachioed Mexican men photos of his daughter. In my case it meant getting into a game called *Let's All Show Our Tattoos*, only to then realise that I was the only person there with a tattoo to show.

Of course what set the evening apart and made it special wasn't the food and drink that they gave so freely... it was their sense of warmth and the generosity of spirit. Family dynamics are always fascinating and unique. Families build their own frameworks. The members of a family create their own shared history and the glossary of shorthand and network of in-jokes they develop forms a kind of protective shield around them. For anyone to invite a couple of strangers into that inner sanctum is truly magical. I know I run the risk of getting schmaltzy here but it's impossible for me to let this evening pass without pausing to share this one blindingly obvious fact with you: nothing could be more in the spirit of Thanksgiving than taking in and feeding strangers. Thanksgiving. Thanks Al.

Looking back it was a strangely bipolar day; a day full of boredom that was then rescued by the kindness of strangers. We didn't know it at the time, but the same was going to be true throughout our time in Kansas.

Chapter 25
Fix or repair daily

Kansas is far and away the most boring landscape I've ever driven through. The place is flat and the roads are ramrod straight. The crops had not long been harvested so every field looked the same. Wherever you looked a dusty yellow crew cut disappeared to the horizon and beyond.

To begin with, the scale of what you're taking in lends it an undeniable magnificence but then you drive and you drive and you drive and three hours later nothing has changed and for all your eyes can tell you, you don't appear to have gone anywhere.

It's the difference between going for a run... and going on a running machine. They both involve the same effort but only one of them actually takes you anywhere. In fact, maybe that's it. Maybe Kansas doesn't exist at all. Maybe that big field is just some clever CGI effect and everyone just takes turns driving on a mile-long stretch of treadmill. It makes as much sense as anything else.

Our journey across the state would take us from Liberal to Kansas City. After losing a day to Thanksgiving we were keen to notch up another state as soon as possible and at around 430 miles it should have been dispatched in a couple of days. As it was it took us three days but if it hadn't been for three acts of wonderful Kansan kindness we might not have made it at all.

★

We met Bill at a rest area set back from the highway. Seduced by the never-ending sameness of the scenery, we'd somehow managed to miss a turn and so we'd pulled off the road and on to this small loop of shingle track in order to consult maps and work out where we were going.

Bill was employed to look after the rest area. He kept the bathrooms clean and tidy and made sure things ticked over. When I saw him approaching our car my first thought was that we were about to get told off or moved on. For reasons best known to himself, Andy had decided to film me as I walked to and from the toilets. The camera hadn't followed me inside but even so I could easily see how that kind of behaviour might arouse the suspicion of a nosey jobsworth, which is what I assumed Bill to be.

For the second time my cynical assumption about a Kansan's motives were unfounded.

'That's a lovely ve-hicle you have there,' he said by way of a greeting. 'You guys sure do know how to ride in style. Hi there, m'name's Bill.'

'Thank you,' I said, shaking his hand through the open window. 'I'm Dave. This is Andy. I think she's pretty special. The car, I mean. Not Andy.'

Bill looked like he was in his early sixties. He was wearing a blue denim shirt and jeans and a dark baseball cap. He had a neatly trimmed white goatee that framed a roguish grin. When I was a kid, I don't think many people of that age wore jeans and I'm pretty sure those that did just looked ridiculous. Baseball caps even more so. But Bill carried it off with ease. Maybe he just had the requisite swagger because of some inherent Americanness, or maybe it's simply that times have changed. But then again, perhaps now that I'm 35 and more than halfway there myself I've started seeing such things with kinder eyes.

'You sound like y're from overseas somewhere... would you be British?'

'Yes. Yes we would.'

'I *love* England. We went to Europe last year. I tell ya, I hated every minute o' Paris. Then we went on that there jet train into

Lon'on and that was great. We ordered a pepperoni pizza in Paris and d'you know, in France, pepperoni ain't meat? It's peppers. Well we refuse' t'eat it. First thing we did in Lon'on was order pepperoni pizza.'

'And how was it?' asked Andy.

'Tch,' Bill chuckled to himself at the memory. 'It was jus' fab'lous. Now,' he glanced down at the map spread out on Andy's lap, 'you two gen'lemen appear t'be lost. Can I help y'at all?'

We tried to explain where we thought we'd gone wrong. We had been following signs to Dodge City but they'd disappeared and we couldn't work out where we were and which turn, if any, we'd missed.

'Well, this'll take ya t' Dodge,' said Bill, 'but it's the long way. I can happily show you folks a li'l short cut if ya like. It'll save you about 12 miles.'

'That would be fantastic!'

I leaned back to give Bill a clearer view of the map but he clearly wasn't interested in showing us in two dimensions, he wanted to show us in the real world.

'Th'easiest thing would be if you jus' follo' me.'

'Really? Are you sure?'

'Jus' wait there a minute 'n when I drive past, you jus' stay on my tail.'

Bill doddered off to his 4x4 and a couple of minutes later we were in convoy. His Dodge 4x4 wasn't as beautiful as our lovely Torino but it was a hell of a lot faster. I had my foot on the floor but his big truck was looking like a tiny speck on the distant horizon. Incidentally, it didn't escape our attention that we were in a Ford following a Dodge, to Dodge, which just happens to be the administrative centre of Ford County, Kansas... it's the sort of thing you notice when the scenery is so very, very dull.

Bill had steered us on to an unmarked road. It had no name, no number and it didn't appear on any of our maps. There were no signs telling us where we were or where we were heading to. Depending on your point of view it was either a brilliant short

cut that only a local would know… or the ideal place to commit
the perfect murder.

Eventually, Bill's Dodge started getting larger and we
realised he'd decided to stop and wait for us. As I pulled up
behind him, he slid out of his car and swaggered over to us,
crouching down and leaning on the driver's side window.

'Ya want to take a right here,' he explained. 'And that's
gonna take y'all the way to Dodge.'

'Thank you, sir. That was very nice of you and it's very much
appreciated.'

'It's my pleasure,' he leaned in across me to shake Andy's
hand and then backed out and shook mine. 'I enjoyed visitin'
with ya, and I hope to see ya agin some day.'

'I hope so, too,' said Andy. 'You're a true gent.'

Bill beamed. Then paused. Then said, 'I'm a military
disabled veteran, I'm 80 per cent disabled 'cause I got broke up
in the military.'

'Really?' I asked. I was as surprised by the abrupt change of
subject as I was by the information contained in this decidedly
spry old fella's words. 'You seem to be living life with a smile,
Bill.'

'Well,' he flashed that roguish smile, 'I'll be 70 years old on
my birthday 'n my wife is only 57.'

'Well, you're doing something right,' I said, my words skip-
ping across the top of the chuckle he'd just given me.

'Everybody said I robbed a cradle,' Bill was chuckling too.
'But it's won'erful that I can still go at all y'know, because the
Veteran's Association tried to put me in a wheelchair nine years
ago. But I found remedies to take care o' that.' He paused. 'I
use 'lectric shock every night on my feet.'

This time my chuckle was a much more straightforward
laugh. Honestly, I could have sworn I'd just heard him say that
he used an electric shock on his feet every night!

'I take 110 volts, 20 minutes every night to make my feet
work.'

Oh my God, he had!

'All from a natural doctor that had enough gumption to tell me that he could help.'

'That's incredible!' I said, quite literally incredulous.

'But I enjoy it,' said Bill, who was surely playing some game where every sentence he said had to be more surprising than the last. 'I enjoy every day. If the Lord lets me get up, I enjoy it.'

There was a pause while we all tried to think of something to say... what could follow that self-electrocuting revelation. Eventually, it was Bill that broke the deadlock.

'You guys have a safe trip, now. And we'll be seeing ya once again some day.'

And then, with an affectionate pat of the car he made his way back to his ve-hicle and continued with his infectiously cheerful, miraculously electrozappy, happy life.

DISCLAIMER

The author of this work would like to make it clear that the inclusion of the above dialogue in no way represents a personal endorsement of self-electrocution.

If you decide to try putting 110 volts through your feet (or any other part of your anatomy) the author will not be held responsible for any injury or accidental death suffered.

In the event of a light or humorous injury the publishers reserve their right to use your story for publicity purposes. In the event of serious injury or death the publishers reserve the right to sweep it under the carpet and pretend it never happened.

If you're going to do it, please don't leave a copy of the book lying around where the people who find your body will see it.

Please don't electrocute yourself or anyone else.

What are you? Mental?

On our first day of Kansas driving we got roughly halfway, reaching the town of Hutchinson, where we spent the night in one of our less salubrious motels. It's common for hotels of all kinds to offer a selection of pornographic movies... but it's not common to see that fact advertised in big bold letters on the sign outside. Any port in a storm.[10]

In the morning we made our way to the more gentrified Old Town. I liked the wide avenues and the well-preserved old buildings. The deco charm of the 1930s sat side by side with the solidity of the late 1800s and yet they seemed to get along just fine. There was a lazy Sunday morning feel to the area, which was a shame because it was a Saturday morning and it really should have been busier and buzzier than that. From what little we saw of Hutchinson I'd say its defining trait was faded glory.

We'd found a couple of comfy chairs in a coffee shop full of dark woods, red-brick walls and attractively mismatched furniture and enjoyed a much needed breakfast. The relaxing surroundings were good for us because we were feeling decidedly troubled.

As we'd arrived in Hutchinson the night before the car had started to make some very unhappy noises. Where once she had purred now she was wheezing and screeching. It sounded like some small rodent was trapped inside and was being tortured by every moving part. I'd gone to bed vainly hoping that the problem would right itself by morning but of course it hadn't. Instead we woke to find the car had left some pretty unpleasant stains underneath the engine, which is odd because there were no movie channels available in the parking lot. It took longer than normal to get her started and when she did, the smoke that billowed out of the exhaust was more bilious and acrid than ever before. She was definitely poorly.

Our desire to fix the car was tempered by our desire to keep moving and both were undone by our own stupendous ignorance. I confidently predicted we needed an oil change but only

---

[10] was the title of one of the movies offered.

because it sounded like the right kind of thing to say and even though Grant had shown me every dipstick under the hood and explained how to read them and how to process the information revealed, I'd forgotten all of it.

Which is where John, our second Kansan hero, came in. John was one of the coffee shop's owners and he'd overheard a snippet of our conversation.

'I don't wanna butt in,' he said with a smile that was almost a hug, 'but I know a little about cars so I might be able to help y'all out. What appears t'be the problem?'

'I think she's low on oil,' I said, with an apologetic yes-I'm-an-idiot grimace. 'She's definitely low on something.'

Sixty seconds later we were standing outside and John, still wearing the scarlet apron of his coffee shop duties, was showing us around our own engine.

The more knowledge John displayed, the more embarrassing our lack of it became. Why do all men of a certain generation know about cars? I suppose there was a time when owning a car was pretty much impossible if you didn't at least have some basic mechanical know-how in your noggin. Back when our Torino was made (which is shortly before I was made) cars were expected to go wrong and so running one was only afford-able if you learned how to fix it.

Mind you, when I hear men of that generation talking about engines it doesn't sound as though it's stuff they were taught. I'm always left with the impression that it's the kind of knowledge that just sprouted inside one's brain with the onset of puberty. Which only makes me feel all the more inadequate.

The thing is, when you lift the bonnet of a modern car you don't really see any moving parts. You see a sealed unit with no way in. These days engines are far less likely to go wrong and when they do all you can do is take it to a local garage where a teenager in overalls can't diagnose the problem either although he can introduce the engine to a laptop that can.

As the engine has evolved into this secretive sealed unit, so our brains have devolved towards greater mechanical idiocy and mush.

'I see it's a Ford,' said John, snickering to himself. 'D'y'know what the F.O.R.D stands for?'

'No.'

'You got, *Fix Or Repair Daily*... or *Found On the Road Dead.*'

I laughed nervously and lifted the hood.

'Hooo-wheee!' John sounded impressed. 'You got a 351 engine and tha's a good motor... now, let's take a look at your dipsticks...'

Andy and I shared a guilty smirk because we both knew where the two biggest dipsticks were. John moved methodically around the engine, taking every measurement and talking us through the findings. He was constantly tactful and never tried to make us feel stupid despite the mounting evidence to that effect. But there was no getting away from the fact that we ended up being chastised by kindness. As John explained how to test the power-steering fluid it felt like we were a pair of dissolute parents whose GP was going through the motions of politely explaining how to bath a baby, all the while aware that as soon as we left the consulting room he was going to call Social Services.

The end result was that we needed every kind of fluid imaginable.

We were barely able to shift our faces into confused gear before John had whipped out his mobile and put a call into a local auto spares store.

'Hey Darren. I'm a-down th' street here an' I've got a coupla visitors from across th' ocean... from the land o' England. They're in need o' some power-steering fluid, some transmission fluid and some good oil... uh huh... uh huh.. yeah... uh huh... you might have to help them put it in, they're not so sure about what they need to do here... okay? Okay. Tha's jus' great.'

Andy and I looked at each other and metaphorically wiped our brows in relief.

'Now,' said John, giving us our final orders, 'Darren's gonna sort y'out an' he's a great guy. I'm gonna give you dire'tions to Darren's and after that, I'm a-gonna give you dire'tions to a couple o' gas stations and that should see you on y'way, all right?'

Of course it was more than all right. It was fantastic. Left to our own devices we could have lost most of the day trying to sort these things out and now it was looking like we'd have it all done in under an hour.

But John had one more tidbit of wisdom for us.

'Now tell me,' he asked, 'why in heaven's name are you headin' to New York?'

'Well... um... I don't know really,' I said. 'We haven't got a reason... it's just where we always said we were going. And, y'know... I like New York.'

'You don't wanna drive to New York at this time 'year. You wanna stay south o' the 70. You really don't wanna be heading north if you don't have to... and by the sound of it, you don't have to. There's a lot of coast south of the 70, y'know...'

Sadly, in spite of John's fantastic directions we weren't able to leave Hutchinson with a full tank of fuel. He'd told us about two beautiful Mom & Pop gas stations but they both turned out to be closed for the Thanksgiving weekend.

'Damn. Maybe we should stay in Hutch?' The words were coming out of my mouth but I wasn't exactly convinced.

'Don't be daft,' said Andy, 'we're not empty, are we? We've got enough in the tank to move on, haven't we?'

'If we do that,' I said, each word only just making it out of my brain in time, 'we're running the risk of running out. If we stay here till Monday we guarantee that's not going to happen. We can fill up first thing Monday morning and that way we'll have enough fuel to get to Independence, whatever happens.'

Andy's face tensed and his lips went white.

'If it was one night,' he said, 'I'd probably agree... but we don't really want to spend a full two days here, do we? Two nights in Liberal, three nights in Hutchinson... come on, Dave, this is Kansas not quicksand... we should push on.'

'Are you sure?'

'Sure I'm sure. We'll find somewhere.'

Only we didn't find anywhere. We drove 90 miles and while Kansas was remarkably well stocked with independent fuel stops it seemed every single one of them was closed for the weekend too.

Throughout the drive I kept a hawkish eye on the dials, watching as our miles crept up and our fuel dropped down. By the time we were down to a couple of gallons I simply refused to push it any further and insisted that we find somewhere to stay for the night.

We came off at the first available exit. There were two places named on the roadsign: Strong City and Cottonwood Falls.

'Which one do you want to try?' asked Andy.

It was an easy choice. I immediately thought of Cottonwood, Idaho and in a split second a memory travelled across three weeks to cheer me up with a vision of Dennis, Frances and their sawdust-speckled smiles. I knew Cottonwood Falls wouldn't have a beagle-shaped B&B... but at least it would remind me of one and that was enough.

It turned out to be a good call and we found two balconied rooms at the Millstream Motel, a beautiful old stone structure that had been hand-built by some old eccentric who'd probably never met an architect and so had individuality in its DNA. These days it's run by Sharon and Richard; two self-exiled Texans who sold up their various businesses and moved to Kansas to slow down and downsize. If you'd told me that before I'd seen the beautiful spot they were in, I'd have thought they were mad. But standing on the balcony and hearing the Cottonwood River flow past it was easy to see the attraction.

Cottonwood Falls was a pretty little town with an almost fetishistic devotion to Christmas. Every building was decked with lights and decorations and the main street managed to look as much like a Dickensian Christmas Card as is possible without snow.

'It is still November, isn't it?' I asked Andy as we crawled past a crowd of carollers.

'The 25th,' he said. 'One month to go.' He paused. 'Anna's second Christmas.'

Oh God. Cottonwood Falls really did look lovely – if it wasn't surrounded by so much Kansas I might even consider going back one day – but suddenly every bit of tinsel seemed to be adding to the pressure. I knew how important it was to get home in time for Christmas and I really didn't need 10 thousand flashing fairy lights telling me on – off – on – off – on – off – over and over and over and over again.

We checked out early on Sunday morning, said goodbye to Sharon and Richard and went on our way... only to return 40 minutes later.

'Hey there,' said Sharon, 'what you forgot?'

'Actually,' I sighed, 'we were thinking of staying another night if we could.'

Sharon looked at me and then at Andy with his face like thunder.

'What's up?'

So I explained that we'd driven up to the local gas station on the corner of Broadway, only to discover that it was closed for the day.

'Shoot,' said Sharon. 'That's too bad.'

'So if you're not fully booked tonight... can we have our rooms again?'

'Now hang on a minute... we can probably get that place opened up for you...'

'Really?'

The storm cloud lifted from Andy's brow.

'Well, I think so. This is a small town. Let me get the phone... I'll speak to Sue at the Emma Chase Café and we'll see what we can do.'

And so the Cottonwood Falls grapevine was set in motion.

Sharon called Sue and Sue said she'd call the gas station owners and told us to come on down for breakfast.

When we turned up at the café we didn't have to introduce ourselves. We weren't from Kansas. We didn't have the rugged outdoorsman look, we weren't wearing cowboy boots and we weren't wearing western shirts.

'You must be Dave and Andy,' said Sue with a smile so reassuring I already knew that everything was going to be all right. 'Now, everything is gonna be all right,' she said unnecessarily, 'I've spoken to the family who own the station and they're sending Chris and Cody over to serve you. They just asked us to give them a call when you leave here... now, what'll you have?'

By this time, Andy's face was a bright, clear, sunny day with a warm evening ahead and the same again tomorrow. He looked like he'd just got the best Christmas present ever. And I suppose he had. Whichever way you slice it, Sharon and Sue had just given him another day with his daughter, the daughter whose christening had been postponed... the daughter whose christening was supposed to be that day.

Breakfast was good. How could it not be when it tasted so happy? We said goodbye and thank you and thank you and goodbye and several more thank yous and then jumped in the car and trundled the 300 yards down the road to the gas station. We were there only moments before Chris and Cody skidded on to the forecourt on their pushbikes and set about opening up.

They looked around 15. With their slicked-back hair and upturned collars, it was like a pair of nascent James Deans had cycled to our rescue.

You could cast one of them as the male lead in one of those '80s movies set in '50s America where a small town's establishment is shocked by the raw sexuality of rock 'n' roll, even though really the kids just want to dance.

Inexplicably, the other lad was carrying a small plastic pet-carrier in which a tiny kitten was mewing so I guess you'd have to cast him as the male lead in a 1980s TV pilot about a young man and his crime-solving kitten. It's a terrible show. If you ask me he should get a better agent.

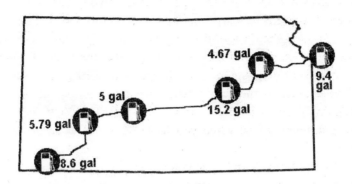

Thanks to the combined efforts of Sharon, Sue, Chris and Cody, we pumped more than 15 gallons at that station which made it far and away our most necessary Kansan fuel stop. We wouldn't have got far that day without it. We wouldn't have had our high-five moment as we finally crossed the state line.

'Toto,' I said in my best Judy Garland voice, 'we're not in Kansas anymore.'

'Goodbye Kansas,' said Andy. 'You were lovely... but I don't want to look at you ever again.'

Chapter 26
I don't know what they believe in but I'll give them 10 out of 10 for their architecture

Some things are destined to be impenetrable. Some things are destined to remain beyond your grasp. You can try all you like. You can ask intelligent questions and receive clear and concise answers but somehow, instead of clearing things up for you, you find your mind is more clouded than before.

For me, Kansas City is one of those things. Actually, it's two of those things. Which is my point. There are two cities called Kansas City. One is in Kansas and the other is in Missouri and they are side by side.

But they're not the same city. Oh, no. They're two separate cities... that just happen to be standing side by side and just happen to have the same name.

I thought maybe Kansas City had existed as one entity before the state lines were drawn up, I thought maybe it had been sliced in two by some letter-of-the-law political procedure, like a more benign version of the two Berlins of old. But apparently not.

Kansas City, Missouri is the original. Located at the confluence of the Missouri and Kansas rivers, it was founded in 1838 as the 'Town of Kansas', taking its name from the river. I suppose they could have named it after the other river but they probably thought the 'Town of Missouri, Missouri' sounded a bit silly. It was incorporated as a city around 1850.

In 1854 the Kansas–Nebraska Act established, as the name would suggest, the territories of Kansas and Nebraska, opening them up to white settlement and a few years later, in 1861, Kansas entered the Union and became a fully fledged state.

Now, 30 years after someone in Missouri thought it would be a good idea to start a town at the confluence of the two rivers someone in Kansas decided to do the same on their side of the border and they gave it the same name. Kansas City, Kansas was founded in 1868 and incorporated as a city only four years later.

How the hell was that allowed to happen? Didn't anyone from Kansas City, MO object? They wouldn't have needed to make a phone call, they could just shout at them from across the street.

'Hi… um… it's about this new city you're founding… um… it's just, the thing is… we're already called Kansas City and it might be confusing so… if you wouldn't mind, do you think you could, y'know, call it something else?'

'Hmmm… I'm not sure about that. I mean, I could mention it to the others… but, well, I know they're all really keen on the name. Steve, especially.'

'Really?'

'Yeah. I don't know if you know this but it's actually the name of one of the rivers…'

'Yeah, we know that. That's what we went with. The river.'

'Really?'

'Yeah… you know when you're standing at the junction of the two rivers?'

Yeah?'

'You know if you look up you can see a load of buildings?'

'Yeah?'

'Well… that's Kansas City. That's us.'

'Really? What a coincidence!'

'No. It's not, is it? It's not a coincidence. Because you do know that we exist. We're right next door! You can't miss us! We've been here for 30 years. We're Kansas City.'

'Yeah, we've been meaning to have a word with you about that.'

'About what?'

'About your name. We think it's a bit, kind of... cheeky.'

'What is?'

'Calling yourself Kansas City when you're not actually in Kansas. I mean... we're Kansans, we live in Kansas... don't you think we should have first dibs on the name.'

'But you didn't even exist when we started. We're named after the river.'

'Really? So are we?'

'Look... I'll tell you what... why don't you name yourself after the other river. It's a bigger river. It's more important.'

'What? You mean call ourselves Missouri?'

'Yeah?'

'Hang on let me think about that. So, we'd end up being called Missouri, Kansas and you'd be Kansas City, Missouri?'

'Yeah.'

'Won't that be confusing?'

'Not as confusing as having two cities called Kansas, no!'

'I've got it! I'll tell you what we can do. If you think Missouri is such a nice name you can change your name to Missouri instead?'

'We can't do that!'

'Why not?'

'Because we've got headed notepaper already. Besides, we did think about that at the time. Everyone thought Missouri, Missouri sounded a bit silly. You can't go around saying Missouri, Missouri... it sounds like you've got a speech impediment.'

'Does it?'

'Or a cold.'

'Really? Missouri, Missouri?'

'Bless you.'

'You've lost me.'

'It's like a cold. Missouri, Missouri.'
'So you are changing your name?'
'What?'
'To Missouri?'
'No!'
'Well, make your mind up.'

The street names don't help either.

Pick a number from 1 to 140. Any number you like. Ask the person on the train next to you if you like[11]. Fifty-five, you say? Right... I'll just refer to my map of the two Kansas Cities... where I can see streets named: North 55th St, South 55th St, East 55th St, West 55th St, North East 55th St, North West 55th St, North 55th Terrace, South 55th Terrace, East 55th Terrace, West 55th Terrace, North East 55th Terrace, North West 55th Terrace, West 55th Place, North 55th Drive and North 55th Court. Welcome to Kansas City: now get lost.

We really were delighted to have left the state of Kansas behind but we were far from thrilled by our first glimpse of very urban Missouri. It was a tale of two cities. It was the best of drives. It was the worst of drives.

To all intents and purposes the city of Independence has become little more than a suburb of Kansas City, Missouri, having been swallowed up by the urban sprawl of that particular metropolis. So while technically we could claim to have driven through Kansas City and then through another Kansas City and eventually into the city of Independence, from behind the wheel of our station wagon it didn't feel like three separate places at all. It was one big car-horn blaring mass of a place.

It sounds trite but it really was a shock to the system. I hadn't been anywhere as recognisably urban as this in over two weeks and without knowing it I'd subtly grown accustomed to the slower pace of life in those small towns.

[11] If you're not reading this on a train you must have the wrong edition. It's a mistake at the printers. Sorry.

'This is horrible,' said Andy, aghast.

'I thought it was going to be like Independence, Oregon,' I said apologetically. 'It's not though. It's like... it's like... everywhere else.'

It was as well. As we cruised up one of the main streets, 23rd I think, we could have been pretty much anywhere in America – a country that isn't built with pedestrians in mind. Only motorists can really get by in towns like this. It's one long straight road taking us from one traffic light to the next with each block home to maybe three or four retail units – shops isn't the word – and all of them the same. The big, bright signs clamoured for attention but really it was just a wash of white noise. Why had we come here again? Because it was called Independence? Was that it? Because Billie Kay had told me that the people who settled Independence, Oregon had travelled from here? Hmm? It might well have been a starting point for thousands of pioneers who headed west but no matter how important a role it has played in American history I really couldn't see us finding any inspiration here. It looked and felt like precisely the kind of town we'd set out to avoid.

'Do you want to just keep going?' I suggested. 'We don't have to stop... we could just keep heading east if you like?'

'Maybe we should give it the once over...'

'Really?'

'Look, no one wants us to keep moving more than I do, but we've been on our way to Independence for a week. I can't spend a whole week trying to get somewhere and then just drive through it, that's just... wrong.'

I smiled to myself at the memory of Stef and I driving straight through Independence, California. At the time we'd deemed our first Independence too small. We thought there was nothing there, that it was too insignificant to warrant our attention. I was regretting that now. My mindset had changed. But back then we'd only been on the road for a couple of days and I don't think we'd yet tuned in to the small-town vibe. With hindsight we hadn't really tuned in to anything at the time, least of all each other. We were still feeling our way through the process and working out where the join was between film and life. And we were still judging things with our city-dwelling eyes. It felt like a lifetime ago.

'Okay,' I said, 'let's find a hotel somewhere. If we stay the night, things might look more charming in the morning.'

There were motels aplenty on that particular strip but all of them cookie-cutter, chain affairs and when we ventured two or three blocks away from the main drag there seemed to be no businesses of any kind. Eventually we drifted into a different part of town with a completely different feel.

Instead of being a busy, bustling, ugly, low-rise chain-fest, this part of town felt like a staid university campus outside of term time. The place had character but appeared to have no life; it felt more like we were driving through a museum exhibit than a community.

The reason for this soon became clear. Independence's most famous son turns out to be the 33rd President of the United States: one Harry S. Truman. He wasn't the most popular of presidents during office but history seems to have judged him kindly... not that he needed history on his side in Independence. He was their boy and they were proud of him. There were monuments and statues and roads named after him and everywhere one looked his austere silhouette seemed to be present. The house where he used to live – a beautiful big old thing with porches and gable roofs sprouting from it in all directions – had been preserved, as had the office where he'd once worked. There was the Truman Depot, the Truman Memorial Building and the Truman Presidential Library and I wouldn't have been at all surprised if the stray dog we saw wandering through Truman Square wasn't actually the Harry S. Truman Memorial Stray Dog. Incidentally, what is it with ex-presidents and libraries? They're obsessed. If a British politician wanted to open a library and have people walk through its doors they'd have to make sure it was well stocked with a lot of Robert Ludlums and the complete works of J.K. Rowling.

Enjoyably at odds with this nineteenth-century aspic environment was a dramatic, modern church or cathedral of some
kind, its narrow, fluted, stainless steel spire piercing the sky like
some giant drill bit. It belonged to a denomination known as
The Community of Christ.

'I don't know what they believe in,' I said, still scouring the
roadside for a hotel of any kind, 'but I'll give them 10 out of 10
for their architecture.'

'I don't know what *they* believe in,' said Andy four or five
minutes later, as we idled at a stop sign, 'but I'm only giving
them two out of 10 for *their* architecture.'

I looked around to see what he was talking about. To our left
was a boxy 1970s building. It was a few stories high and
there was a huge expanse of wall with no window. It looked like
a municipal college or community centre, functional, cheap
and apologetic.

'Yeah... it is a bit drab,' I said, as unexcited by the course of
the conversation as I was by the bricks and mortar I was
looking at.

'I mean, it doesn't exactly scream "hotel", does it?'

'What?'

'Well... it doesn't look very hotelly, does it?'

'It's a hotel?'

'Yeah... look, Olive Branch Hotel.'

'Oh yeah,' I smiled. 'Well spotted!'

It didn't feel very 'hotelly' on the inside either. When the
young man who checked us in gave us directions to our rooms –
'you just take the lifts to the third floor and take a right...' – I
was half expecting him to go on and say, 'and if you could,
please be quiet as you're going past 405 because Mrs Dawson's
Year 9s are sitting an exam this afternoon.'

'This hasn't always been a hotel, has it?' I asked.

'No,' he said. 'It actually used to be an office building... but
don't worry, the rooms are very nice.'

He wasn't wrong. Well, I might quibble with the 'very' but
what they lacked in comfort they made up for in space. You

could have fitted a 20-strong typing pool in my room, no trouble at all.

'Do you want to take 10 minutes to clean up and then go out and grab some food?' asked Andy and in the nanosecond that elapsed between the end of the word 'food' and the start of the question mark that followed it I suddenly became the hungriest man in the world. I hadn't been remotely hungry before he asked the question... but suddenly I was famished. I suppose we had skipped lunch.

'Absolutely,' I said. 'Let's take 10.'

I closed the door behind me, then flopped on to the bed and surveyed the enormous space. Just as I hadn't known I was hungry until food was mentioned so I didn't realise I was tired until I felt a bed beneath my back. I closed my eyes for a few moments' rest and could feel my brain drifting towards sleep. My belly didn't like what my head was doing so it rumbled violently, shaking me awake. Determined not to let myself fall into slumber, I lifted my feet from the bed, span round and planted them firmly on the floor.

Leaning forward, I used the heels of my hands to wipe the sleep from my eyes. Still cradling my head in this fashion I turned to glance at the bedside table where something caught my eye. I don't really know why it grabbed my attention but somehow in this position, with feet splayed, elbows on knees and cheekbones on palms I just seemed to be the perfect height to find my focus locking in on the back of the telephone.

It was the tiniest of details. It was just a small sticker. I could see that it said, 'Property of...' but while I couldn't make out what followed I could see enough to know that it didn't say 'Olive Branch Inn' or anything similar. It wasn't long enough for a start. It was just one word. Maybe an acronym?

Perhaps it was O.B.I.? That would make sense. No... it started with an R. Frustrated with my attempts to crack the code, I leaned closer: 'Property of R.L.D.S.'

That rings a bell. (No phone-pun intended.) R.L.D.S.? R.L.D.S.? R.L.D. bloody S.? R sodding L cocking D bloody S?

Where had I heard that before? What could it stand for? It's normally a Royal-something-or-other... but then I'm normally in Britain. It wouldn't be Royal-anything over here.

But somehow that thought succeeded in making things clearer. Having divorced the R. from the L.D.S., I suddenly saw those three letters in a new light. I saw them for what they were: Latter-day Saints. Mormons! *Cra-zy Mor-mons, Wah! Wah!*

I leapt up and dragged my laptop out of the bag. I don't know why it was important. But it was. My computer wouldn't turn on quickly enough for me but eventually it chimed hello. A few seconds later and I was online and googling R.L.D.S.

A-hah! The *Reorganized Church of Jesus Christ of Latter-day Saints*... who changed their name to the *Community of Christ* in 2001. Ahhh... so that's who worships inside that upturned drill bit down the road, is it?

I clicked and I read and I clicked and I read and I opened new windows and read some more.

Here we go again. So... back in the 1830s when Joseph Smith was telling the world about the book he'd found/made up[12] not everyone was especially happy about what he was up to.

Smith had founded the church in New York but ridicule and persecution led them to up sticks and move on... something he was going to have to do on several occasions during these turbulent times. At some point he identified Independence, Missouri as an ideal gathering point for the church but as always they managed to upset the locals and were forced out.

Eventually, they settled in Illinois where Smith bought some malarial swampland besides the Mississippi, drained it and started building a city that he named Nauvoo. By the mid-1840s the population was in excess of 10,000.

Smith was understandably keen to avoid the persecution they'd experienced elsewhere and somehow he managed to negotiate a city charter that seemed to grant them the freedoms they desired.

[12] delete as appropriate.*
* clue: he made it up.

Nauvoo was run by a mayor and a council and everyone knew that the mayor did whatever Joseph Smith wanted him to do because... well, because Smith was the mayor of Nauvoo. So essentially Smith ended up with his own little fiefdom. He was running his own city and his own religion and even had his own little army too. Every community had its own militia back then, but Nauvoo's was different because it didn't have any allegiance to the state.

I suppose it would be easy to twist these facts and use them to characterise Smith as some kind of power-crazed loon but I think it's important to keep things in perspective. Let's remember, it was just a little place called Nauvoo, it's not like he was running for President of the United States, was he?

Oh. It turns out he was. In 1844, Smith announced that he was running for the presidency of the United States. The man was clearly a power-crazed loon.

Certainly that's what some residents of Nauvoo thought. There were people who felt he simply held too many positions of authority and that he was abusing the inherent privileges. Others were upset with him because he'd married their wives.

So what did they do? Did they march on city hall or sack the temple? No. They set up a newspaper – *The Nauvoo Expositor* – with which they aimed to expose the wrongs of the church leaders. They managed only one issue because a few days later the Nauvoo City Council, aka Joseph Smith and friends, issued an ordinance against the paper and had the press destroyed.

This was the straw that broke the camel's back. You can run your own town and start your own faith, you can even marry a lot of women but when you disrupt the freedom of the press, by golly sir, you are in trouble. Joseph and his brother Hyrum[13] were imprisoned in Carthage, Illinois to await charges.

On June 27, 1844 the two of them met brutal deaths. A mob stormed the jail, and the Smith brothers were shot. Murdered. A mother lost two sons, several sons and daughters lost their

[13] Don't you wish he'd had another brother called Fyrum?

fathers... and several wives lost their husbands. Martyred. Thousands of Mormons lost their leader.

They weren't leaderless for long. Various people staked their claims with varying degrees of success. Splinter groups came into being and offshoots of the religion were created – many of which exist to this day. But because history is written by the victors and because the Church of Jesus Christ of Latter-day Saints now has 12 million members they get to make the strongest – and by 'strongest' I mean 'loudest' – claim on the title of true successors.

They're the ones that ended up in Utah where they were led by one of Joseph Smith's lieutenants, Brigham Young; a confirmed racist who fathered 56 children and had 51 wives. Way to go Mormons! I shouldn't judge him too harshly. I know it's a lot of wives but it's worth bearing in mind that he did marry a lot of Joseph Smith's widows. Any friend would have done the same.

The second-largest offshoot was the Reorganized Church of Jesus Christ of Latter-day Saints and today they number roughly 250,000, albeit under their new name the Community of Christ... which brings us up to date with me staring into my laptop screen, unable to drag myself away from the unfolding story.

While the majority had followed Brigham Young west to Utah this lot stayed in the Midwest. They believed that Joseph Smith's son – also Joseph – should lead them, which was problematic at the time because young Joseph was only 11 years of age. So they pootled around, twiddled their thumbs and waited until eventually, in 1860, young Joseph decided he was up for the job and became head of his father's church.

In fairness it's worth pointing out that there were significant differences in doctrine from the get go. This branch of the church was opposed to the practice of plural marriage from the start with many of them – young Joseph included – refusing to accept that Joseph Smith had practised it himself. (This despite the fact that young Joseph met many of his dad's exes who tried to persuade him otherwise.)

Many members of what became known as the R.L.D.S. were keen for the church to make its home in Independence, Missouri to establish the Zion that the first Joseph Smith had prophesised and towards the end of young Joe's term of office it finally happened.

Unlike his father, Joseph had only three wives and none of them concurrently – he just kept outlasting them. He fathered 14 children, continuing to pop sprogs out right into his late sixties. Three of his sons, Frederick M., Israel A. and W. Wallace took on the mantle of Church President in turn, meaning that remarkably the church was still being controlled by one of his kids as late on as 1978. Imagine that! Imagine being W. Wallace Smith in the late '70s! In a world where *Grease* was on at the movies and punk had exploded a man was running a church based on the teachings of his own grandfather, who'd been murdered as long ago as 1844! How ridiculously elastic is time? How can three generations really stretch that far?

In fact, there was one more generation in the pipes and it wasn't until 1997 that the church appointed a leader who was not directly descended from Joseph Smith. Perhaps predictably, this was too much for some people to take and they branched out yet again, forming another smaller splinter group with a name so lacking in confidence it's remarkable: the Remnant Church of Jesus Christ of Latter-day Saints. The Remnants! Who's going to join a group called The Remnants? Their leader might be a maternal second great grandson of the original power-crazed loon Joseph Smith but I don't think he's quite got the family's gift for PR.

It was at this point that I stopped myself from digging any further. I didn't want to know if there was a Reorganised Remnant Church run by a third cousin twice removed or a Remnant Reorganised Remnant Church run by a second cousin thrice removed or for that matter, a Second Remnant Remnant Church run by a third cousin twice reorganised... the whole thing was already bubbling over with more than enough madness for me.

As indeed was I.

With every word I read I could feel my Salt Lake City madness returning; swelling up inside me, growing, spreading... taking over. It was in Salt Lake City that my dolour had really taken hold; that was the funk that eventually led to the mania of Moab. I didn't want to revisit it. I didn't want to revisit *him*. But he was there. Knocking inside my head, asking to be let back in. I told myself not to let it happen. Rationally, I knew there was no need for it. Andy's presence had steadied the ship, so why allow something as trivial as this to throw me off balance now?

Sod it. There was an easier way. An irrational, intolerant, cowardly way admittedly... but it was so much easier. But then what am I supposed to do, tell you about the rational choice I should have made, or tell you what actually happened?

I picked up the phone and dialled Andy's room.

'Hello?'

'Andy, it's me.'

'Where the hell have you been?'

'Nowhere, I—'

'We said 10 minutes! It's been over an hour! I knocked on your door and you didn't answer...'

'Did you? Shit. I didn't hear it. Sorry. Look. I've been... thinking...'

'What?'

'Have you unpacked anything?'

'No.'

'Good.'

'Why?'

'I don't want to stay here. Come on, we're checking out.'

Chapter 27
Old and tired and
...Kaput

Our waitress tipped the coffee pot nonchalantly to pour first Andy's second and then my third refill of the day. She cleared the empty plates from our breakfast spread and then with one hand she deftly slid the paper chit for our meal on to the table, skilfully wedging one corner of it under the ketchup bottle-cum-impromptu paperweight saying, 'There ya go guys.'

'Thanks,' I said... but she was already across the room, pouring someone else's coffee.

I picked up the piece of paper and took in the amount she'd circled. I threw a casual I'll-get-this shrug in Andy's direction and reached into my jeans pocket for the cash.

'So...' said Andy, 'do you want to tell me what last night was about?'

'What do you mean?'

'I mean... do you want to tell me why we checked in to a hotel, spent less than two hours there and then sneaked out like a pair of naughty schoolboys. I'm not used to renting hotel rooms by the hour, Dave, I'm not that kind of guy.'

'Oh... that.'

'Yes. *That.*'

'I just had to get out,' I said.

'Dave... we checked out of a perfectly nice, if strangely officey, hotel and ended up staying in a scuzzhole of a motel

with windows so thin I couldn't just hear the traffic on the I-70.
I could taste the sodding exhaust fumes. What do you mean,
"you just had to get out"?'

'Okay,' I sighed. 'Y'know I told you about spending three
days in Salt Lake City? How I went a bit... mental?'

'Yeah.'

'Well, it was like the ghost of cities past came to haunt me
last night. I started going a bit Salt-Lake crazy and I, um, I...
just had to get out.' Andy stared at me, clearly unsatisfied with
my less than complete answer. He was trying to work out
whether it was wise to push me for more. I knew I owed him
more. 'It was the phone that did it,' I said weakly.

'The phone?'

'Yeah. It had a sticker on the back of it.' I took a deep breath.
'The sticker said "Property of R.L.D.S." and so I thought...'

Explaining the ins and outs of my Latter-Day Saints reading
from the night before took us through our fourth and fifth
refills but eventually I think I'd said all there was to say.

'So,' said Andy incredulously, '*we* left the hotel because *you*
were worried about Mormons?'

'No. I was worried about *me*,' I said. 'But if you think about
it, I reckon it means the hotel is part of a chain so, y'know, we
did the right thing...'

'How does that follow?'

'Well, the hotel is owned by the Community of Christ, right?
And they have churches in 50 countries. Well, that's a chain in
anyone's language. They're all branches of the same business...
it's just their business happens to be *believing in Joseph Smith's
proprietary brand of hokum.*'

'But how do you know they own the hotel?'

'Because the sticker says...' I started... but my words faded
away as I realised I hadn't really thought this one through.

'You have no idea who owns the hotel. Maybe it was an
R.L.D.S. office building that got bought? *Maybe* they used to be
the office phones? *Maybe* they didn't bother peeling the stickers
off the back of the phones because they had better things to do

and because it never occurred to them that anyone would be idiotic enough to leave because of the Mormon telephony! Did you ask reception?'

'Um... no.'

'You daft bastard.' Andy shook his head in disbelief. Then he smiled. Then he laughed. Then he picked up a sachet of sugar and threw it at me, hitting his target dead centre. Bullseye. Man's nose. 'You stupid, stupid, stupid cock.'

'Sorry,' I said.

'What are you?'

'I'm a stupid, stupid, stupid cock.'

'Right. Now...' Andy clapped his hands together in a gesture of *that's-that-ness* '... let's work out where the hell we go next.'

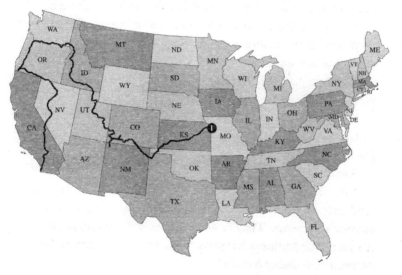

We unfolded our map on the table and studied our position. The two Kansas Cities were at the centre of a spider's web of interstate highways. They were circled by the 435 beltway and bisected by both the 35 – heading vaguely north to south – and the 70 – heading from east to west.

It was the 70 that had kept us awake last night. It was the 70 that we could hear rumbling now.

'Well,' said Andy tracing his finger along its paper path, 'that was our mistake right there…'

'Where?'

'There… look where Independence is… it's eight or nine miles north of the 70.'

'So?'

'Don't you remember? In Hutchinson? John asked why we were heading to New York? Remember his advice: stay south of the 70. Remember?'

'Yeah.'

'Y'know at the time I foolishly thought he was warning us about the weather but I get it now. He was warning us about you. North of the 70 and you turn into a stupid, stupid, stupid cock.'

Another sachet of sugar hit me on the nose.

'So we're staying south of the 70 from now on, are we?'

'We most certainly are,' said Andy.

I tutted with tutty regret.

'What's up?'

'Well… I know we don't have a great reason why it has to end in New York… but I did kind of like the idea.'

'Yeah… and you liked the idea of starting in LA as well and that didn't happen…'

'I know… but actually it's *because* we ended up starting in Coronado that I like New York so much. Coronado is an island. Manhattan is an island. That's as coast-to-coast as it's possible to be. That's from *beyond* one coast to *beyond* the other. No one could ever say I hadn't been from coast to coast then… there'd be no room for error.'

'Dave,' another sachet of sugar caught me. On the chin this time. 'Do you really think anyone cares? Do you *actually* think you have to drive right up to the sea and get the car's feet wet before people will accept you've gone from coast to coast?'

His tone of voice was so derisory that I had little choice but to join in and scoff at the literal ocean-to-ocean notion.

'No,' I said, 'of course not.' I was lying.

'Right... so let's work out where we go from here.' Andy turned his attention back to the map. 'Now... if we go down *this* way we could...'

He froze mid-sentence. I waited a moment for him to carry on but he didn't. I wondered if I was going to have to reboot him.

'What is it?'

Nothing. This time it was my turn to throw a sachet of sugar. He swatted it away before it landed but at least it jolted him back to life.

'Um... I can't quite believe I'm going to say this,' he said. 'D'you want to go back to Kansas?'

'What? Are you mad?'

'Look,' he said. 'Just take a look.'

I followed his eyes to his finger and his finger to the map. He was pointing at a town in the south-eastern corner of Kansas. It was only 10 or 20 miles from the border with Oklahoma... and it was called... Independence.

'You are mad.'

'No... I'm not... you've got to admit it has a sort of... karmic balance.'

'Does it?'

'Yeah. Think about it... when you were with Stef you went to an Independence you didn't like and then decided to go to another which you did. So obviously now *we've* been to an Independence you didn't like, we should go to another one as well. Because you'll like it.'

'Obviously?'

'Yeah. Obviously.' We both reached for packets of sugar but neither of us launched. 'Besides... it's actually a pretty good route. It takes us south and if we scooch east from there, we can nip under the Appalachian Mountains and hit the coast in South Carolina or Georgia.'

'I'm just checking that you're actually suggesting this. This isn't my idea... this is yours. Mr Missing-his-wife-and-child is suggesting a detour to a town called Independence?'

'It's not much of a detour.'

'It involves going west!'

'Only *slightly*. I'm not suggesting we stop there for the day. Unless there's a Taylor's closing there too. But we can get there by lunchtime, grab a bite, tick it off the list and then move on. We can be halfway across Arkansas by teatime.'

'Toto,' I said, in my best Judy Garland voice. 'We're in Kansas again.'

'Y'know for a straight bloke you're surprisingly camp at times...'

'It's funny you should say that...'

'Is it?'

'Yeah.'

'Why?'

'Because,' I took a deep breath to fill my lungs with song, thought about which member of the Village People I was about to be, decided it didn't matter and then went for it: 'We didn't stay at the R-L-D-S – we didn't stay at the R-L-D-eh-ess... they believe Joseph Smith, was not taking the pith... and that ma-ade me want to scarper... We didn't stay at the R-L-D-S – ba-da-ba-da-bada –

R-L-D—'

'Stop! Stop, stop, stop, stop!'

Pause.

'Young man...'

'I will kill you.'

'I think we're doing the right thing,' I said. We were nudging a little ahead of the speed limit, going strong with an empty road ahead of us. 'Take a look behind us.'

Andy turned to see what I'd already taken in with the rear-view mirror: an angry slate grey sky. Up ahead it was clear and blue.

'That looks horrible,' said Andy. 'I told you, heading south was the thing to do.'

'I think your route is a good'un,' I said. 'I'd been thinking about Independence as a kind of halfway point... but going this way, I reckon we've got less than a week to go.'

'Really?'

'Four or five days if you think about it. We get into Arkansas today... then we've only got Mississippi, Alabama and Georgia to get across. I reckon they're a day each, easy.'

'So long as we find gas.'

My blood ran cold. My heart stopped. I froze. The intensity of the silence told me that Andy had frozen too. We shared a nervous are-you-thinking-what-I'm-thinking look, confirming for ourselves that we were indeed both trapped in the same paranoid moment. When did we last fill up and why had my mind gone blank? I took a deep breath and glanced nervously at the fuel gauge...

Oh the relief. Joy of joys we still had three quarters of a tank.

'Phew... you had me worried then,' I said. 'I thought this was going to be one of *those* conversations.'

'Same here,' said Andy. 'Let's not tempt fate, eh?'

'KADUNK,' said fate, making one of the many horrible sounds it can make when tempted.

The noise was so sudden and the jolt it gave the car so pronounced my first reaction was that someone must have lobbed a lump of concrete at us. It startled me into that fight or flight level of hyper alertness; a meerkat-like straight back and wild-eyed, intensely focused stare.

'What the f—'

But the noise hadn't stopped. This time I definitely heard something hit the hood, but from underneath – *KADUNK* – it was followed by a bang as sudden and sharp as gunfire and then a kind of *BUKK-A-CHU-KUKKA* as something heavy ricocheted around inside the engine space then down and under us, skittling across the road surface and clipping our back wheel – *WHONK* – as it went.

I was going to just pull over on the hard shoulder but we were only a hundred yards from a slip road, leading up a slight embankment to an overpass and it seemed wise to *go somewhere* instead of stranding ourselves on an almost empty highway. We easily had enough momentum to carry us up the gentle slope where we could see precisely one building. It was only a couple of hundred yards away and while the engine clanked angrily at being asked to do anything at all we limped our pitiful way into its concrete parking lot. The sign on the simple white building said: Antiques and More. Maybe they'd want to buy our antique car? One careful owner. And then one not so careful owner.

I rested my head on the steering wheel. Andy said nothing. There wasn't very much either of us could say. I was hoping that the antique shop would transform itself magically into mechanics specialising in 1970s Fords... but when I lifted my head it was still selling antiques.

'What do you think it was?' asked Andy eventually.

'I don't know but it definitely wasn't a fucking hubcap, was it?' I snapped. I looked around at the unpromising surroundings. 'We're screwed, aren't we?'

'Not necessarily,' said Andy. 'We'll be able to get some help here and then we...'

'Here? It's a bloody antique shop!'

'Yeah... but you're forgetting one crucial fact: it's in Kansas.'

He was right as well.

I think you're already aware that both Andy and I are mechanical dunces so, while we did try to examine the problem for ourselves, lifting the hood and taking a sniff around, I hope you won't mind if I spare you the 10 minutes of embarrassingly ill-informed blather and guesswork that accompanied it and instead skip straight to our conclusion: 'I think a spinny-wheel-thing has fallen off.'

Oh yeah. We were nothing if not technical.

Now meet Fred, our local, neighbourhood antique dealer. Fred was tall, angular and bespectacled and I'd guess he was in his late thirties. So, about our age then. He said that he 'wasn't really mechanically minded' but volunteered to take a look anyway. Compare and contrast his diagnosis with our own:

'Okay... so there's a bracket here that mounts on top of th'air conditionin'... it looks like it's some kind of idler pulley. Let's see... you got three belts. There's one on the generator and the one that runs the water pump is okay which is good news. If it was the water pump you'd be in trouble. Yup. It looks to me like you lost your idler pulley on th'air conditionin'.'

Which if I check my Kansan/English dictionary means, 'You've lost a spinny-wheel-thing.'

The idler-pulley/spinny-wheel-thing had simply fatigued with age and sheared off, bouncing around the engine briefly and then disappearing for good into the wilds of Kansas.

If Fred was right and it was only running the air-conditioning then that was good news. Even if we couldn't fix it the car would still drive. The angry clanking noise we'd experienced as we limped on to Fred's lot had been caused by the loose fan belt hanging down and getting caught up in the machinery but that was nothing we couldn't sort out with a Stanley knife.

But Fred thought he could do better than that.

'Let me put you in touch with Dennis,' he said. 'He's a good guy and he'll let you know fo' sure what you're dealin' with. He can prob'ly fix it.'

Forty-five minutes later we'd driven gingerly through the suburbs of Ottawa, Kansas to an estate – half sited trailers and half more permanent homes – where we found Dennis and his work-from-home workshop.

Dennis had silver hair, sparkling Paul Newman eyes and a stainless steel tankard of coffee that was never far from his lips. When the coffee wasn't there, a *hyuk-hyuk* chuckle was.

'It's a nice old 70-mark Torino,' he said in his singsong accent. There really was something musical to Dennis's voice, his pitch rising and falling with every syllable, always ending on a high. 'I'll tell you what... it's been a while since I've seen one of these. I'm used to all this fuel-injection stuff, *hyuk hyuk*.'

I lifted the hood and he had a look inside. It would have taken Andy and I a lifetime to work out what was wrong. Fred had taken a couple of minutes. Dennis confirmed the result in 10 seconds.

'It's the tensioner pulley,' he said. 'It jus' runs the air-con. Lookee here, it goes crankshaft, idler, AC, tensioner... so it's not running anythin' else, which is good news.'

What a relief. We were worried she was going to need a liver transplant and it turned out she'd just performed her own appendectomy. It would be nice to have air-con, but we *could* live without it.

'So it *is* just the AC?' I asked. I needed to have the good news confirmed; I wanted to make doubly sure. It seemed so unlikely that a problem could announce itself with such violent noises and then turn out to be harmless. Such sound and fury.

'Oh sure,' said Dennis, 'It's jus' the AC.'

'Well, that's a result,' I said. 'I guess we can survive without that...'

'Let's jus' see if we can fix it,' said Dennis, reaching for his phone, 'I don' think this is gonna be an easy part to get but I might as well find out for ya.'

He pressed some digits and then, holding the phone in place with his shoulder, he took a slug of coffee. When someone picked up at the other end I was surprised by the way they cut straight to the chase. Not that the absence of small talk seemed impolite in any way, it seemed to be more the product of good-natured familiarity than anything else. With barely a hello, Dennis launched straight into the haiku-cum-lullaby that described the particular component he was seeking.

'Brad. I got a 70 model. Torino. Station wagon. With a 351 four barrel. Big block Cleveland. Air conditioner. Adjuster. Pulley. Assembly. Apple. Wallpaper. Hole-punch. Safari. Delta. Foxtrot. Madeley. Finnegan.'

Okay... I admit it, I made the back end of that sentence up. The list actually ended at somewhere round about 'assembly' but I was enjoying the sound of Dennis's voice so much I just wanted him to keep talking. Besides, for all the sense it was making he might just as well have just been singing random words anyway.

He paused, waiting for Brad to respond. Andy and I leaned

in, hoping to hear the news even before Dennis could relay it. There was no news. There was only silence. Dennis raised his eyebrows as it to say, *cuh, still waiting!* We both raised ours as if to say, *yup!*

When it became obvious that Dennis was going to be on hold for an indefinite period of time, he shrugged and renewed our face-to-face conversation instead.

'So, tell me,' he asked, 'what're two English boys like you doin' in a 70 Torino with California plates?'

Between us we ran through a brief explanation of our journey. I was surprised by the way it seemed to so obviously hit a nerve. We didn't ask Dennis any leading questions – in fact we didn't ask him any questions at all – but at the mere mention of our all-Mom-&-Pop, no-The-Man™ agenda it was as if a little seed of righteous anger flowered inside him.

'You know, we used t'have grocery stores all over this town. There used t'be a bunch of Mom and Pop stores in every neighbourhood but they're all gone now. The big people are taking over. Now we have two grocery stores: Walmart and the place across the street from them. A lot o' places in downtown Ottawa have closed down since Walmart came to town.'

'D'you think it's…'

Dennis raised his hand to silence me. His phone call was finally resumed and it was far more important that he heard whatever it was Brad had to say.

'Uh huh. Uh huh. Yeah. Okay… tell me somethin' good, Brad…' There was another lengthy pause. 'Really? You can get that by tomorro' mornin'? Man! Let me jus' ask these two gen'lemen…' he held the phone away from his ear for a moment and asked, 'are you gonna stay in town?'

'Well,' I looked to Andy for guidance while trying not to commit, 'I guess we shouuuuuuuuld…'

'Don't worry,' Dennis was ahead of the game, 'we have independent motels…'

'Then the answer's yes.'

'Brad,' said Dennis, the phone at his jaw once more, 'go

ahead an' order that for me, sir. But I need these things first thing in the mornin' you hear, these gen'lemen are from out o' town and we want to help 'em on their way, all right? All right. Speak to you tomorro'.'

The phone went down.

'I'm amazed,' I said. I was as well. 'Why would an obscure part like that be so easily available?'

'I don't rightly know, *hyuk, hyuk*... someone must be looking after you. So, is nine in the morning good for you?'

Fussily we both reassured him that it was very, very good for us.

'Dennis,' said Andy, 'you're an absolute gent.'

At which Dennis threw his head back and laughed a full and hearty laugh that put all his previous *hyuks* to shame.

'Man,' he said, 'I jus' *love* your English accents, *hyuk hyuk*. This is a crack up. I remember listenin' to The Beatles talkin' when I was younger and man, that accent o' yours is somethin' else.'

'Y'know,' I smiled, 'to our ears, your accent's pretty exotic too.'

'Git outta here! Man, listen to you!'

'This is all well and good chaps,' said Andy – his 'chaps' made both me and Dennis laugh – 'but shouldn't we sort out a hotel now we know we're staying?'

'We can fix y'up,' said Dennis. 'We got a lot o' independent motels here for sure.' He retrieved a copy of the *Yellow Pages* from the back of his garage and started flicking through. 'We don't have a Holiday Inn here that's fo' sure...'

'Good.'

'We used t'have a Holiday Inn Express but they got bought out and I think that's now a Best Western...'

'Well, we won't be there then...'

'Here we are,' he said, settling on the correct page, 'let me see now, yeah that's now a Best Western, like I say, then there's a Super 8 out there and a Travelodge too. We got a... shoot, we got a Day's Inn... man, a lot of these didn't used to be chains...

oh y'know, I thought we had a lot but it looks like there's jus' the one...'

'We only need one,' said I.

'With two rooms,' added Andy.

'The only thing about the Village Inn,' Dennis frowned, 'is you won't find it since they've screwed with the highway... but that's okay,' his face brightened, 'cos I can show you where it is. In fact, I tell you what I'll do; I'll drive out and y'all can follo' me and we can stop off on th' way at a Mom and Pop gas station too. How does that sound?'

'It sounds great,' I said, 'but we really don't want to be any trouble so if you've got things to do I'm sure we can find our way around...'

'Trouble? You kiddin' me? I *love* talkin' to the two of you! I could listen to that accent o' yours all day!'

The Village Inn felt like it was on its last legs. It was in such a remote spot and surrounded by so much darkness that from a distance the dimly lit motel appeared to just float in the night sky.

Pulling into the potholed parking lot it felt like we were being written in as late arrivals to a Stephen King novel. The porch lights that barely illuminated the outside of the building were presumably meant to make us feel safe as we walked from car to door... but in reality they just added to the sinister air. They rocked gently in the breeze, casting mysterious shadows that twisted and turned round corners, drawing the eye to imaginary assailants. There was just enough light to fool the eye, not enough to reassure it.

As a business it seemed doomed to failure. If you didn't know it was there you'd never think to look for it... and if you did know it was there, you were probably too scared to look closer. In this location they didn't really have a chance. If I didn't know any better I'd think it was their own dumb fault for building it where they had. But I did know better. I thought back to the conversation I'd had in Cottonwood, Idaho. The motel next door to the B&B beagle had gone out of business and Dennis had explained how all the town's businesses had been affected by the improved highway that now carried motorists past and not through the town. It looked like the same thing was happening here. Once upon a time this had been a good location for a motel. But not anymore.

No wonder the place was looking a little tatty. At less than $30 a room, what could they do about it? That's 15 quid!

And yet the rooms were great. It was like an optical illusion. The outside of the building seemed to suggest bad plumbing and peeling wallpaper, but instead it was surprisingly cosy, comfy and warm. It wasn't exactly the lap of luxury… but it was more than enough for our needs.

I lay back on the bed and flicked through some TV but my mind was too busy churning over the day to focus on any of it. I couldn't work out how I felt. Had the day been lucky? Or unlucky? Was it bad fortune that the spinny-wheel-thing had decided to give in or was it good fortune that it was *only* the spinny-wheel-thing? What would have happened if it had been worse? Everyone was very relieved that it was only the air conditioning and not the water pump… but what if it *had* been the water pump? How serious would that have been? Had we come close to ending the journey prematurely?

I muted the TV, picked up the phone and called Andy in the room next door.

'Hello?'

'It's me.'

'No.'

'No what?'

'No, I'm not checking out. I'm in bed already. It's nice here. If there are stickers on the phones ignore them. I'm not budging.'

'It's all right,' I said, 'I wasn't going to say anything like that.'

'Good. You have to stay rational. We're south of the 70, remember.'

'Yeah. So… I was just thinking about today and… and do you think we're lucky or unlucky?'

'Um... lucky.'

'Why?'

'Honestly?'

'Yeah.'

'Because I thought it was what you wanted me to say,' he paused. 'Dave... what's up?'

'What do you think would have happened if it had been worse? What if it wasn't just the air conditioning? What if it *was* the water pump? What if we couldn't drive the car and Dennis couldn't fix it?'

'You can *always* fix a car.'

'Well, what if it was going to take three weeks? What if it was going to take us through Christmas? What if it was a write off? What if it was going to cost us more to fix than the car was worth?'

'Then I guess the journey would be over. I guess that would be the story.'

'Shit...'

'Dave... you were going to do this journey by yourself, weren't you? No film. Just you, right?'

'Yeah.'

'So if you were by yourself and it happened... if it was just you and the car was screwed... would you have been able to just buy another one and carry on?'

I thought it through. Of course I knew the answer. There would have been no chance.

'No,' I said. 'I wouldn't.'

'So it would have been over, right? And like you've always said... we're making a film about your journey... so if it ends, it ends and that's what we get.'

'Right.' There was silence. 'So we came close to ending today?'

'Well... not really, Dave. It *wasn't* the water pump. It *was* the air conditioning. It's not like the car did a coin flip to decide which part of it should break... the weak part broke. That pulley probably hasn't been used for years. Since you had the heating fixed in Moab it's suddenly been pressed into service and it's old and tired and… kaput. But Dennis'll fix it. We'll be on our way by 10 a.m. It's all good.'

'You're right.' I wanted to believe him. 'It's all good.'

'Good night, Dave.'

'G'night.'

I put the phone down and looked back up at the TV. It looked like news footage. They were showing minor car accidents on icy roads. Maybe it was one of those *World's Worst Drivers* shows. I watched as drivers applied their brakes only to find themselves sliding a hundred yards into unavoidable collisions. At least that wasn't happening to us, I thought.

I un-muted the sound to find out more.

'Motorists in Kansas City have been advised not to travel unless their journey is absolutely necessary,' said an arch, knowing, female voice, 'but city authorities still expect to see more scenes like this.'

Kansas City? That was barely an hour away! Can it really have been so close? Was that *really* happening in Kansas City? The news had moved on to another story but I wanted confirmation so I started flicking through the channels, in the hope that I'd find a rival station's coverage of the same. I did better than that: I found the Weather Channel.

I picked up the phone and dialled.

'Now what?'

'Turn on the TV. Go to the Weather Channel.'

'What number?'

I told him.

'Shit!'

'It's not good, is it? Kansas City has been hit by an ice storm. There's no way we'd be able to get out of there… look at it! If we were still there… we'd still be there. They're expecting it to last a week!'

'Well, there's your answer then: I feel lucky. Lucky we got out of there when we did.'

'True enough.'

'And we're definitely heading south tomorrow. We're driving away from that. The minute the car is fixed, we're on our way right? Heading south, deal?'

'Deal.'

Chapter 28

The best guitar player around

Dennis didn't let us down. He fitted the new pulley with cheery efficiency in less than half an hour and by 10 o'clock we were waving him goodbye and hitting the road south.

I don't know if watching the Weather Channel the night before had made us paranoid but it definitely felt like things were turning. The air was chilly and the sky was full of dark, oppressive clouds. It felt like the world was closing in and getting angrier. A vicious wind was licking its way across the plains, buffeting the car from side to side and unsettling her joints. Suddenly, the windows didn't feel tight in their seals, the doors didn't seem as flush as before and anything that could rattle did.

The worst offender was the roof rack. Right at the back it had a horizontal brace, fashioned like some minimalist spoiler. It was held in place by a network of rusted screws, two or three of which were missing. If I drove at the wrong speed it started to vibrate rapidly, making the most annoying *digadigadigadi-gadigadiga* sound imaginable. It sounded like the Devil was drumming his fingers on the inside of our brains while at the same time God was contemplating whether or not to whip the wind up further. With a really good gust he could probably use that roof rack to peel back the car's lid and suck the pair of us from our seats and, who knows, throw us all the way to Oz.

The rattling roof rack was so unbearable it ended up limiting our speed. Every time I got near to 70mph it would go crazy and the only way of making it stop was to ease my foot off the gas. Sixty-three? Okay. Sixty-five? *Diga-dig* pause *diga-dig* pause. Sixty-seven? *Digadigadigadigadigadiga.* So back to 63 we'd go.

Even so, it was around half past 12 when we finally crossed the Verdigris River and rolled into Independence. My fourth. Andy's second.

We weren't intending to stop. We didn't want to give the weather the chance to catch us up and consume us. Independence was no longer a destination. It was simply enough to say we'd been. The horizon was still promising blue skies and while we never seemed to get any closer to them, they were always going to be worth chasing.

Even so, it was satisfying to see that the place ticked a lot of boxes. Within a minute of passing through the *'Welcome to Independence'* sign there was a 200-yard stretch of road that delivered three independent businesses: first a motel, then a diner and finally a gas station; the three things that most embodied our trip. Of course, we did stop long enough to refuel. We were never going to turn down chain-free gas.

'Hey there, whereabouts in California are y' from?' asked the station's owner as he came out to serve us. It was an old-fashioned gas station with old-fashioned service. He had a raspy, reedy, vibrato voice that seemed to be blown about on the wind every bit as much as our roof rack.

'The car's from California,' I said. 'But we're from London, England.'

'London? Cool! I'm a big Thin Lizzy fan. My name's Tommy. I play music professionally, too.'

Tommy had long bleached hair streaming out of the back of his baseball cap and a Muppet-like energy fizzed through everything he did. I thought about pointing out that Thin Lizzy were Irish but there didn't seem to be any point and besides, I don't think Tommy was going to leave a long enough gap in his monologue.

'They've done an article on me in the local paper,' he said, apropos of nothing in particular. 'I've played music for 25 years. I've been to California and played out there. I lived in Sacramento for about six years. But I'm from this area and I got kids now. But I still play.'

'That's cool.'

'Yeah. Man, I love all the English rockers. They're all getting older now but then so'm I. I'm a big Thin Lizzy fan. And Ozzy too. Y'know when he first came out with that *big* sound. He wants to go back to that. My wife always says I'd be the perfect replacement for him! But that's the thing, ain't it? I'll never get that chance livin' in the Midwest.'

I assumed Tommy was joking. Certainly the idea that it was only geography that had prevented him from replacing Ozzy Osbourne made me chuckle. But when I looked into Tommy's tinted glasses I got the distinct sense that his words were tinged with a genuine sadness.

'I played over a thousand gigs,' he said, 'so I can hold my own with any o' those guys. It's just I'm stuck in a little place.'

It was actually heartbreaking.

'But you like it here, right?'

'Oh yeah.'

'I can tell this isn't just a job to you, Tommy. You *like* doing this. You're on stage right now. You're performing right now.'

'You're absolutely right,' he said with a big smile. 'I'm on stage here all day every day and I love it. I've been here, running this, for six years and I love it.'

'How'd you get into it?'

'I played baseball with this guy and he called me up one day and offered it to me... said I'd be perfect. I said, "what about my looks?" and he said, "agh, don't worry about it – your personality sells!"' The pump cut out, Tommy looked to the dials. 'There you go,' he said, 'you got $18.'

'Y'know, Tommy,' I handed him a 20. 'I'm inclined to agree, your personality does sell.'

'That's nice of you, sir. Now... just you tell the folks in England that you met the best guitar player around, y'hear?'

'You got it.'

With the car fuelled up on Tommy's gas and the two of us fuelled up on Tommy's energy we headed back on to the long and windy – but not winding – road. We wanted to head south-east but this being Kansas that wasn't really an option... it had to be one or the other. So we went south for a bit, then east for a bit then south, then east and finally, for the second time in three days, we left the state of Kansas behind.

There was always a celebratory mood in the car when we crossed into a new state. Well, maybe not on the two occasions when we drove into New Mexico by accident... but whenever we did it on purpose it definitely lifted our spirits. Each state line acted as a marker; proof that progress was being made. We were definitely happy to leave Kansas and enter Oklahoma... even if it was exactly seven days since we'd crossed the same state line going the other way.

But our buoyant mood wasn't going to last long. The town of Picher soon saw to that. It's not that anything bad happened to us there it's just that the place was so depressed it made our happiness feel indecent. Picher was a place that made you feel guilty for smiling.

It used to be a mining town. The evidence of its former life is plentiful with enormous great grey heaps of slag all around it. The earth seems barren and scorched. It was heavy metals – zinc and lead – that once made the place rich and between the two World Wars the population rose to around 16,000 people. But the mines closed in the '70s. When we passed through, stopping to refuel at the Picher Express, they reckoned there were fewer than a thousand people remaining and by the time you read this it might well be down to zero. Picher has been poisoned.

The slagheaps we saw around the place – known locally as chat piles – mean there is lead dust in the air. It's in the ground-water too. And the people. Many of Picher's children have toxic levels of lead in their bodies and the incidence of learning disabilities is higher than average. According to the United

States Environmental Protection Agency, it is officially one of the most toxic areas in the country.

To make matters worse, the extensive mining has left much of Picher's infrastructure in danger of physical collapse. Big rigs are diverted around the town because of a legitimate fear that the roads will cave in beneath their weight.

Actually, this hasn't really made matters worse at all. In a strange way it might have made things better. It seems like it's only since the threat of collapse has existed that the authorities have stepped in and decided to do something about it. Kind of.

What they're doing is paying people to leave. Literally. Picher has been scheduled for closure. Local residents are being bought out with the government making non-negotiable, take-it-or-leave it offers on their homes.

We filled up and moved on, while trying not to breathe the air. Driving past abandoned homes; we saw broken windows, missing doors and front yards covered in junk; the flotsam and jetsam of discarded, damaged lives.

The taint of depression was still with us as we passed through the town of Miami (a place that will only resemble its more famous namesake if Florida finds itself plunged into a nuclear winter) and it wasn't until we were halfway across a huge long modern bridge over the Grand Lake o' the Cherokees that we started to feel we'd shaken it off.

The lake was created in the 1940s when the Pensacola Dam was built to generate hydroelectric power. It's a vast expanse of water that has transformed this already beautiful part of the world in the foothills of the Ozark Mountains into something of a tourist destination. Lots of businesses were catering to boaters and anglers and the like and suddenly there were plenty of places to stay too. We were growing weary and it was certainly tempting to take some lakeside lodging but, determined to get across the border and into Arkansas, we ploughed on.

We made it, eventually pulling into the sudden urbanity of Siloam Springs just as the night started to draw in. We'd done around 260 miles, seen Kansas, Oklahoma and Arkansas, filled up in Ottawa, Independence and Picher and while the time of day meant we never quite caught up with the blue sky we were chasing we did seem to have got away from the worst of the weather. It was definitely time to call it a day and the hunt for a motel began.

We found ourselves driving down an unappealing strip of non-stop, brightly lit neon commerce that seemed unpromising for our needs but somehow, from amongst the sea of signs that vied for our attention, Andy was able to pick out the one that read: The Stone Inn Motel.

'What do you reckon?' I asked, as we nosed into the parking lot.

'It's a motel like all the others,' shrugged Andy. 'We're knackered. It'll do.'

We didn't know it yet but we'd landed on our feet.

It might have looked like an average motel and it might have cost no more than an average motel but when we opened the doors to our rooms we got much more than we were expecting and we were both instantly thrown into fits of manic laughter.

The rooms were themed. Mine was called 'African Queen' while Andy had scored 'Little Tokyo'. In mine the walls were adorned with golden wallpaper that depicted lions patrolling the veldt, the chairs were upholstered with exotic animal prints and large (plastic) palms spilled out of an outsize colonial planter. In Andy's the walls were austere and white, the furniture simple, elegant and black and there were oriental throws and faux-silk bed linen.

In truth, it was all a bit tacky – the rooms looked like they belonged in a cheap bordello as much as anything – but that didn't matter. They were funny and they were different and when you've seen a lot of motel rooms back to back the fact that somebody has made an effort to make theirs different really does count for something.

I wouldn't want to live in that environment – I've never asked a decorator if they can recreate that 'cheap porn' look – but for one night, they were just what we needed: a laugh.

'That was a good drive today, Dave. Well done,' said Andy. 'Now, how about we have a coffee and see what the weather's doing back in Kansas City? We can congratulate ourselves on getting out of it.'

By the time I returned from the bathroom with a coffee jug full of water, Andy had already flipped through the TV stations and found the Weather Channel.

I opened the packet of coffee and poured it into the cone of filter paper.

'What's it look like?' I asked.

'Not good.'

'Really?' I enjoyed a mischievous chuckle. 'Go on, how bad is it?'

'No.' Andy wasn't chuckling. 'I mean it's bad for us.'

'What?'

I stopped what I was doing and tuned in to the information on screen instead.

The weather was bloody following us. The ice storm that had engulfed Kansas City the day before was *still* right behind us and was expected to hit Siloam Springs the next day. It was going just as fast as we were.

'Right,' said Andy, 'come with me.'

He strode purposefully out of the room and towards the car.

By the time I caught up with him he was at the back of the car with a screwdriver in his hand.

'How the hell do you do that?'

'What?'

'Make tools appear from nowhere?'

Andy furrowed his brow.

'I don't know what you're on about... now, hold this.' He passed me a torch. 'Give me some light, will you?'

'Where d'you want it?'

'On this bloody roof rack. If we've got to run from the weather I want to be able to run as fast as we can and this thing is driving me nuts.'

Chapter 29
Roadsign poetry

Keen to be on our way we started earlier than normal the next morning. Being well-brought up boys, we performed our usual car-loading routine on tiptoes and with whispers so as not to disturb anyone in the nearby rooms. Sadly, I fear our efforts were in vain because the car did not share our sense of tact. She roared grumpily to life with a coughing, spluttering series of false starts that might well have roused the whole town and not just the Stone Inn Motel. She obviously wasn't a very well-brought up girl. At least we tried.

As we left Siloam Springs in the pleasantly hazy, early morning half-light we looked to the skies to see if we'd woken the weather too. Nothing was moving. Maybe we'd got away with it.

We took Highway 412, a beautifully scenic route due east that carried us around the skirts of the Ozarks, hugging their gently undulating contours.

When we'd crossed the Rockies it had felt like a fight. Not a mean-spirited fight in a pub carpark, more a challenging session on the judo mats, but a fight all the same. The kind that ends in a draw, leaves you with a few bumps and bruises and sees you parting company with a firm handshake and the promise that one day you'll meet again.

By contrast, crossing the Ozarks was a dance. And not a drunken dance at a pub disco either. More a delicate turn around the ballroom floor, perhaps a Viennese Waltz. The kind of dance that sees you parting company with a chaste kiss and the hope that one day you'll meet again.

There was something about this part of Arkansas that felt utterly familiar. At times the rolling green fields and sturdy old trees, the grazing livestock and weathered barns looked as if they'd been plucked from some pastoral English idyll and deposited here just to make us feel at home. Perhaps that's why we danced so well together. Because I already knew the tune.

There was certainly a recognisable rhythm to it. For much of the journey thus far it was common to find 50-, 60- even 100-mile stretches of emptiness between one town and the next. Now new towns and villages were cropping up every 5, 10 or 20 miles and because that's similar to the rhythm and pace of driving I've grown up with it felt right and I felt comfortable. It also created some nice accidental roadsign poetry as two or three place names would huddle together on one sign. I think my favourite linguistic triptych was Yellville, Flippin, Gassville, three towns that appeared within a 20-mile run but which we adopted as our own in-car slang intensifier.

'Are you happy?' one of us would ask.

'Yellville *Flippin* Gassville, I am.'

Well... you do have to make your own entertainment in situations like this.

The quick turnover of places made life more cheerful in a more important way too because it helped to allay some of our routine fears about gas. Discovering that Town A doesn't have an unchained gas station doesn't arouse quite so much fear when you know that Town B is just around the corner.

And gas was relatively easily found too. In fact there was even one stretch where we passed no less than three unbranded gas stations in the space of 30 miles. By that time our confidence was so high that we even felt able to drive straight past one of them, choosing momentum over a half-gallon fuel stop. It was the first and only time that Grant's Destroyer tactics were not employed.

Our first taste of Arkansas gas came at a tiny little ramshackle station in the tiny little ramshackle village of Marble. It was a remarkably tatty place – almost peeling away from the earth at its edges. Its continued existence was all the more remarkable for the presence of a shiny new Conoco gas station less than 200 yards down the road.

The Marble Store's proprietor, the not-ramshackle-at-all Theresa, was in no doubt as to how they were surviving.

'It's God's will,' she said, rearranging her cerise blouse but not her forcefield of stoicism. 'He brought me here and it's His will that I stay here. God brought me to this area 24 years ago. God brought me to Eureka Springs for the Great Passion Play. While I was there I saw an advert in the paper for this store, I bought it and I've been here ever since. It's my destiny.'

'Wow!' I said because I didn't know what else to say and it really was one hell of an impulse buy.

'You see the sign outside?' said Theresa. 'It was damaged in a fire 20 years ago. I haven't bought a new one because people told me I'd be crazy spending money on it when the authorities were only going to tear it down.'

'Really? Why would they...?'

'They want to widen the highway. They say they want to take it all the way to my pumps. If they do that the pumps will have to go. But by the grace of God I'm still here. I've been fighting this for 20 years with His help.'

Well done Him. Now if only He could have a word with her about the clutter. The stores shelves really were something to behold. There didn't seem to be any kind of system to it, goods just seemed to be stashed wherever they would fit. Goods were stacked up on the floor, hanging by hooks from the ceiling and sitting one on top of the other if that's where they'd ended up. I'd put money on there being some things on those shelves that have been there longer than Theresa herself. I don't think she knows *how* to throw things away. The principle behind the shop seemed to be 'well, let's leave that there for now... you never know, someone might want it one day...'

The sunglasses on sale at $2.99 had been in and out of fashion at least three times and they were clipped on to a cardboard display stand so yellowed it was almost a sepia photo of itself. Three wire baskets hung from the ceiling by the till and spilling out of them was a chaotic mess of hair clips, highlighter pens, clothes pegs, biros, badges, golf balls and more. There were second-hand books, herbal medicines, huge sacks of potatoes, dog leads, key fobs, plastic crockery, religious pamphlets (naturally), greeting cards, firewood, playing cards, unidentified bits of wire and a 1980s cassette deck still in its box.

But the most remarkable stock wasn't in the store itself. It was just outside and round the corner. Arranged at random on a couple of trestle tables and a portable clothes rack were dozens of dresses, skirts, overcoats and shoes. There was a toaster, a small desk lamp, at least three teddy bears and a pushchair faded by the sun from red to orange. And there was a handwritten sign that said: 'All Items Free'.

'I hadn't been here long,' explained Theresa, 'when someone suggested I should have a garage sale. Well, I don't have time for that and God says, "give and you shall receive" and that's the right thing to do and so that's what I did. I just left some things outside and invited people to shop for free. And people came and some of those people had need and so they shopped. Within a couple of months, other people were donating things as well and it's just kind of grown from there.'

I adored the way Theresa referred to it as 'shopping'. Not taking. Not charity. Free shopping.

'So people just leave things they don't need?' I said. 'It's the ultimate in recycling.'

'We've had furniture. We've had washers, driers, shower stalls, sofas. I truly think it's awesome. We had a woman come about three years ago. She said she'd moved from California with her family and they had nothing. She was living in Huntsville, that's about 20 miles away. Well she came into the shop and asked me if it was true that people could shop for free. I said of course. She asked, "Even me... I'm not from here and

I live 20 miles away?" and of course I told her she could. And I still see her. She still shops here. I think it's wonderful.'

'So do I,' I said. And I do.

When we'd paid for our gas Andy and I went outside and found ourselves just standing and staring at the amazing collection once more. Theresa might have her eccentricities and the store itself might be overcrowded with junk but there was no denying that it was also stocked with love. We couldn't really ask for a more perfect example of a Mom & Pop store that gives to its community in a way that the chains just simply can't do.

It surely won't be long before they do get to widen that highway and Theresa and The Marble Store are forced out of business. People will be able to buy gas thanks to the Conoco down the road but I doubt they'll provide a free shop for the woman from Huntsville.

'How many times have you seen me go running?' I asked.

'What?' Andy was understandably surprised by my left-field enquiry.

'You heard me. How many times have you seen me go running?'

'Never.'

'Exactly. I brought some running shoes with me. Every time I open my bag to get a new pair of kecks out they just get in the way. I'm embarrassed by their pointlessness. I think I ought to leave them here.'

'Really?'

'Why not?' I said, already on my way to the car. 'That way someone else with size nines can feel embarrassed about the fact that *they're* not running.'

I lowered the tailgate and fished inside my bag, reaching through the pile of dirty washing. A couple of bits of underwear spilled out as I yanked the trainers free. I stuffed my sweaty socks back inside the bag – leaving those would be an act of cruelty – and then returned to the Free Shop, trainers in hand. I walked to the back of the display and placed them next to the other pairs of shoes. I enjoyed a wry smile at a nearly forgotten memory. I'd left my shoes behind in foreign countries before but this was the first time I'd done it on purpose. It was better this way.

As I turned to return to the car a flash of shiny metal caught my magpie's eye. Behind the clothes rail and almost out of sight was an old broken up gas pump. I pulled the dresses to one side to take a closer look. It was a big lump of metal and its rusted innards were spilling out on to the floor. Leaning against the base was a large white panel of enamelled metal. I pulled it out. It was dusty and dirty and rusted where the coating had chipped.

What I was holding was the pump's fascia; essentially, the bit you'd look at when you wanted to see the wheels turning, telling you how many gallons you'd pumped and how many dollars it was going to cost you.

'Do you think this is meant to be in with the free stuff or do you think it's just been put out of the way?' I asked.

'Does it matter?' said Andy.

'I think it'd be a nice souvenir,' I said. 'I've spent this whole trip searching for gas stations – having a small part of one on the wall at home seems kind of fitting, don't you think?'

Andy shrugged. 'You'd better ask her,' he said. 'I can't imagine anyone else is going to want it...'

'I'll offer to buy it,' I said. 'It might be tricky getting it home but it's worth a go.'

I wandered back into the shop.

'Forgotten something?'

'Actually,' I said, 'I was just looking at the Free Shop and I saw this,' I held up the dirty, white, metal panel, 'and I was wondering if I could give you $10 for it.'

'If it's outside it's free,' said Theresa with a patient smile.

'I know... but I don't really *need* it,' I said. 'I'd like to give you $10 for it.'

'It's free.'

'Well then I'll take it,' I said, 'and I'll leave $10 here for you to put in a charity tin, should you have one.'

'Well then, thank you,' said Theresa, 'that's very nice of you.'

I put the $10 bill on the counter. As I did so I noticed a sheet of paper that had been sticky-taped to the back of the cash register. I can't believe I hadn't seen it before but then it was obviously easy to overlook things when there was quite so much to look at.

There were two words that really drew my eye: 'Boycott' and 'Walmart'.

This had to be interesting. Was this some small sign of a grass roots revolt against the giant chain? If nothing else it would surely make me smile in the same way that the 'Friends Don't Let Friends Drink Starbucks' bumper sticker had done when I saw it on Dave's till in Moab. I paused, leaning in closer to properly take in its content:

There will be a NATIONWIDE BOYCOTT led by the American Family Association against WALMART STORES on the two (2) days after Thanksgiving.

Due to Walmart's promotion of homosexuality and other perversions. If you are not already boycotting Walmart, please consider taking this temporary stand for righteousness.

Oh. Oh dear. How confusing. My poor little brain was thrown into turmoil trying to work out who was the bigger enemy here. I looked at the $10 bill that I'd set down on the counter. Was taking it back the right thing to do? I couldn't, could I?

I had no idea what Walmart had done to inspire this particular protest but I'll bet they weren't actually *promoting* homosexuality. I'll bet they weren't using their in-store public address systems to make pro-homosexual announcements. No one ever walked into a Walmart to hear, 'Can the driver of a red

Mustang please move the vehicle because it is causing an obstruction. Heterosexual relationships are for squares, get down with the same-sex lovin' cos that's where it's at… it's gggggrrrrreat!'

This was Walmart for crying out loud! This is the store that has magazines like *Vogue* covered up for being too racy and refuses to stock CDs by artists whose lyrics they deem too suggestive, so it's not like they're known for pushing back America's cultural boundaries. (Or if they are, they're perhaps pushing the wrong ones in the wrong direction.)

Besides, I didn't need to know exactly what Walmart had done to know what I thought about this campaign. The phrase 'homosexuality and other perversions' made clear the AFA's bigoted agenda.[14]

It wasn't just the wrong-headedness of the campaign that was offensive. I found its limpness offensive too. A 'temporary stand for righteousness'! Imagine being so committed in your bigotry that you're prepared to protest something… but only temporarily! There was me thinking that righteousness (even, or perhaps especially, misguided hate-filled righteousness) was the kind of thing that would inspire a more permanent stand.

Surely anyone so confident in their own moral compass as to feel they know righteousness from wrongeousness (with such certaineousness) would want to live it 365 days of the year, wouldn't they? Otherwise what's the point?

Okay. I'm sorry about this but I feel the need to stop myself before I say something I'll regret. I'm reading the words on the screen as I type them and I'm afraid I don't really recognise myself in them. I'm aware that I sound pious and self-righteous

---

[14] It turns out that the American Family Association have had many spats with Walmart over their so-called 'promotion' of homosexuality. The reasons are varied, ranging from Walmart joining the National Gay and Lesbian Chamber of Commerce to selling *Brokeback Mountain* on DVD. Lunacy.

myself and it's making me uncomfortable. I can only apologise if it's made you uncomfortable too. I'm going to stop for a moment. I'm going to go and make a cup of tea. I'm going to go away and think about things and then return when my head is clear and I feel better able to express on the page what it is I really want to say. I won't be long. In fact from your point of view it won't take any time at all. I'll be straight back at the start of the next paragraph. Here I come...

Told you. Right, here's the thing. I have a confession. I enjoyed meeting Theresa and I enjoyed discovering that the love she so evidently poured into The Marble Store was that old-fash-ioned hate-y kind of love. There, I've said it now.

I don't agree with her views and I was certainly disappointed that what had seemed so lovely was suddenly tainted but I can't pretend to be shocked or upset about it when I know that deep down I was thrilled. I know that's not nice of me but I also know that I wasn't happy pretending otherwise.

The thing is, if they ever produce an *I-Spy* book of *'Things to Experience in the Southern States'*[15] I'm pretty sure that 'right-wing, Christian bigotry' would be in there. It's one of the clichés that characterises that part of the world and what are clichés for if not for ticking off a list?

It was satisfying in the same way that it would be if you went to Paris for the weekend and saw a man in a beret saying, 'oo la la'. It was an encounter that left me thinking, 'wow, these kind of people really do exist!' and isn't that exactly the kind of experience that makes travelling so exciting?

In a way it was exactly what I was there for. Let's not pretend there was any higher purpose to my trip. I was doing this unchained thing for purely selfish reasons. I think travelling should be about difference. I think the chains spread sameness. I'd spent four months on tour in the States being depressed by

---

[15] Note to self: I could make a million with these things!

the sameness. This trip was simply my way of returning there and immersing myself in difference.

Which means that meeting Theresa and her naïve, dodgy beliefs was a result.

It might be more chilling to hear the same views expressed by a politician, a church leader or a teacher, say. But Theresa was none of those things. Theresa was an eccentric lady of advancing years who was running a run-down gas station in the belief that God had called her to do so. Eccentricity Factor: 7. Chill Factor: 3. Set phasers to stun.

Oh... and in case you think I'm judging Theresa harshly based on the one piece of paper that she'd taped to the till, I should say that as I left I picked up a handful of the religious pamphlets that were prominently displayed and they were evidence of more of the same. I suppose they might have been left there by someone else, but I doubt it.

They made for fun reading. They were all in the same comic strip format. They were about five inches wide and three inches tall and maybe 20 pages long. By and large each story ended in one of two ways. The central character might go to Heaven or – and this was far more likely – Hell. Occasionally, there'd be a twist on this formula and there'd be a couple of characters involved and guess what? Yup. The one who made the right choices would get to go to Heaven and the silly sinful one would be sent to Hell.

In the small selection I picked up there were dozens of suggested paths to the bad place. There's a page in one of them that depicts the hordes all trudging towards Hell. There are speech bubbles emerging from nine or 10 of them which are presumably there to give us clues as to the wrongs they've committed. Some of them are comically naïve. For example, one of them actually says, 'I love my sin'! But then there are also speech bubbles saying things like, 'We've shacked up for years...' and even 'Allah be praised.' Gulp.

But my favourite pamphlet (and by that I mean the pamphlet that I enjoyed disagreeing with most) was called

Flight 144. In this one a young man called Ed gets to sit next to a couple of famous Christian missionaries on a flight from a fictional African country back to the US. The three of them discuss their lives, and we learn that the two missionaries have devoted theirs to good works. They've spent 50 years in Africa during which time they've fed and clothed thousands as well as building five schools and four hospitals.

Ed's life has been somewhat different. He killed a man in a drunken bar brawl. I know! It's good, isn't it!

Anyway, while Ed was in the slammer he found the Lord and turned to the path of righteousness. He even managed to lead his former cellmate to Christ too. Well done, Ed.

But Ed was embarrassed to be sitting next to such wonderful people when he'd only managed to save one soul and he wonders aloud about how many sinners his new travelling companions have rescued. He's surprised to learn that they haven't saved any souls – just thousands and thousands of lives.

Which turns out to have been a big mistake when the plane crashes and everyone on board dies. The missionaries, having foolishly wasted their lives bringing healthcare, education, food and shelter to the needy, are cast into the burning flames of Hell for all eternity and Ed, the bar-brawling killer who's repented, made his peace (and crucially saved a soul) is transported to his beautiful mansion in Heaven. And they all lived happily ever after. Apart from the missionaries who lived in never-ending pain and suffering.

Lovely. Welcome to your friendly neighbourhood store… you're all going to Hell.

Our final taste of Arkansas gas was rather different. It came under a pitch-black sky in the town of Portia. It was Robert's Service Center, a business named not for a Mr Roberts but for a Mr Robert Shelton. It was a Mom & Pop store in the truest sense of the phrase with Robert's wife, Fern, filling the Mom role to his Pop. Between them they ran a tight ship of a place; an old-fashioned, full-service, service station where they don't just pump your gas but wash your windscreen, check your oil and warm your heart too.

We almost drove straight past it because they'd turned many of the lights off and were in the process of shutting up shop but I saw it at the last minute and turned tightly to nose our way on to their forecourt.

'Hey, how y'doin'?' said Fern with a cheery smile. 'You looking for gas?'

'Yes please, fill her up.'

'You got it.'

By the time we'd got out of the car, Robert was already washing the windscreen – which was good news because we seemed to have squished an extraordinarily high number of bugs on this leg of our journey. (Andy was getting worried that unless he could find a company that distributes insect snuff-films, most of what he'd shot that day would be useless. It's a very niche market.)

Robert and Fern had been running their gas station for 28 years but Robert had been pumping gas in these parts for far longer than that.

'I've been on this highway since I was 13 years old,' he said. He was tall, with a thin face, silver hair and a droop of a moustache. His words were always more animated than his face. 'I'm 58 now – so I've been here a while. My family owned a station about 2 miles away, at Blackrock. That was an Exxon station. My brother bought that place in... I think it was '76. He got killed in a car accident in '86. Then I bought the station and we was there for two or three years before we moved here.'

'Do you want me t'check your oil?' asked Fern. She was short, constantly smiling and had a pair of glasses perched on her button nose.

'Yes please,' I said. 'Y'know, I don't think I've ever seen a full-service station back at home... it's lovely.'

Fern leaned across, almost at full stretch to get to our dipstick.

'There's not too many of us left in the States either,' she said.

'They're pushing us out.' She pulled the dipstick out and then had to lean back into the light to read it. 'Uh huh... you're down a quart of oil. D'you want me to get that?'

'Yes please.' I said.

Andy and I exchanged worried glances. It had only been five days since we'd added a quart back in Hutchinson.

'Actually, I think we'll take another quart with us as well,' I called out. Better safe than sorry.

'The thing with a lotta gas stations these days,' said Fern as she returned with our oil, 'is they add in so much else like the convenience stores and all so they don't need to make all their money on the gas...'

'Would you be tempted to go that way? Have you ever been offered one of those deals? Has one of the majors ever come to you and offered to brand your station as one of their chain?'

Fern giggled. 'We're not fancy enough to be one of those,' she said. 'We used t'be Exxon a long while back.'

'Really?'

'That's right,' said Robert, joining the fray. 'They told us about 10 years ago that we either had to buy the station or git out...'

My jaw dropped lower and lower as Robert explained their story. When the two of them had first taken the station 28 years earlier they were renting it and it was part of the Exxon chain. Eighteen years later Exxon must have decided that the store wasn't really in keeping with their corporate image. They decided to close it down but gave Robert and Fern an option on buying the place first. Here's the truly amazing part. When Robert decided to buy it, they then told him that he needed to spend $120,000 in order to make it look like a nice, modern Exxon station.

Isn't that amazing? They were getting rid of the place because it didn't fit in... and when he wanted to carry on with the business – the business he'd spent 18 years building – they expected him to spend $120,000 to make it fit in with the rest of the chain. Robert was understandably unimpressed.

'I said, no I don't have to make it look pretty for Exxon... I'll buy this station, I'll change the name and we'll be independent. And we're still here. They been tryin' to squeeze us out for 10 years.' He smiled. 'I'm stubborn.'

'He sure is,' said Fern, looking up into her husband's eyes with nothing but love and admiration in her own.

In that brief moment the pair of them looked just like the high-school sweethearts that I imagine they'd surely once been.

'When we first started here, 28 years ago,' said Robert, 'there was approximately 25 full-service service stations in about a 25-mile radius of us. Proper Mom and Pops, too. People told us we weren't gonna last cos we're too small and all the quick shops and convenience stores were takin' over. I said, "No. The convenience stores will not take over if someone wants to work... and I want to work." There's too many businesses where the boss wants to wear a white shirt and drive around in a limousine. Well *this* boss wants to work.'

'Good for you,' I said vapidly.

'We're not wealthy... but in a way we are because we got our health and each other and we got our own business and we work here and we like it and then we take off and go and do what we wanna do...'

'And we've arrived at closing time so we should let you get on...'

One of the difficulties with travelling unchained is that a lot of places tend to close a little earlier. In a chain gas station there might be a minimum-wage teenager serving people through a hatch at 1 a.m. but if the only people who work at your business are Mom and Pop then you need to have a home time. Robert and Fern work from 7 a.m. to 6 p.m. Tuesday to Friday and from 8 a.m. to 2 p.m. on Saturdays, taking two and a half days a week off.

Mom & Pops might be hard enough to find at the best of times but after dark they become even rarer than before which is why we normally started looking for a motel not long after nightfall.

But because we'd caught the last throw of the dice at Robert's Service Center we had a full tank of gas and that gave us the confidence to push on. We had a great incentive too. For an investment of 130 miles – or about half of our full tank of gas – we could cut across the corner of Tennessee into Mississippi and turn our one-state day into a three-state day in less than three hours. That had to be worth it.

'Are you up for it?' asked Andy.

'Yellville *Flippin* Gassville, I am!'

'Good.' Andy rubbed his hands together with eagerness. '*This* is why we should start early.'

'What do you mean?'

'Well, think about it. We started at least an hour earlier than normal this morning. If we hadn't done that we wouldn't have found Robert's. If we hadn't found Robert's we wouldn't have a full tank now and if we didn't have a full tank now we wouldn't be contemplating another two and a half hours of driving. We'd have to stop. So by adding an hour on at the start of the day we've also been able to add on two and a half hours at the end of the day. Starting an hour early gives us the chance to make this into a three-state day... that's brilliant, isn't it?'

'Yellville *Flippin* Gassville it is.'

Pause.

'I think we can probably stop that now, don't you?'

From: Jake Lingwood (Ebury Publishing)
Subject: Re: Chapters 24 to 29
To: Dave Gorman

Dave,

Thanks for the new chapters.

Just checking… there's a bit in 29 where you stop writing
and make a cup of tea. Do you mean to leave that in?
Thought you might want to go back and rewrite the bit
before it? Or do you want to keep it in?

Jake

PS: I know you were happy with the cover but we've had a
rethink. Thoughts?

From: Dave Gorman
Subject: Re: Chapters 24 to 29
To: Jake Lingwood (Ebury Publishing)

> *Or do you want to keep it in?*

Yellville Flippin Gassville I do.

Dave

PS: The new cover is better.

There really isn't much I can tell you about our time in Tennessee. We were there for less than 40 minutes and it was dark. All that we saw were headlights. Even crossing the Mississippi River was unspectacular. There was no fanfare, no showy bridge and no illumination to speak of. We couldn't see the surface of the water, indeed the only real clue that we were crossing the river came when the hum of the road beneath our wheels changed pitch.

Memphis is lodged in the south-western corner of Tennessee like a billiard ball wedged in the jaws of a pocket so in crossing the city we crossed not just from Arkansas into Tennessee but also from Tennessee into Mississippi.

There was real conviction in our high fives. We had only three states to go before we hit the coast: Mississippi, Alabama and Georgia. It was exciting.

The minute we were into Mississippi we began our hunt for a motel. When the first town we came to was called Olive Branch – the same name as that taken by the hotel in Independence, Missouri that had tripped my switches a few nights earlier – we should have realised it was a bad omen.

Olive Branch felt newly built and antiseptic. We cruised up and down a couple of broad avenues and while we saw many motels not one of them was unchained. It seemed bigger and more sprawling than we imagined it would be. I don't know if we missed some obvious signs or were just tired and starting to misfire but Olive Branch didn't seem to have any definable centre to it. It felt like it was all suburb and no town, and because it felt aimless as a place, our search felt more aimless too.

Eventually, after 40 or 50 minutes of fruitless to-ing and fro-ing we pulled on to the forecourt of a chain gas station. We obviously weren't going to give them any money but we wanted to stop, gather our bearings and change our tactics. We wanted to look in the phone book and we were happy to ask for help.

With hindsight, asking for help might have been a mistake. I don't think the words 'helpful' and 'Mississippi' are very common bedfellows. In fact I think Mississippi might well be the yang to America's Kansan yin. Where Kansas had been defined by its kindness, Mississippi's hallmark turned out to be its meanspiritedness.

We would be in the Magnolia State for less than 24 hours but even in that short space of time there would be three acts of Mississippian meanness that would make my blood boil. That's an alarmingly high hit rate. (Especially when you consider the fact that for nearly eight of those hours I was alone in a motel bedroom.) The first of these incidents came from a small-town cop.

It had soon become apparent that Olive Branch had little or nothing to offer. The girl in the gas station didn't know of any independent motels but you could hardly blame her for that because the phone book didn't know any either.

'You could prob'ly get somewhere if you went int' Memphis,' she suggested.

I winced at the idea. 'We've just come through that way...'

'Well you're only 15 miles from Byhalia...'

'And do you think there's a motel there?'

'Prob'ly.'

It was as good a guess as any and so we stretched our day a

little further and headed for Byhalia. It was small – I think the population was around 800 – and it was dark. Byhalia appeared to have gone to bed.

We cruised slowly through the sleepy streets, pausing every now and then to stare at a business in the hope that it would turn into a motel if we scrutinised it for long enough but none of them ever did. There were no neon signs blinking through the darkness here in fact there were no bright lights at all.

And then suddenly there were lots of bright lights. Red, white and blue ones. They were flashing in my rear-view mirror and they were accompanied by the heart-stopping *bwerp-bwerp* of a police siren.

I pulled over to the side of the road. The police car pulled in behind me. Nobody moved.

I turned to Andy.

'What did I do?' I asked with panic in my voice. 'Have I done something wrong?'

'I don't think so…'

'Are you sure? I haven't gone through any traffic lights, have I? You *can* turn right on a red light here, can't you?'

I looked in the rear-view mirror and saw two cops still sitting in their patrol car and the lights still flashing. I didn't know what I was supposed to do next. Driving away seemed like a pretty bad idea. Getting out of the car seemed like a really, *really* bad idea. What else was there?

'Maybe they're waiting for you to turn the engine off,' suggested Andy, who was busy burying his camera under the passenger seat. 'Maybe they want to know you're not going anywhere before they get out…?'

It made sense. I turned the key and the Torino shuddered into silence. It turned out to be the wrong thing to do.

'Take the next right and *then* pull over!'

The words came through a loudhailer. They were so loud and so authoritative I'm surprised 800 Byhalians weren't leaping out of bed and obediently rushing to their cars. The loudhailer is not a friendly medium. You could use one to tell someone you loved them and it would still sound angry and officious. Put someone who actually *is* angry and officious behind the mic and it becomes absolutely terrifying. I don't care where in the world you come from, foreign police are always so much more frightening than your own. They just know the script so much better than you do.

I did as I was told, taking the bend nice and slowly. I rolled forward far enough to give them room to pull in behind me and then stopped. One of the cops got out of their car and sidled his way towards us. He'd shaved his head completely, which meant judging his age was difficult. He could have been anywhere from his mid-twenties to his early forties.

I wound down my window, frantically turning the handle over and over as fast as I could. A small fart emerged. Andy giggled. Giggling didn't seem like a very good idea.

'Hello, sir,' I said.

I tried to smile but found myself unsure as to how to pitch it. Too much and I'd look cocky. Too little and I'd look guilty. Instead I looked constipated… which is certainly not how I felt.

'Good evening.'

If he was trying to smile he was making an even worse go of it than I was. My guess is he wasn't trying to smile.

He shone his flashlight in my face and then at my hands.

'Sir,' he said, 'we've stopped you on account of a faulty stop light.'

'Really?' I asked. It seemed highly unlikely but then he'd been behind us and I hadn't.

'Yes sir.'

I've seen this in the movies. This is the bit where he takes a stroll to the back of the car and uses his nightstick to break the stop light. I checked that Andy had stashed the camera out of sight and that *this* was not in the movies.

'Would you mind telling me what you're doing here at this time of night, sir?'

'Um… we… um…' Why was my throat so dry? What kind of useless defence mechanism was this? And why did I really need a pee all of a sudden? What possible evolutionary purpose had this ever served? Why, when challenged by an authority figure, would all the liquid in my body abandon my throat where it was needed and make its way to my bladder where it was most definitely not? What possible use had this ever served mankind? What would my ancestors do in this situation, dry cough and piss on him? 'Um… we were just looking for a motel…'

'And what motel would that be, sir?'

'Um… not a particular motel. We're just looking for *a* motel, *any* motel. Or hotel.'

'Can I see your driver's licence, sir?'

I reached into my jeans' pocket, pulled out my wallet and then my licence. He took it from me and examined it by torchlight, pulling a concerned face when he saw its foreign pinkness. He continued to examine my licence while asking for our vehicle registration and insurance documents. Grant had explained how important it was to have these to hand so we'd stashed them under the driver's seat from day one. I reached under and pulled them out. They were coated with a thin layer of old, crusty seat foam that had fallen from the underside of my chair with age. I blew the dead stuffing off the A4 sheets of paper and handed them to the officer. He took them in silence, strolled back to his car and handed them to his colleague.

'He's lying about the stop light,' whispered Andy through the corner of his mouth. 'I know he's lying.'

I was about to respond but our friend had returned to my open window.

'Sir, what is this licence?' he asked.

Surely a trick question. It was my driving licence. It had the words 'Driving Licence' written on it. But if I said, 'It's my driving licence', wouldn't that sound sarcastic. Wouldn't it sound like I was calling him stupid? Maybe he was asking me what *kind* of driving licence it was… but then that was no better. All the clues were there. And when I say 'clues' I mean it had 'UK' written on it. Surely he didn't need me to explain this one! Surely he could put two and two together and get four. Actually it was even easier than that. When you put two and two together to get four you do have to do *some* maths. (Or math in his case.) But putting 'UK' and 'Driving Licence' together to get 'UK Driving Licence' involves no maths whatsoever. You literally *just put them together*. It's as easy as putting two and two together and getting two two.

'It's um... my driving licence,' I said. 'I'm from the UK.'

I could hear his colleague's walkie-talkie chattering away in the background. Our documents had been run through the computer and the results were in. I heard my own name. Then Stef's. Then Andy's. Which was strangely scary.

'Sir, I'm afraid this driver's licence is not legal.'

I felt the blood drain from my face. Had it expired? Surely not.

'Is it not?' I asked nervously. 'Is there something wrong with it?'

'It's not a US licence, sir. It's not legal here.'

'Now hang on a minute Mr Policeman sir, but you're being ridiculous. That is plainly a lie! Of course my driving licence is legal here! I've used it to hire cars in this country on many occasions. Or maybe *I'm* wrong! In which case, surely someone should tell Messrs *Avis* and *Hertz* about this immediately! They must have aided and abetted *thousands* of criminals only this week! I'll tell you what, Officer Bullethead, I think you've got bigger fish to fry. If I were you I'd make my way to one of the various hire-car companies you'll find at Memphis International Airport immediately. If you hang around for a few hours you could make dozens of arrests! Put your back into it and you could be looking at an Officer of the Year award. Especially if you stop being a lying piece-of-shit dipstick!'

... is what I wanted to say.

'Really? But I've used it to hire cars before?' is what I actually said. But I think he knew what I meant.

'Well it may be legal in some states, sir, but it is not legal in Mississippi.'

'But...'

'Now... I'm not gonna give you a hard time over this... but I am gonna strongly recommend that you do not hang around in Byhalia any longer, do you read me?'

'Um... yes?'

'And get that stop light looked at first thing in the morning, all right?'

He handed me back my paperwork and swaggered back to his car, leaving Team Unchained in a state of stunned silence. They flashed their lights, *bwerped* their siren, pulled out and cruised past us.

'That was strange,' I said. 'Do you want to check the stop light?'

Andy jumped out as I started the engine. He ran round the car checking all the bulbs while I danced through all the pedals. All was present and correct.

'He was just making that whole thing up, wasn't he?'

'Yeah... I reckon he just got nosey,' said Andy. 'Old car, Californian plates. He wanted to know what was going on.'

'What about all that driving licence shit? He didn't know what he was on about! He was just making shit up because he didn't want to admit he didn't know what he was on about.'

'I think he wanted the strangers off his patch just in case.' Andy grinned. 'We're freedom fighters! We're being run out of town by the cops!'

We did find ourselves a Holly Springs motel. It wasn't much to write home about. (Which is a shame given what I'm doing at this precise moment.)

If I tell you that the motel had a strictly enforced policy of only allowing one person into reception at a time and that in reception packets of condoms could be bought for a dollar a pop I think that pretty much gives you the measure of the place. Really. It was that charming.

It was hard to believe this day had started in Siloam Springs. We'd driven nearly 400 miles. When we'd left Robert's Service Center we thought we were committing to another two and a half hours of driving but it was now more than five hours later and midnight was fast approaching.

You'd think that 400 miles was enough to give the bad weather the slip... but apparently not. It was still on our tail. A severe weather warning had been issued for the next day with thunderstorms, high winds and a temperature drop of up to 30 degrees all on the cards. We knew we couldn't afford to hang around. We had to get up and go. If we didn't get out of there in time we might end up having to spend another night in that motel – and that wasn't happening.

We got up early but this time the rain was out before us. Rain – stupid big rain with drops the size of your fist – was falling. We loaded the car with a relay race of mad dashes but no matter how mad or how dash we were, there was no way of not getting soaked. It was the kind of rain that didn't just get through your clothes... it got through your skin. Stiff, sodden denim clung to the back of my knees and my shoes squelched with every flex of the sole.

'You know what I could have done with today?' I said.

'What?'

'A spare pair of shoes. If only I had, say, a pair of running shoes that I don't really wear that much. I could have worn *them* this morning and kept my normal shoes dry.'

'So could I,' said Andy. 'And do you know what makes that really annoying? I saw a pair yesterday that looked all right... and they were being given away for free!'

'Ha bloody ha. Come on, let's get the hell out of here.'

I slid the key into the ignition, pumped the gas a couple of times and then turned the key. She'd never been quieter. Not a cough, not a splutter, nothing.

Literally nothing. Not even the faintest sign of life. The battery was flat. It was the kind of rain that didn't just get through your clothes and your skin... it got through your car as well.

We asked for help at reception (one at a time, naturally) but got no joy. Mine was a strange conversation. When it started he had a car but didn't know what jump-leads were but then somehow the ground shifted and he did know what jump-leads were but didn't have any and then all of a sudden he didn't even have a car. At which point I gave up pursuing the issue in case he decided that electricity didn't even exist as a concept. That kind of thing could really screw us up.

I emerged from reception to find Andy waiting with a big, stupid grin on his face. Something was up so I gave him a condom and asked him what it was. He walked me a few yards out beyond the front of the motel and then turned me round to face it. It was a thing of beauty. Attached to the motel building was a garage. Problem solved.

'Come on,' I said, 'let's go and ask.'

The closer we got to the door the more uncertain we started to feel. It looked like a garage. It smelled like a garage. It *was* a garage but it seemed to be lacking a certain garageyness. I'd had to visit a few mechanics in the last few weeks. They'd all had some reassuring quality to them. They were all places that exuded a 'please-don't-worry-because-we're-here-to-help' vibe. I don't quite know what they did to create it but I do know that it was absent here.

There was no one on the shop floor and the door to the office was firmly shut. I knocked. I felt like a naughty schoolboy who'd come to take his punishment. This was the headmaster's study and he was inside, flexing his cane.

My rather tentative knock was met with silence. I tried again but with a bit more force. Silence. A third time. Still nothing. We didn't have many options left so I thought I might as well try the door. It opened.

Suddenly, the place didn't smell like a garage at all. It smelled like a strip club ashtray. In a strip club where nothing's been cleaned in 20 years. Including the strippers. Who, incidentally, all smoke cigars on stage using parts of their anatomy that were not designed with cigar smoking in mind. A thick fug of foul smoke hung in the air. There were seven or eight men there all sitting around the outside of the room and I think all but one of them was smoking these repulsive, stubby cigars. It was this wonderful bunch of men – this cabal of stogie smoking grotesques – who were to deliver the next act of Mississippi meanness.

The group's body language made it clear who was in charge. You know that notional *I-Spy* book of *Things to Experience in the Southern States*? Well, let's just say I could now put a tick next to: 'A person so big you wonder how it is they're still alive.'

He was huge. One of the largest men I've ever seen. He'd wedged his enormous, corpulent, toad-like figure in behind a large, heavy wooden desk and it wasn't unreasonable to wonder what would happen to the desk if he tried to stand up. Maybe he'd end up wearing it as a bib. He looked like he'd been drawn by Hogarth to illustrate some cautionary tale on the theme of gluttony... and it looked like Hogarth's editor had come back five times asking for him to be made bigger.

There were two or three black guys in the gang but King Toad and the rest of them were white... although these terms do nothing to describe the unhealthy deathly spectrum of true hues on display: they were pinks, purples and puces, blues, greys and greens.

We weren't greeted warmly. In fact we weren't greeted at all. They just carried on with their conversation as if we didn't exist. They spoke in low growls and with accents so thick that I didn't have a chance of divining the meaning of any of it. In all honesty, I couldn't even make out words. Imagine hearing Scooby Doo doing an impression of Elvis Presley. Got it? Now slow it down to one fifth of the speed. Okay? Now make Scooby drunk. *Now* you're close. At one point I couldn't even work out which one of them was speaking. The sound seemed to be coming from the beaten-up sofa to our right, which meant there were two likely candidates... but I swear neither of them were moving their lips. The sound was so low I think I must have been hearing it more through the vibration in my bones than through my ears. And yet the others seemed to be giving it their full attention. Maybe there was a subwoofer hidden inside the sofa and it was pumping out some mind controlling bass beat that I'd learn to appreciate if I only gave it some time.

Eventually, there was a brief lull in the growling so I tried to seize the opportunity.

'Excuse me…'

But the lull was briefer than I hoped and the growling soon picked up exactly where it had left off.

If we hadn't *needed* their assistance we'd have walked straight out… although that's an utterly pointless thing to say when it's obvious that if we hadn't needed their assistance we wouldn't have walked in there in the first place.

Three 'excuse me's went unanswered but eventually Baron Greenback deigned to turn his fat face the quarter inch needed to acknowledge us. It was the first time any of them had even made eye contact. He barked something in our direction. I didn't have a clue what it was but as the rest of them were all looking my way I knew I'd been granted another turn and so I ploughed on.

'Hi… we're parked up at the motel just here… and we have a flat battery… so we were wondering if it was possible to get a jump start from you. We'd really, *really* appreciate it.'

Silence. Then some growling. Then some barking. As one of the men started to stir in his seat the boss made a superhuman effort to make himself clear. For the first time I understood what he was saying.

'That'll be $6. You can pay him.'

Six dollars! It was obvious he'd just made the number up so how on earth did he arrive at six? Six? Why not five? Or 10? I'd have admired the man more if he'd said 50. It was obvious we were over a barrel so he'd have got away with it if he had. Six bucks was like charging us and not charging us at the same time. It was a token amount but what was it a token of? Presumably just the idea that doing anything for free was somehow offensive to him. It was *only* $6 but somehow it magnified his meanness so much more.

Are you kind or mean? Let's take a fun test to find out.

Imagine you're at a bus stop with an elderly lady who has a large suitcase. The bus comes and she asks you to help her lift the case on to the bus. Do you answer: A: *Yes*, B: *No*, C: *I'll do it for 40 quid*, or D: *I'll do it for two quid*?

If you answered A you're kind. Well done. Answers B and C are the same answer. They're just different ways of saying no. If you answered B or C, you're mean. If you answered D however you are a truly despicable oaf. You've decided to put a price on kindness … and surely that's the meanest thing of all.

The worst thing about mean-spirited behaviour is that it infects its victims. You emerge from it feeling angry and bitter and you have to make a conscious effort not to pass it on down the line.

'That was just *horrible*,' said Andy as we finally made our way on to the rain sodden streets of Holly Springs. 'I don't think any of them smiled. Not once!'

'I know!' My grip on the steering wheel was more intense than it needed to be. My knuckles were white. 'And the guy who ended up giving us the jump start… he can't have said more than three words throughout!'

'Were they words? Honestly? What a bunch of rude bastards! There is nothing nice to be said for this place.'

'Well, we're getting out of it as soon as we can.'

'Oh! You don't know how good that sounds,' said Andy. 'Come on… let's goooooowwwwaaaaaggggghhhh!.'

'Aaaaaagggggghh!'

My foot slammed on the brakes.

'Aaaaaagggggghh!'

The road was wet and we started to skid.

'Aaaaaagggggghh!'

The van – the van that had pulled into the road in front of us without bloody looking – had now just stopped making his already stupid move even stupider. First he goes through a stop sign and on to a busy road without looking and then, instead of completing the turn and getting out of our way, he sees us, panics and hits the brakes, planting himself even more firmly in the firing line. The idiot. I was almost tempted to drive straight into him on purpose. Almost.

We were still sliding and there was nowhere else to go so I yanked the steering wheel to the right and turned our nose that way. I closed my eyes and waited for the bang. It didn't happen.

When I opened my eyes our two vehicles were less than a yard apart. We were both angled at 45 degrees to the line of the road – the van because he'd frozen halfway through a 90-degree turn and us because I'd been forced to try and steer our car around his stupid cocking van.

'Shit!' said Andy, pausing to catch his breath. 'My God. Well done. Seriously. You okay?'

'What a fucking idiot!' I yelled. I was feeling very far from okay and I couldn't stop the words from falling out of me. 'What did he think he was doing? I saw him! I thought he was going a bit fast, I thought he wasn't going to be able to slow down in time and then, bosh, the idiot doesn't stop and he's there. Right there! What the hell was he playing at?!'

I reached for the door handle and started to get out of the car only to be restrained by the seat belt I'd forgotten I was wearing. It was a good job too because just as the Torino was wrestling me back into my seat, the van's passenger side door slid open to reveal two men who instantly made me want to stay right where I was.

Describing them is easy. One of them looked like Eminem and the other one looked even more like Eminem. They had bleached blond, short-cropped hair, T-shirts, jeans and attitude. I'll be honest, I might be getting them all wrong. It's entirely possible that I was judging them through a pop-culture filter that they don't subscribe to and that actually we'd just had a near-miss incident with twin albinos. Who knows? I probably didn't spend enough time taking in the smaller details because I was too busy focusing on the pistol that one of them was holding. HE HAD A BLOODY GUN! Now to be fair to the man, he wasn't actually pointing it at me, it was more that he was making a point of showing it to me... and did I mention that HE HAD A BLOODY GUN!

Unreal Slim Shady 1 smiled as Unreal Slim Shady 2 pulled the door closed. There was a brief pause and then they carried on their journey.

And we carried on ours, even more desperate than before to get out of Holly Springs and Mississippi.

I-Spy book of *Things to Experience in the Southern States.* Guns. Tick.

Once we'd left the threatening, gritty, beaten up streets of Holly Springs behind there was less than a hundred miles needed to get us out of Mississippi.

Outside of the towns Mississippi seemed to be mostly trees and churches. The road we took sliced through a blanket of evergreens, punctuated by the odd rust patch of something more autumnal and then suddenly, there'd be a patch of open land and set back from the road would be an enormous, gleaming white Baptist church.

They were mind-bogglingly big places and I couldn't help but wonder where on earth they drew their congregations from. We might drive through a community with a population of less than 400 people and then two or three miles later find ourselves driving past a church that could surely seat 4,000. And then 15 miles later we'd pass another one.

These churches weren't relics of the past. They looked new and shiny – white palaces not white elephants – so presumably they'd been built to satisfy demand. Either that or someone put the decimal point in the wrong place when they filled in the New Church Order Form a few years back. Oops.

Whichever way I looked at it I just couldn't make sense of the vast capacity for worship. There didn't seem to be enough people or homes around to make the numbers add up. Maybe the people of Mississippi are really good at hiding? Or perhaps all those trees go to church and nobody told me.[16]

The landscape didn't change much as we crossed the border

---

[16] He was a carpenter after all.

and hit Alabama but the mood in the car certainly did. Mississippi had tried to hold on to us but we'd finally shaken the bugger off.

But we had to get realistic. Our Mississippi blues had cost us too much time. The bastards had stolen away our vital early start and that meant we were going to have to pull up short for the day or risk ending up in the suburbs of Birmingham, Alabama low on fuel and late at night.

When we'd put our heads down for the night in Holly Springs, Mississippi we thought we might be two days from the coast. Frustratingly, when we put our heads down for the night in Winfield, Alabama we were still two days from the coast.

Chapter 31
Brilliant

When you look at a map and see a town called Brilliant you simply have to go and take a look. And if you are a town called Brilliant you simply have to deliver. It did. Brilliant, Alabama had an unbranded gas station. Which was brilliant.

And that's the problem with visiting a town called Brilliant. Once you've been there you can't stop yourself from using the word and half of what comes out of your mouth soon starts to sound like a poor attempt at a bad joke.

When you first get to Brilliant and you see your first sign saying something like, 'Brilliant Elementary School' you're bound to have at least a snort of laughter in you. You wouldn't be human otherwise. But when you drive past 10 similar signs in the space of half a mile the joke inevitably wears a little thin.

I suppose if you live there you must build up some kind of immunity to Brilliant puns in the same way that the people who work in a chocolate factory soon stop helping themselves to sweets.

But in the short term, this sudden overexposure to the word 'brilliant' infects your brain. Once the Brilliant virus has wormed its way in, it starts to eat away at what scientists call your 'superlative store'. This is the part of the brain where you keep words like, 'fabulous', 'fantastic', 'superb', 'amazing', 'magnificent', 'great', 'marvellous' and even 'fandabidozi'. Suddenly, these words start to be overwritten and the next time you reach for one the only superlative you can access is 'brilliant'.

Which would have little impact under normal circumstances but when you're in or around the town of Brilliant (and good things are happening to you) you end up sounding like you're cracking bad gags whether you want to or not.

The Brilliant virus first struck while we were pumping gas there. Andy shoved the camera in my face and asked me what I thought of the place and all I did was speak my mind.

'This is brilliant!'

It was only when I saw Andy cock his head to one side with a playful wince that I realised what I'd said.

'Oh... I didn't mean it like that... I... um... I actually just meant... it's... um... *brilliant.*'

Andy chuckled in an *I'm-not-sure-I-really-believe-you-but-I'll-let-you-get-away-with-it-this-time* kind of way.

Ten minutes later we were leaving the town and heading back to the highway. As we did so Andy sat in the passenger seat reviewing the footage he'd just shot, by watching it back in the camera. He was nodding away to himself in a satisfied, dare I say it, smug way.

'You look happy,' I said, pitching my volume up a little to penetrate his headphoned world.

'Yeah... that was brilliant.'

This time it was my turn to scoff and it was Andy who was claiming accidental punnage.

It kept happening.

'Birmingham's not far from Brilliant,' said Andy when our journey there had taken less than an hour.

I was worried about getting snarled up in city traffic but Birmingham was remarkably easy to negotiate and we were through it in 40 minutes. It would have taken only half an hour but amazingly our route took us past an unbranded gas station and we weren't going to turn the opportunity down even if there was an air of violence about the place – the cashier was hidden behind a reinforced door and a thick sheet of bullet-proof glass and when Andy tried to film me at the pumps it was a matter of seconds before a policeman told him not to in no uncertain terms: 'Sir, that looks like an expensive camera and you are not using that thing around here, d'you hear?'

Even with this little slice of unpleasantness it wasn't until we'd got to the other side of Birmingham that we eventually found the definitive cure for the Brilliant virus. When it's the only superlative in your repertoire there's only one way of guaranteeing you can cut the 'brilliants' out of your own conversation... you need to be plunged into a world of utter shitness.

And as luck would have it – that's what happened to us.

It started, as so many things do, with a noise. Something was rattling under the hood. It sounded like the car was violently shaking a not-very-full charity tin. Maybe we'd run over one of the Salvation Army's footsoldiers?

Ch'k'ch'k'ch'k'ch'k'ch'k'ch...

'Now what!'

Ch'k'ch'k'ch'k'ch'k'ch'k'ch...

'It's never made that noise before,' said Andy with a heavy sigh. 'Shit! Shitting arse. Shitting, shitty arse. We're going to have to stop, aren't we?'

'Ngggghhhh!' I yelled.

That's what it sounds like if you lay every swear word one on top of the other and say them all at the same time.

'I can't believe this is happening! We're only two days away. Two days!'

I pulled into a shopping plaza's parking lot. Wearily, we sloped out of the car and I lifted the hood. The two of us stared at the mysterious metal jigsaw while the engine hummed. And rattled.

It was coming from somewhere towards the front of the engine, near the radiator but apart from that we were obviously clueless. Even if we had been able to identify the problem component it's not like we would have been able to fix the thing.

'It's like it knows we're getting near the end of the journey,' said Andy.

'It's not an elephant on its way to the sodding graveyard!' I snapped. 'It doesn't have to die when we get there. In fact it'll be really quite inconvenient if it does.' I turned the engine off. 'We want to sell the bastard, don't we? Why are we even looking at this? We both know we haven't got a clue what we're looking for.'

'It's always worth lifting the hood,' said Andy. 'It lets people know you're in trouble. It's like a little cry for help.'

'Nice theory,' I said, 'but I don't think it's worked this time.' I closed the lid. 'I certainly can't see anyone coming to help us.'

'No.' Andy pointed over my right shoulder. 'But I do see someone coming to have a look.'

I turned and sure enough someone was making a very definite beeline towards our car. She was forty-something, short and had a bubbly mop of red shoulder-length curls.

'Hey there,' she said in a squeak of a voice, 'I just wanted to say that you have a bee-yootiful car!'

'Thanks.'

'Y'know, my folks used to have one of these. Same colour, same model. Practically the same car!'

'Really? Wow.'

'*Man*!' She smiled to herself at some secret reminiscence. 'We used to have the best vacations in that thing. We went all over.' She stopped suddenly. She looked at me as if I might be a trick of the light and then said, 'Speak to me.'

'I'm sorry? What?'

'Just speak to me... I wanna hear your accent. I wanna see if I can work out where you're from.'

'Okay... well... um... hello... my name's Dave... and you are?'

'I'm Robyn,' she said. 'What about him? Does he speak?'

'I'm Andy,' said Andy. 'Pleased to meet you.'

'Oh I got it, I got it!' she squealed again. 'You're Australian, aren't you?'

'No. No… I'm afraid we're not. We're English.'

'No! *Really*?' She was suspicious. 'You don't sound English. Are you *kidding* me?'

'No. I promise you. We really are English. Aren't we Andy?'

'Strewth yeah.'

I smiled but it sailed right over her head. I told you she was short.

She pulled her phone from her purse and started fiddling uncomfortably with the controls.

'Would you mind if I took a photograph of your car?' she asked. 'Only my folks are gonna freak when I show them this.'

'Go ahead.' I stepped to one side so as not to block the photo and then said the thing you're supposed to say in situations like this. 'You can be in it if you like… would you like me to take it?'

'No, that's okay,' she said. 'They both know what I look like already!' She made herself laugh, erupting into a fit of staccato laughter that made me think maybe she had the same loose part as our car. 'I've got to take two if you don't mind because I need to send one to my mom and one to my dad. They're divorced.'

'Right… um… feel free to take as many as you like,' I said, 'but I think once you've got a photo on your phone you can probably send the same picture to both of them at the same time.'

'Noooooooo… I *can't* do that,' she said, as if speaking to a simpleton. 'They're divorced!'

'Of course… yes. Silly me.'

'Y'know, when my father bought our old station wagon it was a present for Mom. He bought it because he was about to go off to Vietnam. Ain't that sweet?'

My knees almost buckled with the surprise. I leaned into the car for support. I looked across to Andy, fully expecting him to be registering as much shock as me but of course it wasn't ringing any bells for him because he hadn't been there when Grant had told us his stories.

Me? I could summon a memory of Grant so clear he could have been standing right there with me: '*When I graduated from*

SEAL training, I was given a platoon on my way to Vietnam and my then wife said she wasn't going to let me go there unless I got her a new car so... there she is.'

I looked at Robyn. Was she the right age? Could have been. It couldn't be... could it? Was it possible? Had we really driven this thing 6,000-odd miles across America from father to daughter?

'Excuse me,' I asked, suddenly nervous, 'your father... um, his name wouldn't be Grant, would it?'

She looked startled by the question.

'No,' she said. 'Where'd *that* come from?'

'Um... I... well, we... well actually, not me and Andy but me and someone else... we... um... I just had a funny feeling that's all.'

'Well then you're strange, ain't you? Now, tell me, what are two strange Englishmen doing drivin' this old thing through Alabama?'

'Well we're going from coast to coast,' I said. 'Or at least we're trying to. We were hoping to finish up in Georgia tomorrow.'

'Shouldn't be a problem...'

'You're right. It *shouldn't* be. But she's just started making a very odd noise.'

'Really? Hmm. Well, if you like, you can pop the hood and I'll take a look?'

'Seriously?' I asked. She clearly was. 'Does *everyone* in America know about cars?'

'Not everyone.' She shrugged. 'But, I do. Married at 22, divorced at 29. Two kids and no job. Mommy had to do something to put food on the table. So I trained as a mechanic.'

I know there's no real reason why a short, squeaky woman with red hair shouldn't be a mechanic but there's no point pretending I wasn't surprised. I was. She really did seem a most unlikely candidate.

With the hood up, I slipped into the driver's seat and turned the key.

Ch'k'ch'k'ch'k'ch'k'ch'k'ch...

'Hmmm... It doesn't sound good,' she said. And then the words that chilled my blood, 'I think you're gonna need a new water pump.'

The water pump. In Ottawa, Kansas when we'd lost the idler pulley from the air-conditioning unit everyone was at great pains to tell me how lucky we were that it wasn't the water pump. Well we weren't lucky anymore. We were in trouble. I think it was at this point that the Brilliant virus was completely eradicated.

'That doesn't sound good,' I said.

'It's not. First of all you've got to get the part and that isn't going to be easy on a car of this age.' Robyn peered into the engine space, craning her neck, trying to catch the best light. 'And even then there's no guarantee. These bolts are old and rusted. Taking the old one off is going to be tricky. If one of these old bolts snaps it ends up inside the engine and then the whole thing is done for. It's a 50/50... you really want to take this to a specialist.'

'Really? So it's not the sort of thing you'd do?'

'Me?' The staccato laughter burst out once more. 'If you brought this thing to my shop I'd sure give it a go... but I don't think you want to bring it to my shop. Even if I did fix it, you'd be hundreds of miles off course given that you're heading for Georgia. I'm not from around here, I'm just visiting with friends...'

'Really? Oh. Where're you from?'

'Kansas.'

I should have seen that coming. Of course she was from Kansas. She was helping strangers.

'I don't suppose you know of any local garages?'

Robyn shook her head.

'When did the noise start?'

'Today.'

'Less than an hour ago,' added Andy, 'we pretty much pulled straight in.'

'Well,' she sucked some air through her teeth, 'you *might* get away with it.'

'What do you mean?'

'I had an old Toyota a few years back that had this same problem and I drove it like this for five months before it went.'

'Five months! Really?'

'Yes, sir.'

Something about that didn't ring true. Why would a mechanic drive a car in that condition for five months? Wouldn't you just fix it? You don't hear doctors saying, 'The strange thing is, my leg was bleeding for days before the infection set in.'

My confusion didn't last long however. Robyn was soon answering my questions before I could even ask them.

'The thing is,' she said, 'that car wasn't a beauty like this. In fact that car was a worthless piece of crap. It would have cost more to fix it than the car was worth. Believe me, I drove that thing till it died and I didn't even go to the funeral.'

'I don't want this car to have a funeral.'

'You're in real trouble if it's leaking... and it isn't. If I were you I'd keep going... but please, when you see an auto shop, take it in.'

We headed tentatively back out on to the highway – *ch'k'ch'k'ch'k'ch'k'ch'k* – 50mph max – *ch'k'ch'k'ch'k'ch'k'ch'k* – eyes peeled on the lookout for garages at all times – *ch'k'ch'k'ch'k'ch'k'ch'k* – there were none – *ch'k'ch'k'ch'k'ch'k'ch'k* – there was nothing.

While the car kept chattering Andy and I were silent. There was only one thing on my mind but I didn't want to talk about it because I didn't want to tempt fate. Instead, cogs turned silently. I was calculating the odds that we could get away with it. I was working on the assumption that Robyn's Toyota had stretched good fortune to its outer limit, which meant that the chance of failure in the next five months – or 150 days – was 100 per cent. So the chance of it failing in the next 75 days was 50 per cent. And so on. If my maths was correct that meant the chance of the water pump failing in the first two days was going to be *less than 2 per cent*. We had a greater than 98 per cent chance of success! Didn't that compare favourably with the 50/50 chance of a rusty bolt falling inside the engine and bollocksing everything up? Wasn't it wiser just to keep going? Maybe everything was going to be okay.

These were the thoughts that span round my head but I didn't dare risk vocalising them. That seemed like a sure-fire way of bringing the bad stuff on. I didn't want to get cocky. Cockiness is exactly what the evil gremlins look out for. And the gremlins were there for sure. They were in position. They had the spanner in their tiny, clammy gremlin fingers and we all knew *the works* were in range. All it needed was one reassuring sentence, one confident word and they were going to release the spanner. I didn't want to give them the satisfaction.

But I forgot one crucial thing. Those bastard gremlins can read your mind.

In truth it wasn't the most dramatic of noises. Sort of a *pfffft*. As sounds go it had nowhere near the violence that had accompanied our other car crises. But the effect was far more dramatic. The engine just died. We lost power immediately and all I could do was steer us off the road and into the verge.

It wasn't just the car that made less noise this time… so did we. There was swearing – of course there was swearing – but it wasn't as explosive. It all just felt too serious for that. We were enveloped in the feeling that this time it might turn out to be final.

The water pump wasn't just leaking, it was spilling its guts. Rusty brown water gushed out, staining the white gravel where we'd come to a rest. And then with a pathetic final squirt, a dribble and a splash, it stopped. The car was dead.

We checked our mobile phones and discovered we had no reception. We were well and truly stranded. We were right by the junction of two huge long straight roads. Whichever direction we looked the road stretched on for ever and there appeared to be nothing else up ahead. No phones, no transport and nothing to walk towards. No hope.

We were roughly 400 miles from the coast.

'I woke up so excited this morning,' I said. 'I knew it was two days away. Not anymore it's not.'

'We got close,' said Andy.

'You're right. We were close.' I held my finger and thumb up to show him how close we were. '*This* close. On the map.'

I looked down at the ground, more to avoid the camera's gaze than anything else but what I saw there made me recoil in surprise. There at my feet was the delicate frame of a dead sparrow. Peaceful, unbloodied but dead.

You see. The car had made less noise this time and so had we and now... so had the metaphors. No need for the blood and guts of the I-84 Idaho road of death. No need for the macabre disembowelled cat of La Veta... a simple, elegant bird in a state of permanent rest was all it took. No struggle. No violence. Just a peaceful acceptance that it was all over.

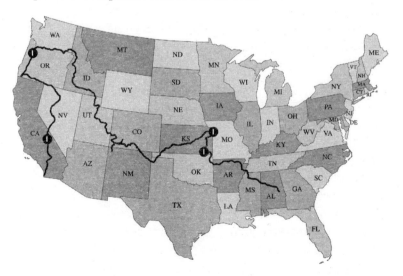

Chapter 32
Just stand on the damn things

'Are you guys okay?'

The voice came from a deep blue Chevy pick-up truck. Or rather the driver of a deep blue Chevy pick-up truck. He was wearing a deep-blue baseball cap, a deep-blue jacket and a deep-blue shirt.

'No. No we're not,' I said. 'We've broken down. We can't get any phone reception and we don't know where we are.'

'There's a garage about four miles this-a-way... you ever been towed before?'

'No, sir. No I haven't.'

The way he sighed made me regret my honest reply. He looked to the heavens as if to check that he really was supposed to go along with this Good Samaritan malarkey and when the message came down that yes, that was the general idea, he exhaled deeply before saying, 'Well okay... let's hook y'up and see what we can do.'

He obviously wasn't thrilled by the idea of towing a novice towee. Which made me wonder precisely how much skill being towed really required. I mean, it's not water-skiing, is it?

He pulled up a good distance in front of us, jumped into the back of his pick-up – he was wearing deep-blue jeans as well – and fished out a long, sturdy chain. Once he'd attached the chain to both vehicles he came over to give me my first towing lesson.

'Okay... now when I motion like this,' he moved his left arm up and down like an arthritic seagull, 'that means we're gonna slow down and I need you to put your foot on the brakes. I need you to slow down for me, y'hear? We want to keep the chain taut at all times. Otherwise we end up jerking the shit out of it and you end up piling into my rear end. You got it?'

'I got it.'

'When I do this…'

'I hit the brakes.'

'Good.'

We climbed into our respective cabs. My palms were sweaty. My heart was pumping. He'd put a good dose of fear in me. Which was probably no bad thing. He gave me the signal so I put my foot on the brakes and waited for the chain to become taut as we pulled away. It didn't happen quite like that. I think the technical term for what happened is we 'jerked the shit out of it.' He stopped immediately, got out of his truck and came striding back towards us. I lowered my window and tried to get my defence in first.

'I had my foot on the brakes, I swear.'

'Really?'

'Really.'

'Hmm. Looks like you got them power brakes.' He checked with the heavens again but luckily either the line was busy or he was told to persist. 'All right,' he said, 'I'm gonna need you to stand on them things as much as you can, okay? Just stand on the damn things because I don't want you hitting my rear end.'

'You got it,' I said. 'Let's just take it nice and slow and we can…'

But Blue was off and in his truck already. I put my full body weight on the pedal and still we got off to a bumpy start.

What followed was one of the scariest rides of my life. To get where we were going we had to make a left turn into a major highway crossing four lanes of traffic. There were no traffic lights to control the junction and with his truck, the chain and us we were three cars long. Once he entered that turn we were all committed.

After a not-quite-so-bumpy jerk start, we eventually got up to a steady speed with a taut chain. Blue gave me the signal in reverse, which I assumed was his way of telling me to ease off the brakes… so I did. We crept up from 10 to 20mph. Then 25. Then 30. The left turn was approaching, there was a stop sign I'm sure we should have been obeying but it was obvious we were going to do no such thing.

We cruised through and in one long, steady arc we got across the highway and into the right-hand lane. It was like water-skiing in a major shipping lane. But the fear wasn't over yet. Now that we were on a major road Blue decided to put his foot down. Of course I did whatever he asked me to do.

Pretty soon we were doing 65. That wasn't taking it nice and slow. We were a freewheeling, two-tonne lump of metal being driven by his bad-tempered left arm and my shit-scared right foot. Why weren't we pootling along at 20? Why was he putting us all through this? Wasn't this just making us all the more likely to end up parked in the back of his truck?

That left arm started to flap so my right foot pressed hard. His signalling grew more frantic but there wasn't anything else I could do. I could smell our brakes burning. Memories of Mount Whitney zinged back to haunt me. I swatted them aside. I had more urgent matters to attend to.

We were slowing but surely we weren't slowing fast enough. He started indicating for a right turn. My arse was off the seat as I tried in vain to put more force down. He turned. We followed. We left tarmac. We hit gravel. We left the hum. We hit the crunch. The chain snapped. Clunk.

We'd made it.

My heart was pumping. There was a film of sweat on my brow. I've never been more convinced I was going to have a car crash. And when I say that, I include the time when I was 23 and had a car crash.

'The chain snapped,' said Blue as we stepped out of the car. His tone was accusatory. It was my fault. I should have been able to brake harder in my car with power brakes and no power.

'I'm really sorry,' I said. 'Our brakes were burning. You can smell them from here. Is there anything we can do for you... how much would a chain cost because we can...'

'It don't matter.' He was sulking.

'We're really grateful for your help. I don't know what we'd have done without you.'

'Okay,' he said, barely able to hide the obvious disdain he had for the two incompetent foreigners and their piss poor tow-ability.

What a peculiarly grouchy saviour he was. And what an odd combination of gratitude and fear he'd instilled in me. We were truly grateful for his intervention and without him I really don't know what we'd have done... but as he left and I offered him a handshake a part of me thought he was going to give me a right hook instead.

'The thing is,' said John across the counter, 'it's not really the kind of work we do.' He smiled an apologetic smile and pulled one of the six biros from his top pocket. He didn't need a pen. He just needed something to play with. 'We tend to work with modern cars. We *could* order the part and it might take two or three days to get a hold of. But even then we got to take the old pump out and that's kind of a specialised job.'

'Yeah, I know... the bolts are kind of rusted...'

'Exactly. And if one of them snaps and ends up inside the engine then the whole thing is screwed and to be perfectly honest with you... I'm not sure that's a responsibility we want to take on.'

'But we could...'

'I honestly don't think we're gonna be able to help you...'

'... but I can put you in touch with another company who might.'

'That would be great.'

'They're only about 10 miles away and they're used to dealing with older vehicles. Here, let me find you their card and you can call them yourself.'

I was feeling exhausted and harassed by life. It was only the middle of the afternoon but I'd long ago reached the end of my tether. The car wasn't dead she was in a coma. I just wanted to know whether she was going to live or die. I was tired of not knowing. While there was still hope I couldn't give up but that just left my emotions in a state of suspended animation and my nerve endings in tatters. If she was going to the Old Fords' Home in the sky I wanted to get it over and done with. I was weary of being in limbo. I wanted to celebrate or grieve.

The card John returned with was for Gill's Service Center.

'Here you go,' he said. 'Just give them a call.'

I looked at the card. I looked at the phone. I took a deep breath. And then I looked at the phone again. I wanted to pick it up and make the call but I could feel the tension inside me and I didn't want to carry that into a fresh conversation. I stared at the phone and took another deep breath. I just needed a few moments to compose myself and find an inner calm. From John's perspective I must have looked very odd. He'd given me the number. The phone was right there. Why wasn't I dialling already? Two men. A desk. A phone. A number. And nothing happening. Was this real life or an extract from one of Samuel Beckett's less successful plays?

John cocked his head to one side and studied my expression. Perhaps he was trying to work out whether or not I recognised the telephone. Nervously, he twiddled his biro. My brain had frozen. I hadn't reached the end of my journey but mentally I'd reached the end of the road. John placed the pen down on the desk with a sense of deliberate precision and then slid the phone three inches closer to me.

'There y'go...' he said.

'Thanks.'

'Let's see... it's Friday afternoon now,' said the cheery voice on the end of the line, 'so if we order the part right away we should get it on Monday morning. How does that sound?'

It sounded like a friendly and efficient Alabaman mechanic offering to do a professional job in a timely fashion. And it sounded terrible.

I wanted to cry. I just wanted someone to tell us they were on their way and they were going to fix it. I wanted someone to take control of the situation so that I didn't have to continue wrestling with it any more. Given the seriousness of our mechanical failure I knew that wasn't going to happen... but that didn't mean I knew how to deal with any other outcome.

'Hello? Can you hear me? I said we can probably get the part for Monday...'

A weekend's delay gave us a serious problem that my weary, addled brain simply couldn't handle. We were by the side of a busy highway and at least 10 miles from the nearest town. We had a car that wouldn't go and a carload of luggage that we couldn't afford to leave unattended. We had to find a hotel. And we had to find a way of getting ourselves – and our belongings – to that hotel. I know it's not the trickiest of problems. With a clear mind there is an obvious solution. But I didn't have a clear mind. I had a mind clouded by six weeks of stress and folly. I stared out of the window at our useless, comatose car and felt a cold sweat engulf me.

'Sir? Would you like me to order that part for you, sir?'

'Sorry,' I said, jolting myself back into the moment, 'um… yeah, yeah… I think you better had…'

The *car-luggage-hotel-distance* cogs were still turning. I knew there was an obvious solution. There had to be. We couldn't change the luggage. The nearest hotel wasn't going to get any nearer. The only thing that could be changed was… the car. Of course! A taxi! Wow. If it had taken me this long to come up with that, my brain really was in meltdown. What a relief! A taxi! I couldn't believe I'd been sweating so much over something so easily dealt with. A bloody taxi! Amazed and faintly amused by my own stupidity, a small, embarrassed tickle of a laugh escaped my lips…

'Are you okay, sir?'

'Yes,' I said. I was already aware that I was breathing easier. 'I'm sorry… I was getting a bit panicky for a moment there. You know what it's like when your car breaks down.'

'So we're going to order the part?'

'Please do,' I said. 'It's fine. I guess we're just going to have to find somewhere to stay for a few days. I don't suppose you could recommend an independent hotel and a local taxi firm, could you?'

'A taxi? Hmmm? A taxi? Y'know… I don't *honestly* think there is a taxi company in Harpersville. Haven't you got another ride?'

What? My little spell of confidence evaporated, my heartbeat quickened and the cold sweat returned. What did *that* mean? *Another ride?* What? Were we supposed to keep a spare car with us in case of emergencies?

'Um… um… no,' I said, 'no, we don't.' I concentrated on breathing for a moment or two. 'Look… I know this isn't your problem but I think we're kind of stranded so… um… is there any chance you could come and pick our car up *today*?' If I'd been *a bit panicky* a few moments ago, I was *a lot panicky* now.

My brain was slow but my words were quick. 'If there's any way that you could store it somewhere safe for the weekend then we wouldn't have to empty all our stuff and at least then we could just take what we need for a couple of days, I mean really it's just our washbags and a change of underwear and then...'

'Whoa... okay... slow down... let me just see,' said the voice. 'You just hang on there while I take a look and see if Tommy's around.'

I didn't know who Tommy was or what he did but I didn't care. I just wanted him to be around. He was.

'Okay, I'm gonna send Tommy out to pick y'up. Let's get this car o' yours in here and then let's see if we can't sort y'out, okay? He should be with you in about half an hour. How does that sound?'

That sounded fabulous.

'I can't believe this has happened,' I said, still slumping in the front seat of Tommy's tow-truck. We were at Gill's Service Center and the car was being winched down but I hadn't yet summoned the energy to climb out of the cab and face the next phase of our ordeal. 'Only two hours ago I thought we were dead and buried. I can't keep up.'

Andy rested his hand on my shoulder. 'We're lucky bastards,' he said. 'I thought it was over too... but we're still going. Now, come on, let's get out, smile and be nice to these people. They've saved our bacon. Or is it my bacon and your tofu-burger?'

I smiled at his silly joke. But then the mention of food made my stomach growl and I growled too. We hadn't eaten all day. Why hadn't we had a Brilliant breakfast?

I tried to persuade my legs to move. I told myself that things were good. Okay, so our broken water pump was going to cost us a weekend in Harpersville, Alabama but compared to where we'd been before Blue had come along, surely things were going better than we could realistically have hoped.

The water pump wasn't the kind of thing that could be

custom built like our San Diegan tailpipes. And it wasn't the kind of thing that anyone was ever going to have in stock. So really, the fact that we'd already found the people who could fix it and that we only had to wait a couple of days for the part to arrive was a best case scenario. In fact, for a bad day, it really was going very well indeed.

I unslumped. Uncoiling my body slowly, I straightened my back one vertebra at a time, energising myself as I went.

'Come on,' I said, 'let's get out and get on with it. We still need to find a hotel, let alone anything else…'

The two of us shuffled along the padded bench seat and jumped down from the cab.

'Hey… which one of you is Dave?' said a familiar voice. 'I spoke to you on the phone,' he said as we shook hands, 'I'm Bim and I've got some good news for you…'

'That's nice to hear,' I said. 'This is Andy. So if you've got good news I'm hoping you've spoken to a hotel…?'

'Nah… it's better than that.' Bim smiled. 'We found a water pump!'

'What? *Really?* A water pump for a 1970 Ford Torino? No way! I don't believe it!'

'Must have been on the shelf for a long time,' said Bim. 'Prob'ly over ordered one years ago.'

Surely this was too good to be true! How on earth was this possible? I couldn't take it in. Until I'd seen it with my own eyes I refused to believe a word Bim was saying. Which is why it wasn't long before Bim was holding the new water pump in front of my eyes.

It was exactly what he said it was. The thing was still in its box. The box had faded with age and had clearly been sitting on a shelf for the best part of 40 years untouched. It was ridiculous. It was beautiful. Now all they had to do was fit the bloody thing.

For a small town, Gill's seemed like quite a sizeable organisation. In a couple of large industrial sheds there were maybe a dozen bays where cars were being worked on by a busy, buzzy crew of blue shirted mechanics. But there was a vacancy and with a bit of huff and puff we soon rolled the Torino into place.

Like open-heart surgery what followed was both brutal and precise. Incisions were made, parts were disconnected and a metal life hung in the balance. Was that the *bip... bip...* of a life-support machine or was someone, somewhere taking a hammer to an anvil? Our surgeon was Scotty, while the boss, Bim (his real name was James Gill), was on hand as a consultant. I played the role of the nervous father. I knew there was nothing I could do to affect the outcome so I just bit my lip and tried to stay out of the experts' way.

Half an hour in and the one thing I was really dreading happened. As Scotty was unscrewing one of the old bolts it just sheared in two, the head coming away with the wrench leaving a two inch long rod of rusted, threaded metal in place. Robyn's words echoed through my mind: *'If one of these old bolts snaps it ends up inside the engine and then the whole thing is done for.'* Shit.

Scotty and Bim didn't panic. They just went to work on the bolt, trying first one method and then another to loosen the thing. It was heated and lubed, cooled and shocked but still it wouldn't budge. They tried various tools, each managing to grip the bolt's surface with greater force than the last. But instead of finding the power to turn the damn thing, all they seemed to do was strip away its spiralling thread, leaving behind a smoother, less grippable surface than before.

Deep down, I knew why it wasn't turning. I knew what was making it hold. The bolt passed through a metal plate. For it to unscrew and be drawn out of its hole it needed to be on the level. It needed to be perfectly horizontal. And it wasn't. It was weighed down on this side. By the weight or responsibility. Six and a half thousand miles of road trip rested on that two-inch spur of rusty metal. Six weeks of my life hung in the balance. If Scotty could turn that bolt, I could turn to the next page of my journey. If the bolt was going to seize and snap then my road trip was going to seize and snap with it.

Nobody said it was a last-ditch attempt but when you've

watched two men sweat over one bolt for 40 minutes and then one of them asks for a lump-hammer it does kind of feel like you're entering an all-or-nothing endgame. Not a scalpel, not forceps. A hammer.

Scotty's hand came down. *CLANK*. It didn't move. It didn't snap. *CLANK*. It didn't move. It didn't snap. *CLANK*. It didn't move. It didn't snap. But there was something. A tiny flake of red-brown metal spun off into the air. The thinnest scab, almost transparent, almost not there. Caught on the breeze, it was diverted from its parabolic trajectory, spinning, floating, passing through the harsh beam of the workman's light, flirting with Scotty's sleeve before freefalling to the oil-stained floor below. No one seemed to notice it but me. Could that tiny slither of rust have made the difference? Had the bolt been held in place by a fingernail clipping-sized slither of iron oxide? With a long armed pair of pliers and a great deal of brute force Scotty gripped the bolt once more. His knuckles went white as he tightened his grasp. He angled his body to put a bit more of his weight behind it and... and... and... it turned.

An eighth of an inch? Not even that. But it was enough. In a tug of war you only need a tiny bit of give to take full advantage and once the rust had loosened its ferrous embrace it had no chance of re-establishing itself. The bolt was turned again. And again. And again. And again. And with every turn of that rusty bolt I grew stronger. With every rotation my belief grew. Turn. We could finish this thing. Turn. Everything was going to be all right. Turn. Nothing – and I mean nothing – could stop us now.

Chapter 34
25,200 seconds

What can I tell you about the next day? It was a day defined not by incident but by emotion. If I described all that I saw that day, you still wouldn't understand even a hundredth of what I felt.

I could tell you about seeing cotton fields for the first time in my life. The crops had been gathered and in each field there stood huge rectangular bails of tightly bound white cotton, each one the size of a school bus. Around the fringes and besides the road, where the harvester couldn't reach, straggly little cotton balls still clung on to the brittle stalks.

I could describe Georgia's rolling green pastures or the eerie silence of her mysterious swamps where dark green algae seemed to suffocate the water's surface and climbing plants drooped from otherwise bare branches looking like the skeletons of so many dead apes.

Or there were the sleepy towns with their imposing courthouses and defiantly grand, unapologetic homes. I could tell you about pumping gas under the simple, white stuccoed car port at the tiny, vintage Thomas' Station on the Square in Buena Vista or about failing to pump gas 20 miles later at an abandoned gas station in the middle of nowhere. There, a beaten-up pump stood besides a beaten-up barn so flimsy and close to collapse it was difficult to imagine it had ever been substantial enough to house a real business. How many years had it lain abandoned? Long enough for gas to go up by a dollar for sure. The price on the pump said $1.29. As a time-of-death record surely that was as accurate as a drowned man's watch.

I could discuss the nervous wait at the railroad crossing in the tiny town of Lilly as a huge freight train chugged west – *duga-dugdug-duga-dugdug-duga-dugdug-duga-dugdug* – momentarily keeping us from reaching our final appointment with independent gas.

Maybe I should give you my impression of Savannah, Georgia, the city where we finally reached the Atlantic seaboard. Even late on a December day there was a muggy heat to the place. That would explain the city's evident love affair with shade. Distinctive trees – Live Oaks, apparently – lined many of the avenues, their strong but spindly branches spreading like many-knuckled witches' fingers to create an impenetrable canopy and shut out the clear blue sky. Spanish moss hung from the branches at every joint and every fingertip like a lazy beard designer offering you the same ZZ Top selection he showed you last season and also the season before.

Savannah had history, that's for sure. Unlike most American cities it had been there long enough for once moneyed districts to go to seed and for some once poor areas to become fashionable too. Huge, elegant wooden mansions cried out for a lick of paint, their verandahs and porches propped up on bricks, their lawns unkempt and their gutters weeping. By contrast there were narrow, almost Parisian-style streets lined with scrawny, pastel-hued townhouses. There the wooden shutters creaked and the plaster peeled away from the walls, not because they were unloved but because they'd been artfully distressed by their middle-class occupants.

But no matter how much I told you about any of this it would amount to nothing because none of these sights defined the day. It didn't matter what it looked like. What counted was the way it felt.

I guess I was expecting to feel an explosive moment of euphoria as we reached the finishing line... but it wasn't like that at all. Instead the joy seeped into me incrementally, bit by bit throughout the long, long day. It ended up being almost exactly a seven-hour drive. That's 420 minutes. 25,200 seconds.

What's the happiest you've ever been? Can you divide it into 25,200 perceptible units? Imagine travelling towards it at one unit per second. That's honestly how it felt. It was a dripping tap of Tantric happiness. Hardly noticeable at first, almost impossible to tell the difference from one second to the next and yet, by the end of the day, it was going to flood through me.

I've never been more aware of my own being, of the space I occupied and the oxygen I breathed. As I turned the steering wheel I felt like I could see the air molecules moving through the hairs on my arm. I could feel every nerve ending in my body. Every square millimetre of skin seemed to be tingling. Even the skin concealed within the folds of my belly button seemed to be tingling. Why, as we drove down one of Savannah's tree-lined avenues, did the skin beneath my finger-nails start to itch?

Inevitably, it was a day of reflection, too. When I first set off on this journey the only plan was that there was no plan. No route, no schedule, no itinerary, just some ill-defined and vaguely noble notion about where we were going to spend our dollars. By definition it was always going to be an unpredictable beast... but it had gone beyond the simply unpredictable. The fact that it was Andy and not Stef who was now sitting in the passenger seat was proof of that.

I'd come to try and find the other side of American life but of course it wasn't as simple as that. There was no *one other side*. And wasn't that the point? The homogenous, corporate world I'd been exposed to on my tour of US theatres had been stifling, soulless... empty. On the evidence of that trip, that was all America appeared to be. But in six weeks of travelling I'd met as many different sides to the country as I'd met people.

Larry bends tailpipes in one America and Michael rents treehouses in another. The worlds in which Robert and Fern refuel cars, Dennis and Frances carve dogs and Bim and Scotty replace water pumps are all distinct and different. There's an America where Joe is waiting for Amoco to come and take down their sign and there's another where Sharon calls Sue who calls Cody who comes along and opens up. There's an America where the best guitar player around is pumping gas and another where two strangers are welcomed in for Thanksgiving dinner in a town that smells of death.

How long will these various Americas survive? One of them has passed already. The America in which Billie Kay serves up milkshakes and Marge makes egg salad is no more. What's going to replace it? What will replace the others when their turns come? Twenty years ago a journey like ours would have been easy. I can't help thinking that in 20 years' time it might just be impossible.

It's a shame because these places – the good and the bad – are truer to the American spirit than anything the faceless, bland and acceptably average corporations have to offer. The chains offer us a world in which average things are guaranteed... I'd rather live in a world in which fabulous things are possible. I'll take a rollercoaster instead of a train.

As we passed through Savannah and out to the eastern edge of the city my happiness – still increasing drip by drip – was starting to overwhelm me. We crossed over a bridge and on to Whitemarsh Island and my chest swelled with pride. I'd driven nearly 7,000 miles in order to cross a country less than 3,000 miles wide. It had been a journey with as many ups as downs but in that instant I couldn't summon up one ounce of regret. Not for my Moab madness. Not for any of it.

That was when I knew I hadn't just worked out what it was I wanted America to be... I'd discovered what I wanted *me* to be. I wanted to live my life with passion. I wanted to aim high and make mistakes. I want to *be* a rollercoaster and not a train.

Another bridge carried us further east and on to Wilmington Island. We'd spent just over $9,000 on food, lodgings and gas. Only $97 had been given to The Man™. And most of that was voodoo.

Another bridge carried us out over a narrow stretch of water and on to an improbable ribbon of a road built through some swampland. Was that the Atlantic to our left? Where does a river end and the sea begin? Pretty soon it would be over. I held the steering wheel gently in my hands. Andy knew what half this journey was like. So did Stef. But only the car and I knew what the whole thing was like. Only we had survived it all. I didn't want to let her go. I didn't want to say goodbye.

A final high bridge carried us on to Tybee Island. There was salt in the air. The buildings were growing increasingly relaxed and open. It's the same with all coastal resorts. You have to bring the outdoors in. The road curved round to the right, running parallel with the coastline. The beach was no more than a hundred yards to our left. Any left turn would do. Any left turn would take us to the finishing line. Did I want the finishing line? Did it have to end?

We crawled up a narrow side street and as close as we could to the beach. There was sand under the tyres. I could see the waves crashing. From the island of Coronado to the island of Tybee. From beyond the Pacific coast to beyond the Atlantic coast.

The journey was complete.

I paused.

There was silence. Nothing moved.

The final drips of happiness filled me up and confirmed for me something I'd known since day one. You don't need a convertible to feel the wind in your hair. You don't even need wind. Or hair. It's not a physical sensation, it's a state of mind.

I want to live a passionate life.

I always want to feel the wind in my hair.

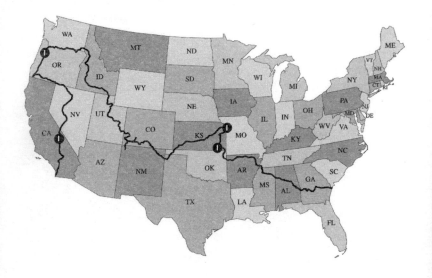

From: Jake Lingwood (Ebury Publishing)
Subject: Re: Chapters 1 to 34
To: Dave Gorman

Dave,

Thanks for the completed manuscript.

In this version you seem to have reprinted some of our emails. I presume you want me to take those out.

Let's meet up for a drink soon.

Jake

From: Dave Gorman
Subject: Re: Chapters 1 to 34
To: Jake Lingwood (Ebury Publishing)

Jake,

Do you mind leaving them in?

Yes, let's.

Dave

The Torino:

The car was sold but has failed to stay in touch. In December 2007 she was advertised for sale on the website CraigsList.com and from the accompanying photos it looks like she has new hubcaps. She certainly has a new price. If you own the car Dave would love to hear from you... especially if you find a pair of socks in the secret compartment.

Stef:

Stef lives in Brooklyn. She no longer wields a camera, is on first-name terms with a chiropractor but is no longer wearing a truss. As well as being an executive producer on a major US network TV show, she is running her own production company. Her hobbies include listening to depressing indie music and eating too much mashed potato.

Andy:

Andy lives in West London. His daughter still hasn't been christened but she has now reacquainted herself with his face. He is a series director on a major BBC TV series. He annoys Dave by consistently beating him at poker although Dave currently has the edge when it comes to Scrabble.

Dave:

Dave lives in East London. He never wants to eat another egg. He has just finished his third book. And if you're reading this in order, so have you.

About the Author

Dave Gorman is an award-winning comedian, storyteller and writer. He has numerous TV writing credits and was part of the double BAFTA-winning team behind *The Mrs Merton Show*. His live shows have won numerous awards and he is the only performer to twice win the Jury Prize for Best One Person Show at America's prestigious HBO US Comedy Arts Festival. As well as writing, producing and starring in two BBC2 series he has made numerous other TV appearances, including *Absolutely Fabulous*, *The Frank Skinner Show*, *The Late Show with David Letterman*, *The Tonight Show with Jay Leno* and *The Daily Show* with Jon Stewart where he has appeared both as a guest and as the show's 'resident statistician'. He is the host of Radio 4's hit comedy *Genius*. His documentary film, *America Unchained*, won the Audience Award for Best Documentary Feature at the Austin Film Festival. He enjoys cycling, poker, photography and cryptic crosswords. His ambition is to one day become a team captain on *Call My Bluff*.

www.davegorman.com

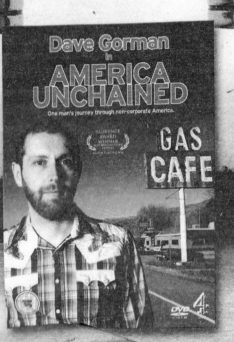